FREE TO BE HOLY

No matter what era of church history you study, you will find strains of doctrine that attempt to "turn the grace of our God into licentiousness" (Jude 4). There have been voices in every generation claiming they are defending the gospel or exalting God's grace while treating holiness as optional. Even now, the absurd notion that divine grace is hostile to obedience is being peddled by people "promising ... freedom while they themselves are slaves of corruption" (2 Peter 2:19). They insist this is what it means to have a gospel-centered message.

But Scripture commands us to "pursue" (*strive* toward, press after, stay on the trail of) "the sanctification without which no one will see the Lord" (Hebrews 12:14). Scripture also says authentic grace teaches us "to deny ungodliness and worldly desires and to live sensibly, righteously and godly" (Titus 2:12). *True* freedom is emancipation from the slavery of sin. And to be freed from sin is to be a slave of righteousness (Romans 6:18).

Jerry Wragg and Paul Shirley unpack that truth in this excellent book, a wonderfully clear and helpful study of what the Bible says about sanctification, the mortification of sin, and the necessity of obedience in the Christian walk. This is a welcome resource—and a much-needed answer to the current flood of confusion about the relationship between grace and practical holiness.

> **John MacArthur**, Pastor-Teacher,
> Grace Community Church, Sun Valley, CA
> President,
> The Master's University and Seminary

Free to Be Holy tosses a lifeline to those who imagine that being saved by grace demands no more than relaxed buoyancy. Indeed, while it is God's *grace alone* that saves us and bears us on into eternity, that same free grace calls for more than treading water. It demands a profound "obedience of faith" that labors to God's glory—as did the apostle Paul, who declared, "But by the grace of God I am what I am, and his grace toward me was not in vain. On the contrary, I worked harder than any of them, though it was not I, but the grace of God that is in me" (1 Cor 15:10). This careful work by Jerry Wragg and Paul Shirley is sure to liberate many from the thrall of antinomianism, to a soaring life of graced Scriptural obedience to God's ever-freeing will.

R. Kent Hughes, Senior Pastor Emeritus,
College Church, Wheaton, IL
Visiting Professor of Pastoral Theology,
Westminster Theological Seminary, Philadelphia, PA

Holiness is not a coincidental byproduct of grace that just happens by passive reflection. John Stott reminds us that "holiness is not a condition into which we drift. We are not passive spectators of a sanctification God works in us." He's right! The lavish grace of Christ makes us free from our sin *and* free to be holy! This profound truth has fallen on hard times. The reason is, I surmise, we've been lied to. Peddlers of cheap grace are leading us to believe that biblical imperatives are opposed to gospel indicatives, loving God's Law is a heretical retreat to works, and liberation from sin means using a veneer of "grace" as a cover to indulge the flesh. Holy striving has been replaced with a modern update of "let go and let God" which, ironically, doesn't make the gospel more appealing but sin more enslaving.

Pastors Wragg and Shirley show us a more excellent way filled with real gospel encouragements. They offer us more than hollow platitudes or shallow quips. From a multitude of angles, the authors help us see that a pure heart, a clear conscience, and a sincere faith do not merely bloom in the Christian life as if it were some wild flower we just happen upon. The true flower of biblical sanctification is rooted by Christ in gospel soil and carefully cultivated by a life of faith enabled by the Spirit's power. I praise the Lord for this volume and pray it will be received by a needy church and a hungry people.

Paul Lamey, Pastor,
Grace Community Church, Huntsville, AL

While there are many areas believers cannot afford to be confused about, the doctrine of sanctification is one of the most important. Although Reformed theology has traditionally been known for its robust understanding of how believers actively grow in holiness, recent trends in some Reformed circles have posited that attempts to grow spiritually by employing the means of grace amount to works-based, legalistic, or pietistic Christianity. These voices advocate for less effort in the pursuit of holiness and more resting in the finished work of Christ, less trying and more trusting, less Law and more grace. This unbalanced understanding of sanctification threatens to derail a believer's genuine, God-empowered efforts at personal holiness. Recognizing this danger, Wragg and Shirley offer a necessary corrective by detailing the New Testament's emphasis on the believer's responsibility to strive for and actively seek sanctification. With insightful wisdom and pastoral care, they re-center the pendulum by carefully noting the balanced manner in which Scripture describes both the believer's positional sanctification and their responsibility to make progress in the Christian life. This book is a must-read for any true follower of Christ who is serious about their holiness!

Todd Dykstra, Teaching Pastor,
Maranatha Bible Church, Comstock Park, MI

While the glorious truth of justification is an incredibly important doctrine for the believer, the doctrine of sanctification may be even more critical. Why? Perhaps it is because this aspect of our salvation constitutes the entirety of the Christian's spiritual life and not merely at the initial declaration of our righteousness in Christ. And while we also await our complete holiness in heaven—important as this aspect of our salvation is to our present and future hope of glory—we must now be occupied chiefly with our dogged pursuit of grace-infused obedience. If you therefore, as a disciple of the Lord Jesus, are looking for sound biblical teaching so that you are wonderfully free to be holy, then read this book!

Lance Quinn, Senior Pastor
Bethany Church on the Hill, Thousand Oaks, CA

Many Christians today are busy unhitching the wagon of sanctification from the horse of justification. And in the place of sanctification (a steady, submissive Spirit-produced obedience), they have harnessed a feelings-dominated, meditative Christianity that is strong on gospel-centeredness, spirituality, and "intermittent emotional flings with Christ," but weak on mortifying anger, forsaking worldliness, and not viewing pornography. Contrary to the thinking of many Christians today, obeying the Bible is not legalism—in fact, it's the normal, Christ-assisted thing for a Christian to do. Wragg and Shirley do an excellent job in this book of covering these issues: they wisely reject unbiblical extremes, such as self-atoning legalism and passive emotionalism, refusing to become "dangerously one-dimensional" in regard to spiritual growth. But more than that, they re-hitch the wagon, explaining the right relationship between justification and daily obedience, and color in the picture wonderfully by explaining the right function of faith, adoration, duty, and commands in the Christian life. Read and be blessed!

Joel James, Pastor-Teacher,
Grace Fellowship, Pretoria, South Africa

Much has been written concerning the extremes of antinomianism and legalism. Some in the church have migrated dangerously close to one or the other of these twin evils. Others, in a misguided effort to avoid them, look for a supposed "balanced" way in the middle. The problem is their definition of "balance"— being a little bit antinomian and a little bit legalistic in the hopes of finding a safe way to live the Christian life. All the while Scripture keeps sounding consistent, timeless principles that clearly outline how God's people are sanctified. In short, the biblical way is faith-based and grace-strengthened and joy-filled effort to obey, grow, and mature so that Christ is pleased and glorified. And that's the way highlighted by the authors in this excellent resource—the way to enjoy both freedom in Christ and growth in Christ.

Carey Hardy, Senior Pastor,
Twin City Bible Church, Winston-Salem, NC

Theological pendulum swings have unfortunately adversely affected the biblical balance that God demands of those professing to belong to Christ. A recent trend has been causing an imbalance to Scripture's clear presentation of the indicative/imperative motif. Concerning the so-called Free Grace movement the biblical imperatives directed to believers are virtually expunged.

In this excellent volume Wragg and Shirley commendably restore biblical balance to this exceedingly vital issue pertaining to God's desire for "lives of holiness and godliness" (2 Peter 3:11, ESV). And most commendably they make their case not through pious-sounding appeals to emotions but through an exegetically-driven theology based upon a host of clear biblical texts.

Since this controversy is not merely a scholars' debate but pertains to the very essence of our sanctification, pastors and lay people alike need to understand the serious practical implications of it. Therefore, this book is a must for bringing God's people back to a biblical balance.

George J. Zemek, Academic Dean,
The Expositors Seminary

Free to Be Holy addresses a subject that is vital for all times but crucial for our time. It addresses a biblical mindset and the biblical means for progressive sanctification in the Christian life. It explains the relationship between justification and Christian growth. It answers popular errors that confuse believers about God's design for living a life of obedience to Christ. Jerry Wragg and Paul Shirley are careful exegetes and faithful pastoral guides on this subject. It is a timely offering, and I heartily recommend it.

Richard Caldwell, Pastor-Teacher,
Founders Baptist Church, Spring, TX

No other topic is more critical to the Christian life than progressive sanctification, and no other book addresses the believer's pursuit of holiness more effectively than this one.

Pastors Jerry Wragg and Paul Shirley have done a great service to the body of Christ in bringing biblical clarity to an issue that is so often shrouded in confusion. Whether you are a brand new Christian just starting out, or a mature believer who has been pursuing holiness for several decades, this book will provide the guidance you need to "work out your salvation with fear and trembling" (Phil 2:12). I couldn't recommend it more highly.

Matt Waymeyer, Associate Pastor,
Grace Immanuel Bible Church, Jupiter, FL

One weakness of many contemporary books about issues of doctrinal and spiritual significance is that they are written by authors who are detached from the practical and pastoral ramifications of those issues. That is not the case with this book! The authors of this book are deeply engaged in the care of souls and leadership of local assemblies, so this book is the fruit of their intense desire to know God's mind on this subject so that they can shepherd God's sheep with His truth. And that order is profoundly clear here—know God's mind first, then help God's people with the truth. The result is a book that is full of biblical truth and spiritually helpful application. This is theology for the church and I highly commend it!

Dave Doran, Pastor,
Inter-City Baptist Church, Allen Park, MI
President,
Detroit Baptist Theological Seminary, Allen Park, MI

What could be more important to the lives of Christians than to comprehend and faithfully conform to the biblical doctrine of sanctification? *Free to Be Holy* helps believers understand this vital doctrine through clear expositions of numerous biblical passages and through its insightful implications from those passages for the daily walk by faith we call the Christian life. This is a must-read for all who want to know the joy and freedom of pursuing a life of holiness.

Bob Whitney, Administrative Dean,
The Expositors Seminary

Survey contemporary presentations of the gospel and you will likely find the accents of forgiveness of sins (justification) and going to heaven (glorification). Usually missing from these majestic truths is the lifelong pursuit of holiness (sanctification). Not only is sanctification so often neglected, it is also terribly misunderstood. New voices are redefining sanctification and misleading Christ's bride to "continue in sin that grace may abound" (Rom 6:1). Wragg and Shirley provide biblically rich counsel that answers this new trajectory with the apostle Paul's "By no means!" This book both corrects and counsels. It will point you to perspective and progress as you understand the lifelong pursuit of holiness.

Rick Holland, Senior Pastor,
Mission Road Bible Church, Prairie Village, KS

I have been in local church ministry for fifty years, and one of the things that greives me most is to see Christ's precious sheep languishing, struggling, and atrophying in their walk with Christ. Sadly, too often, struggling people are given unhelpful and even dangerous ideas on how to remedy their struggle. Jerry Wragg and Paul Shirley by contrast have written a volume that not only rightly diagnoses why people struggle in their walk with Christ, but also offers a thorough and comprehensive study on what it means to live a fruitful and faith-fueled walk with Christ. The church will be strengthened by this work.

Alexander Strauch, Author,
Biblical Eldership and *Leading with Love*

FREE TO BE HOLY

The Liberating Grace of Walking by Faith

Jerry Wragg & Paul Shirley

Grace Immanuel Bible Church, Jupiter, FL, USA

Published by
Grace Immanuel Bible Church
17475 Jonathan Drive, Jupiter, FL 33477, USA.
gibcjupiter.org

*

*

ISBN 978-0-578-44726-1

*

Typeset in 11/14 Adobe Caslon Pro

*

DEDICATION

To the men who have been and will be trained at
The Expositors Seminary,
along with a myriad of faithful pastors
who serve Christ's church.

The best shepherds and the most effective preachers
are men with a clear insight into the realities
and implications of biblical sanctification.

To this end we pray that the truths contained in this book
will develop into lifelong convictions that will guide
your ministry to the church.

CONTENTS

Acknowledgments   xv

Preface by Jerry Wragg   xvii

Preface by Paul Shirley   xxiii

Introduction   1

PART 1: SAVED FOR HOLINESS

  1. Saved to Be Holy   15

  2. Saved to Trust and Obey   33

  3. Saved to Walk by Faith   53

  4. Saved from Sin's Tyranny   73

  5. Saved to Love God's Law   85

  6. Saved for Life in the Spirit   101

PART 2: GRACE FOR HOLINESS

  7. Enslaved by Grace   119

  8. Means of Grace (Part 1)   127

  9. Means of Grace (Part 2)   143

PART 3: DISCERNMENT FOR HOLINESS

 10. Discerning Progress   163

 11. Discerning Assurance   177

 12. Discerning a Way Forward   195

    Appendix 1: How Does God Feel?   211

    Appendix 2: A Puritan View of Faith, Feelings,   221
     and Affections

    Selected Bibliography   231

    Scripture Index   233

ACKNOWLEDGMENTS

I NNUMERABLE friends, colleagues, and mentors contributed to this volume through their encouragement, input, and discipleship. Special thanks are particularly in order to our editors, Whitney Oxford, Matthew Waymeyer, Paul Lamey, Todd Murray, Jon Anderson, and Joel James, who enhanced the clarity, precision, and persuasion of our writing.

Additionally, we are thankful for Anna Scheffer and Amanda Henneman (invaluable behind-the-scenes administrative and ministry support), Daron Roberts and Kenny Hartman (exceptional concept creativity, project oversight, and execution), and many other faithful servants at Grace Immanuel Bible Church who lent hands to this ministry effort. We're also very grateful to Brian Arnold and Kevin Huang for their research work. And a special thank you to Kristin Davis (administrative staff, Grace Community Church, Wilmington) for her diligent labor on this project.

The time and effort necessary for a writing project requires the support and encouragement of an entire team of elders, which both of us have. The elders at GIBC and GccWilm have proven themselves to be faithful shepherds and loyal friends. We are both honored and privileged to call these men brothers and co-laborers for the gospel. Without them we would not be able to devote time and thought to writing.

Furthermore, we are both blessed to serve churches that love the truth and earnestly desire to grow in godliness. Both of our congregations listened to many of these chapters in sermon form before they ever made it onto a written page. It is hard to imagine that this book would have been completed without the encouragement of their diligence to hear the truth, graciousness toward imperfect communicators of truth, and hunger for the grace of truth.

Finally, we are indebted to the loving and sacrificial ministry of our wives: Louise Wragg and Elyse Shirley. These ladies are special gifts of grace for the church and for their husbands. Their support, input, and love for the truth fueled our writing. We are inexpressibly thankful to pursue holiness alongside such godly women.

PREFACE BY JERRY WRAGG

I WAS converted to Christ thirty-six years ago while serving in
the United States military. The Lord had graciously assigned
a passionate Christian to our radar station several miles north
of the Arctic Circle in Alaska. The night I repented and believed
in Christ, I remember making a desperate phone call to my father
asking him to send a Bible and any materials on Christianity
101. I had grown up in the church so I knew the gospel, but I
was suddenly overcome by grief that I had wasted so much time.
Even at the age of twenty-one, I had already spent many years in
gross hypocrisy. My excitement overflowed two weeks later upon
receiving my father's care package. That day, I opened the cover of
my first study Bible, I began to read my first theological work (J.
I. Packer's *Knowing God*), and for the first time as a Christian, I
heard an expository sermon (on cassette tape—remember those?).
Looking back, that moment was life altering.

The clarity of the whole counsel of God, preached right from
the text of Scripture, shaped my ripening appetite for the truth.
Listening to an average six sermons a day, I learned to recognize
the *unity and balance* of God's Word. That first study series in the
care package—from the pulpit ministry of Dr. John MacArthur—
explained Matthew 6:9–13, the Lord's prayer. The grace of my
redemption just poured out of every verse. I was humbled by the
astonishing access I had to the throne of God through Christ ("Our
Father ..."). And another spiritual first occurred: I was introduced
to the sovereign grace that had given me such freedom ("Your
Father knows what you need before you ask Him."). I learned how
to pray, what to pray, and the humility that makes it genuine.

Yet, the second tape series in that package, *The Believer's Armor* (from Eph 6:10ff), equally and dramatically shaped my convictions about how the Holy Spirit worked through my spiritual efforts. There I was, a new believer by grace alone, and the Scriptures were calling me to a spiritual battle. It required the daily regimen of "putting on" spiritual armor (convictions forged in the fires of faith). It called for integrity at the core of my life ("belt of truthfulness") and sure-footed urgency ("feet shod with the gospel of peace"). I was to put on the "helmet" and "breastplate," and "take up the shield of faith" and "sword of the Spirit." The power was all of God, but I was commanded to obediently stand my ground. The Holy Spirit provided strength, and His Word turned my earthly thoughts into the mind of Christ.

So it was the theologically precise exposition of texts that taught me about justification and sanctification. I understood from the beginning that growing in the grace and knowledge of the Lord Jesus Christ was not an option (2 Pet 3:18). Sin's absolute sway in my life was over. Christ had put that bondage to death and my old imprisoned self with it (Rom 6:6–11). But the daily fight of faith to "[put] to death the deeds of the body" (Rom 8:13) was also clearly and frequently talked about on almost every page of God's Word. I cut my spiritual teeth on being a slave of Jesus Christ, living by faith, yielding to the Spirit, and growing in the disciplines of faithfulness. Scripture taught me to entrust myself to the grace of God for "everything pertaining to life and godliness" (2 Pet 1:3). I knew instantly the powerlessness of my own resources, and that I must "be strong *in the Lord*, and *in the strength of His might*" (Eph 6:10) But Scripture also taught me the privileged yoke of "having done everything, to stand firm" (Eph 6:13). God promises to conform me to the image of Jesus, but I have obligations and responsibilities through which He makes it happen.

In all those early studies, I never concluded that my responsibility to "fight the good fight of faith" (1 Tim 6:12) would threaten to nullify the grace that had saved me. I never imagined that the imperatives of Scripture were in conflict with the indicatives. It was simple Bible math for me. Every time I came across a "therefore" in the New Testament, I assumed that the grace of God *before* the "therefore" was the ground and power of commands that followed. I am redeemed solely by the grace of God. He granted me the eyes of faith necessary to see the loveliness of Christ, and he produced in me a repentant heart to turn from self-worship. But He didn't save me so that I would be passive in the work He began. I knew that His riches went beyond pardon from sin. He also made His Spirit to dwell in me, providing power to obey. His commands, therefore, seemed the next logical step in the progress toward being "conformed to the image of [Christ]" (Rom 8:29). He is Lord. I'm His disciple. I'm to observe all that He has commanded (Matt 28:19–20). It never dawned on me that heartily striving to obey *in humility and faith* would be considered by some as a trampling of grace.

Move forward nearly thirty years. In 2010, I asked our pastoral staff to join me in an extensive study of the doctrine of sanctification. By that time, my concern had grown over what seemed to me a dangerous trajectory among younger evangelicals regarding spiritual growth. I began hearing phrases such as "Christians have no obligation to obey commands," "The gospel is not about what we do, but what Christ has done," and "We obey out of love, not duty." A new generation of young believers seemed to be passionately celebrating the grace of justification while ignoring the spiritual means of grace for sanctification. Upon completing our study as a staff, we decided that I would preach a series of expositions on how to grow in the Christian life. It actually resulted in two separate sermon series, one dealing with each feature of the broader doctrine of salvation, and the other dealing with progressive sanctification particularly. Not surprisingly, at least to me, was the fact that our collegians and young singles—today's Millennials—expressed repeatedly that they had never understood the believer's active role in the spiritual disciplines. Victory over sin had eluded so many in our midst, and spiritual defeat was where many of them lived day to day. Finally, through the study of the relationship between our justification and sanctification, our young people were beginning to gain victory over their sin as never before. And it has been thrilling to see! It's as though I have a front row seat to a replay of my early years as a new Christian.

This book is the result of several years of study with our pastoral team, as well as the content from the two pulpit series. Part one sets forth the why of our salvation: to what end did God save sinners? In this section we cover:

- the centrality of holiness as the target in progressive sanctification;

- how justification relates to sanctification;

- the troubling rise of subjective Christianity and its effect on evangelicalism's understanding of spiritual growth;

- the biblical definition of faith and the worthy walk;

- how the gospel empowers us with the grace to put sin to death;

- our relationship to the Law; and

- the death of the old man.

Section two deals with primarily the means of grace given by God for our spiritual growth. The third section deals with:

- properly diagnosing spiritual difficulties in our battle with sin;

- understanding the similarities and differences between eternal security, personal assurance, and the struggle with doubts; and

- forging a balanced path forward in discussions on sanctification.

If the body of Christ is edified in even small ways, and struggling sheep find hope and spiritual victory through this work, it will have honored the Chief Shepherd, for whom we are unworthy slaves doing only what we ought to have done (Luke 17:10).

PREFACE BY PAUL SHIRLEY

VAGUE platitudes won't help you grow spiritually. I learned this lesson as a young believer. The Lord had given me an insatiable hunger to study the Bible. I started reading on my own, attending Bible studies, and taking the Sunday morning sermons much more seriously. One Sunday, outfitted with a new notebook and pen, I sat listening to a guest preacher. Forty-five minutes into the sermon I looked at my notes and realized that the only thing I had written down was the date, the speaker's name, and the Scripture passage announced in the bulletin (which I could not remember whether the speaker had read). At that point I knew the sermon would end soon and I had to write something down. Finally, after announcing three conclusions, he said something I could add to my notes: "Let go and let God." He told us that this was the main point of his sermon, and the secret to the Christian life. I could not believe that no one had ever given me this information before, and I eagerly transcribed his words exactly onto my blank page. But as I did, something happened. Before I could finish writing his words I realized that I had no idea what they meant. I looked back at the speaker to see if he would provide any explanation, but he had already begun the closing prayer.

I left church that day very frustrated that I did not understand the most important principle for the Christian life. After lunch, I got out my notebook and Bible to see if I could figure out this enigmatic statement on a full stomach. After fifteen minutes of praying, studying, and thinking, my desperation dissipated when it dawned on me that I could not wrap my mind around "Let go and let God" because it does not mean anything. It is not in the Bible, it does not teach me who God is, and it definitely does not provide a plausible pattern for Christian living. Sure, it sounds great, but in the midst of a trial can it lead me to faithfulness? Can I fight temptation and pursue Christ with it? Does it help me to worship Christ above all? No! It is a vague half-truth without biblical moorings. If you put it on a t-shirt or greeting card you would probably make a lot of money, but coming from the pulpit it is not sanctifying.

By now, almost everyone knows that "Let go and let God" is basically meaningless and totally useless in the midst of real spiritual struggles. Eventually the phrase went out of style as people grew weary of hearing it repeated and frustrated at its lack of potency. But not long ago, when the guest preacher passionately exhorted the congregation with this slogan, a lot of people thought it was profound. Initially, no one seemed to recognize its vacuous nature. At least, no one warned me about it. Most people were pleased with a catchy slogan and didn't seem interested in discerning its biblical accuracy or spiritual profitability.

My fear is that a whole new set of superficial and basically useless platitudes have crept into the vocabulary of the church today. Many of them sound great; plus, they are perfectly tailored for retweeting and sharing. But upon close examination there is not much truth contained in some of the most common slogans for the Christian life. Theological-sounding mantras seemed to have replaced actual theology.

I am deeply concerned that some of my ministry comrades have settled for an appreciation of superficial methods that are marketed to appear Calvinistic, but have departed from the Scripture-saturated teaching of Calvin. At the same time, many of my dear siblings in Christ are languishing in spiritual stagnation because they do not understand the practical mechanics of sanctification set forth in the Scriptures. In many cases, Christians have been cut off from the sanctifying resources promised in the Bible because they have never heard of them.

Soul-sustaining truth has been rejected and replaced with tweetable musings. As a result, spiritual growth remains a mystery that remains unexplained for many. Some Christians grow rapidly, others do not, and neither knows why. Progress becomes enigmatic, stumbling becomes expected, and the process of sanctification, designed to be edifying, becomes exasperating. In desperation, Christians look elsewhere to fill the void left by this lack of instruction. Sometimes they look for answers from within, and other times they seek direction from the world. Either way, it's not pretty. Instead of proven biblical strategies for spiritual growth, visceral impulses and worldly pragmatism chart the course of sanctification. Along the way, there are no reference points to make sure they are heading in the right direction— except that if it feels right, it must be working.

Thankfully, the solution to the problem is simple: we need to go back to the Book. The Bible paints a detailed picture of what sanctification looks like, and we need to start referring to that picture to put the puzzle pieces of our spiritual life together. How do we do that? We begin by admonishing Christians to abandon unbiblical and "abiblical" models of growth, and accept what the Bible says about spiritual maturity. The wisdom of this world will never produce the sanctification of God because, as 1 Corinthians 3:19 reminds us, "the wisdom of this world is foolishness before God." Christians who seek self-help techniques, pop psychology, and sentimental spirituality of this age should not expect progress in sanctification. Additionally, we need to stop celebrating and settling for the shallowest forms of teaching just because they are marketable and not overtly heretical.

Spiritual maturity flows from understanding, believing, and appropriating biblical truth at its deepest level. In order to be helpful to God's people, teaching requires one indispensable ingredient—truth with clarity. God's Word must be clear and present in order for a believer to experience any sanctifying power. It is the Word of God alone that provides the power promised for sanctification. It does not matter how engaging, articulate, or compelling a method might be, if it does not bring the Scripture with clarity and conform my thinking to the mind of Christ, it will not benefit me spiritually. Vague platitudes won't grow God's people. As a young believer, I hungered for something deeper than platitudes, and I am convinced there are many believers still hungering for the meat of the truth. If this study on sanctification can provide direction, clarity, and encouragement to even one of these hungering Christians, it will be an answer to my prayers.

INTRODUCTION

THE chorus of one of my favorite old hymns says, "Grace, grace, God's grace; Grace that will pardon and cleanse within." Many times I heard the senior saints of my childhood church bellowing those words with gusto. They were just old sounding songs to me at the time. But after my conversion that melody and particular line from the chorus penetrated deep into my soul. The sovereign grace of God alone had drawn me, convicted me of my wretchedness, granted me repentance and faith, and opened my eyes to see the loveliness of the Savior! His grace had indeed pardoned me.

But the second truth of that lyric has been equally thrilling to my soul through the years. The grace of God is also sure to "cleanse within." I'm not only declared righteous before God, but I'm also truly being conformed to the image of Jesus Christ. The grace that purchased my justification also mightily works in my sanctification. Recent books and articles are notably passionate about the doctrine of justification. For the first time many are grasping the truth of *sola gratia*—it is grace alone that saves! New songs about the glory of the cross and our freedom from sin's bondage are being written almost weekly. Young people are rightly praising God for the grace that makes us acceptable in Christ alone. These are amazing days for the church and a testimony to the kindness of God in magnifying His truth with such power and clarity.

But what about the equally vital doctrine of sanctification? We know that a condemned sinner cannot, on his own, bring his dead heart to life. Mercy comes running to the sinner. By

God's sovereign initiation He "made us alive together with Christ … so that no one may boast" (Eph 2:5, 9). But does our sanctification work in exactly the same way? Now that we have been declared righteous and have been set apart unto God, what do we do with the remaining sin that "so easily entangles us" (Heb 12:1)? As God's grace conforms us to the image of Christ, what is our role, if any? Are we passive subjects, transformed by the Spirit, while we make no proactive effort to do God's will? Or should we strive to flee sin and submit to Scripture? Do we simply contemplate our freedom in the gospel, confident that power over sin will simply begin to occur? Evangelicals seem increasingly confused about how to answer these questions. Sometimes called "Gospel Sanctification," a view has become popular that believers grow merely by repeatedly pondering the gospel to generate a grateful, and therefore obedient, heart. Proponents allege that since our justification was accomplished by grace alone through regeneration, our spiritual growth occurs essentially the same way—without the collaboration of human effort. Many today fear that laboring to obey the commands of Scripture is a plunge into the self-atonement trap, trying to do what Christ has already done. There is a growing theological divide along these lines, which is leading to serious imbalance for some and dangerous error for others. With the upsurge of joy over justification have come several misguided ideas about how God's grace operates in sanctification.

JUSTIFICATION'S "INSTANT REPLAY"

Evangelicalism's recent obsession with terms like "gospel-centered" and "grace-driven" is the wonderful fruit of clearer, more biblical teaching on the *solas* of the Reformation. They are great terms. They resonate with all who desire to live for the glory of Christ in response to His grace freely given to us. It's why we slap these terms on book covers, use them in songs, and attach them to almost everything in ministry. Perhaps it's also why we can be vulnerable to over-applying them in ways that foster confusion. Unfortunately, being "gospel-centered" today has become synonymous with being against any kind of holy striving. To put forth human effort in the progress of Christian growth is, they claim, to trample grace and return to the Law. Some popular books on the topic have only added to the confusion by forcing this emphasis into passages of Scripture which emphasize our responsibility in the spiritual growth process. For example, in 2011, one author wrote,

> Think of it this way: Sanctification is the daily hard work of going back to the reality of our justification ... . Realizing this has changed the entire way I read the Bible. Think of what Paul tells us in Philippians 2:12; "Work out your salvation with fear and trembling." We've got work to do—but what exactly is it? Get better? Try harder? Pray more? Get more involved at church? Read the Bible longer? What precisely is Paul exhorting us to do? He goes on to explain: "For it is God who works in you, both to will and to work for his good pleasure." (v. 13) God works *his* work in *you*, which is the work already accomplished by Christ ... . By continuing to place your trust in Christ's finished work, and by learning to do this more and more ... all that is your possession already in fact—now becomes increasingly yours in experience.[1]

This view resonates with massive numbers of people who seem relieved that they no longer need to be concerned with trying to obey God's Word. Being conformed to the image of Christ consists of "hitting the refresh button"[2] on our justified standing—a kind of fresh-faith instant replay to free us from the burden of "trying harder." Paul's command to work out our salvation is not, therefore, a call for holy striving, but a command to remember, contemplate, and believe that Christ has already accomplished everything. The effort we're called to exert is the determination to rest, knowing we're acceptable to God through Christ. To prevent

[1] Tullian Tchividjian, *Jesus + Nothing = Everything* (Wheaton, IL: Crossway, 2011), Kindle Electronic Edition: Chapter 7, Location 94–95; emphases original.
[2] Ibid., 95.

legalism we merely ruminate on saving grace until our affections and passions turn Christward, overwhelming us with holy delight unto obedience.

Upon examination, however, Philippians 2:12–13 does not encourage mere contemplation at all. Paul teaches that our proactive striving "with fear and trembling" is *the very means* by which God's grace transforms us. Grace is the *ground and power* of spiritual change, and faith-filled human effort is the *means of grace* through which Christ's power is always working. Preaching gospel grace "to ourselves every day"[3] is good medicine, provided we understand grace from a biblical perspective. According to God's Word, mentally replaying the grace of salvation is not all that's required to fight sin and generate good works. We grow by grace alone, but God has chosen to dispense His grace as we "work out" our salvation. He is working in and through our efforts. Spiritual change is energized, not by any natural resource we bring to the table, but only in His willing and working in us "for His good pleasure" (Phil 2:13) as we trust and obey.

LAW VERSUS GRACE

Current confusion about sanctification has led also to error about the relationship between Law and grace. Charges of "legalism" and "self-atonement" are quickly being leveled at anyone who describes sanctification in terms of striving, obedience, submission, or mortifying sin. Many see the greatest problem in the church today as the drive to conform. The church seems to be running as fast as it can away from any emphasis on our obligation to obey God. People do not want to think of their growth in Christ as something they "must do" but only something they "want to do." Instead of desiring the freedom and power to strive

[3] This concept was first popularized by Jerry Bridges, *The Discipline of Grace* (Colorado Springs: NavPress, 1994). He meant it as a practical tool for helping Christians who believe they have forfeited God's love because of disobedience. I'm sure he never envisioned that the concept would later become linked with the neo-antinomian idea that sanctification is merely contemplating the grace of justification.

for holiness of life, they want a kind of freedom from holy obligation itself. And this view is fast producing in Christians, not a concern for pleasing God and obeying His Word, but a shocking disdain for His commands. They see the commands in Scripture as having "the Law" hanging over them, which they've been told is the same as being a Pharisee. And so they resist any growth that would require them to obey. That doesn't seem like freedom to them. One popular author wrote,

> The greatest cause for our not getting better is our obsession [over] not getting better. There is a better way of getting better than trying harder. Sanctification becomes a reality in those believers who don't obsess over their own sanctification.[4]

Actually, 2 Peter 1:5 teaches the opposite: "applying all diligence, in your faith supply moral excellence."

We are called, so to speak, to try harder "in … faith." Where sin is concerned, Scripture always places culpability, not on high moral standards or our duty to obey, but squarely on our lack of faith. And even self-atoning tendencies (legalism) are rooted, not in striving to obey Scripture's dos and don'ts, but in *believing that conformity equals spiritual merit.* Martyn Lloyd-Jones was insightful on this issue:

> We must be diligent in our seeking [Hebrews 11:6]. "But," says someone, "your preaching, is it not an inculcation of justification by works?" … The answer to that argument is that it is the Apostle Peter … who goes out of his way to remind us … that we must "add" to our faith these various other things and to give all diligence in the doing of it. Be more zealous, be still more active, he says. And, of course, there is no contradiction at all. The error of justification by works is in trusting to the discipline of your own soul to save your soul; but the opposite to trusting your works is not to do nothing, it is to do everything but not to put your trust in any of it. It is not the works that are wrong, it is the faith in your works, trusting in your works. But what a subtle danger this is. … The opposite to a false trust in works

⁴ Steve Brown, *A Scandalous Freedom* (New York: Howard Books, 2004), 60.

is not indolence, lack of discipline and doing nothing, it is to be diligent and more diligent, to be zealous, and to add to your faith.[5]

It is concerning when someone preaches gospel-centeredness *as an argument against* those who are striving to obey God's commands *in the freedom of the gospel.* We seem to be confused as to what is at the heart of Pharisaism. Striving in God's grace and power does not, indeed cannot, produce legalism. We are free indeed, but it is not a freedom to be unholy until God decides He wants to change our character. Our freedom in salvation comes with divine power embedded in its deliverance from sin.

In conversion we are set free from the death grip of sin and guilt (Rom 8:2), and we have the indwelling Holy Spirit working to give us victory over temptation (Eph 6:16). God has defined the freedom we now have in Christ. It is the freedom and power to obey. His grace alone grants us the ability to overcome sin, and yet the same grace that quickened our dead hearts also teaches and empowers us "to deny ungodliness and worldly desires and to live sensibly, righteously and godly" (Titus 2:12). As long as genuine faith in the Word of Christ and humble submission to Him as Lord are behind our obedience, then there is no danger of being a hypocrite. We morph into Pharisees when we begin to *trust in our righteousness* as the measure of our spirituality. Worse, it is the height of hypocrisy to profess true freedom and a desire to be like Jesus while ignoring His designed path to enjoying that freedom.

If you don't want to fall into the trap of Pharisaism, the safeguard is not demanding freedom from holy obligations, but to keep from looking inward and *trusting in* your own ability to be holy. The classic signs of legalism and moralism are pride in one's own righteousness. If you love to parade your spirituality in front of others to be praised by them, you are a hypocrite (Matt 6:5, 16). If you serve God or others to be admired as uber-spiritual, you

---

[5] D. Martyn Lloyd-Jones, *Spiritual Depression: Its Causes and Cure* (Grand Rapids: Eerdmans, 1965), 210–11.

have become a Pharisee. If you measure your spiritual maturity solely by your disciplined conduct, you are moralistic. These are the sure signs of self-righteousness and hypocrisy. Striving to humbly obey God's commands cannot be self-righteousness. It is neither legalism nor moralism to humbly believe Scripture and yield your will to Christ in obedience. At the very *center* of the gospel is the Holy Spirit of grace who assures us of His power to obey. To be gospel-centered is to live every moment of every day in the conscious presence of Christ. It is to "walk by the Spirit" (Gal 5:16) so that we have victory over "the deeds of the flesh" (Gal 5:19). To live in the power of the gospel is to listen to Christ, to trust Him, to fear Him, to submit to Him, to serve Him, and to adore Him. How can anyone claim to be "gospel-centered" and depreciate the very commandments of Jesus at its center?

But some may ask, *Doesn't the gospel of grace mean that Jesus has done everything for us? If we spend our time striving to conform to the commands Jesus already obeyed for us, won't we quickly slip into mere law-keeping and end up cold, lifeless and disillusioned?* Let's be clear: God has accomplished our redemption by His sovereign grace alone. We were dead in sin when He made us alive, granted us repentance and faith, and delivered us from the domain of darkness into the kingdom of His dear Son. And if we spent our days nurturing unbelief by trying to earn God's love through spiritual-sounding words and behavior modification, we would experience the same guilt and weakness suffered by all self-atoning legalists. Such pride always ends in disillusionment and despair. But if we truly believe the gospel, our submission to Christ will not be for the purpose of adding anything to His cross, but rather to magnify His glory through the display of His power. To live out the gospel is to cherish and appropriate the power of the gospel so that Jesus Christ is fully formed in us (Gal 4:19).

And this is what our Lord emphasized most throughout His earthly ministry. All of us would affirm that the Lord was the embodiment of all that the Father desired in carrying out the work of the church. There has never been anyone more gospel-centered than the Lord of glory Himself! He is the supreme object of all gospel interest and mission. He is the message and the very heart of all true means for carrying out His saving work among the nations. To worship Jesus Christ is to exalt and honor His saving message as the centerpiece of all we do. But what did "gospel-centeredness" mean to the Lord?

JESUS' DEFINITION OF GOSPEL-CENTEREDNESS

Jesus gave us a glimpse of what He would have considered to be gospel-centered ministry when He delivered the Great Commission: "Go therefore and make disciples of all the nations, baptizing them in the name of the Father and the Son and the Holy Spirit, teaching them to observe all that I commanded you" (Matt 28:19–20). Notice that Jesus didn't say "all that I *taught* you." He specifically used the New Testament word for *commandment*. Jesus did instruct. He taught and explained the Old Testament Scriptures to His disciples, helping them to understand the manifold grace of God in the arrival of the Messiah. Over a period just short of three years, Jesus gave His ministry companions a comprehensive soteriology. But He also systematically taught them every other truth needed to carry out the Great Commission. And when He finally launched them as His ambassadors, His blueprint for gospel-centered ministry was simple: make disciples of all nations, baptize every new convert, and begin teaching them to obey all of His commandments.

To put it bluntly: being gospel-centered does *not* mean we talk only of being justified by grace alone through faith alone in Christ alone. Those three *solas* are certainly the heart of the good news—the fulcrum upon which redemption turns. But justifying grace is not the sum total of the forgiveness Christ accomplished, nor did He leave us to speculate on our spiritual privileges and duties—not by a long shot. A life centered on the truths of the gospel is a life under the authority and power of the whole counsel of God! It is a walk of faith, living by every word that proceeds from the Lord. Being truly gospel-centered—if it means anything—ultimately means being conformed to the image of Christ (Rom 8:29; Col 3:1–12). It means striving to be holy "according to His power, which mightily works within" us (Col 1:29). It's about walking by faith in the truth and not being paralyzed by less-than-perpetual emotional highs. Being Christ-centered means obeying and teaching others to obey *all* that Jesus commanded.

For many today, such a description of the Christian life seems humdrum. It doesn't sound to them like a very passion-driven way to live. After all, if we're in Christ by His grace alone, shouldn't we be the most emotionally-overwhelmed-by-love-and-gratitude kind of people on the planet? Isn't that a more gospel-centered life than one of trying to crank up obedience through the almost inevitable drudgery of spiritual disciplines?

The answer to the first question is yes. Because of Christ we should always be overwhelmed by love and gratitude. But deep conviction about the truth is what fuels spiritual growth, not emotionally-charged experiences. In fact, the more we learn from Scripture about our redemption, entrust our lives to the truth, and yield our will to Christ in the power of the Spirit, the more our convictions deepen. And the deeper the roots of conviction, the sweeter and more overwhelming will be the fruit of gratitude. If all you're doing is using thoughts about grace to stir up thankful emotions, you'll eventually end up disappointed. Emotions—especially of fallen sinners—are not to be trusted until they, too, are sanctified as a result of obedient faith. Love and gratitude toward God are always proven through humble faith and conformity to His will. Thus, to be gospel-centered requires us to live in the power of gospel grace, learning to obey the commands given to us by that same grace.

Back to the second question above: aren't spiritual disciplines destined to become lifelessly external? Not at all. Spiritual disciplines aren't drudgery—not if they are pursued through a robust faith in the truth. We can't replace the discipline of grace with thankfulness for grace since gratitude itself is a practiced discipline. Gospel-centeredness is therefore defined by the "obedience of faith" (Rom 1:5; 16:26), not bare thankfulness (Heb 11:1–40). If your walk with Christ isn't producing a love for His commands, your "gospel-centeredness" is way *off-centered.*

GOSPEL "OFF-CENTERED"

If your desire to obey Christ is dependent on whether you feel strong emotions toward Christ, you've become dangerously one-dimensional in your spiritual growth. Living a life centered on the gospel will always reflect far more than intermittent emotional flings with Christ. It will result in a growing faith and conformity to His righteous will. Anyone claiming a gospel pulse can't have thoroughly clogged arteries to the will of Christ. The danger of becoming out of balance necessitates deep and honest self-examination. You are gospel off-centered if:

- you think worship is primarily about emotional "closeness" with God.

- your walk with Christ is mostly about "sensing God's presence" rather than knowing and trusting in the Word of God.

- you're convinced that fearing God is not a biblical motivation for obedience.

- you believe that grace nullifies all moral duty to Christ.

- you think that union with Christ means spiritual growth "just happens" without actively killing sin.

- you've assumed that emotional sensations *always precede or accompany* obedience.

- you think saying no to the flesh should never be a spiritually painful battle.

- you think self-discipline and striving to be holy are inherently legalistic.

- you believe true conversion doesn't always involve separation from the world.

- your Christian life is driven by subjective experiences rather than humble faith in God's Word.

This list can help you determine if you have drifted from the biblical center. A thoroughly biblical view of sanctification is absolutely crucial to flourishing in the Christian life. Thankfully, the doctrine of justification has returned to its former pre-eminence in contemporary evangelicalism. It is my fervent prayer that this volume is a careful examination of key questions, and that the biblical doctrine of sanctification is clarified, reaffirmed, and passionately celebrated, bringing greater balance to the new excitement over justification so prevalent today.

PART 1: SAVED FOR HOLINESS

CHAPTER 1

SAVED TO BE HOLY

I N the midst of a difficult trial, has someone ever said to you, "God is far more concerned with your holiness than your happiness"? Upon hearing it, did you recoil, wondering why God would not care about the joy of His people? And aside from the person's good intentions, if he meant that the believer's joy and gladness in the gospel is of no ultimate interest to God, he would have been mistaken. Within every believer is an undercurrent of unshakeable joy that can never be taken away (John 16:22). In that sense, God is concerned with our ultimate "happiness" because He defines what it is and how it is to be enjoyed. Yet the assertion about holiness is still valid. God's highest aim is "the peaceful fruit of righteousness" (Heb 12:11) cultivated in His people. Why? Because His beloved Son is righteous, and we have been "predestined to become conformed to the image of His Son" (Rom 8:29). Indeed, that is what it means to glorify God in all that we do (1 Cor 10:31). We are God's "workmanship, created in Christ Jesus for good works, which God prepared beforehand so that we would walk in them" (Eph 2:10).

God's agenda is, and always has been, that His people would be "created ... in righteousness and holiness of the truth" (Eph 4:24). We have been redeemed and set apart—sanctified—so that we might "put on the new self who is being renewed to a true knowledge according to the image of the One who created him" (Col 3:10). In a word, we are saved to be holy. And make no mistake: being conformed to the image of Christ in thought, word, and deed *is the path to true happiness and eternal communion with Him!* There is no real joy without freedom from sin's penalty, and no lasting happiness without the power to live a righteous life (Ps 45:7; 51:7–10). Holiness and true joy in the Holy Spirit are core features of God's future kingdom (Rom 14:17), and therefore should be the intense pursuit of every believer.

God is as concerned with holiness as He is with forgiveness; the two cannot be divided. No man can survive an encounter with God while still bearing the stain of sin, and no man can enjoy unhindered daily communion with God in this life apart from a vibrant pursuit of practical holiness. This is why every aspect of our glorious salvation is aimed at holiness in Christ. Christ redeemed His people for holiness (Col 1:21), and the Spirit calls His people in holiness (1 Thess 4:7–8). Holiness is not an addendum to gospel grace; it is at the heart of it. To study the doctrine of sanctification is to discover its central theme: holiness.

The hard reality is that while we await the glorious return of our Lord Jesus Christ, God's redemptive priorities are not always reflected in us. We are free to be holy, but we do not always live like it. Though new creatures in Christ, we are accustomed to serving the "god" of our old fleshly appetites (Phil 3:19). Growing in holiness involves confronting the vestiges of remaining sin and putting them to death (Rom 8:13), even when it is agonizing to do so. Sinful appetites—no matter how ravenous—are starved when we submit to the Spirit (Gal 5:16–24). Our old disposition must be increasingly conformed to the mind of Christ (1 Cor 2:16)—no matter how deep that old logic might be entrenched. If we delight ourselves in the Lord, we must detach ourselves from the lustful pleasures that so easily entice us. Because God is holy, those who profess His name should reflect who He is (1 Pet 1:14–16).

Despite the Bible's clarion call to holiness, we often neglect or misunderstand these simple principles. The slow, painful process of spiritual growth, combined with the strength of sinful desires, can easily discourage us and stall our pursuit of holiness. As J. C. Ryle observes, "These are they who cannot find it in their hearts to quarrel with their besetting sin, whether it be sloth, indolence, ill-temper, pride, selfishness, impatience, or what it may. They allow it to remain a tolerably quiet and undisturbed tenant of their hearts."[1] With enough time and inertia, neglect turns to contempt for the commands of Scripture that demand holy living.

With alarming frequency, people are circulating deficient views of holiness in many churches. At one extreme are those who conceive of holiness as gained through following man-made rules and preferences rather than grace. Swinging the pendulum to the opposite extreme, some confuse any exhortation to holy living with Pharisaical legalism. Under the banner of grace, they have come to resent the idea of personal holiness. One extreme distorts the pursuit of holiness while the other ignores it altogether.

But holiness and grace are neither unrelated nor opposed. God provided gospel grace *so that* His people could become holy. As John Owen explained, "Holiness is nothing but the implanting, writing and living out of the gospel in our souls."[2] In other words, sanctifying power is never missing from gospel grace. The same grace that frees the believer from the guilt of sin also frees the believer to be holy. Holiness is impossible without grace, and grace always produces holiness. Thankfully, the Bible articulates a clear and thorough understanding of holiness that rises above the din of confusion today. Scripture alone defines holiness and reveals our relationship to it. We must not grow complacent, satisfied with a diminished view of God's holy nature, sin's offense, or the call to holiness in the gospel. Indeed, holiness is the great goal toward which God is moving all of His redeemed (Eph 1:4). It is a primary means through which lost souls are awakened to the gospel as they observe the radiance of a holy life (Matt 5:16; 1 Pet 2:11–12). And since the cross of Christ

---

[1] J. C. Ryle, *Holiness*, (Hertfordshire, England: Evangelical Press, 1979), 149.

[2] John Owen, *Works, Vol. 3: The Holy Spirit* (Edinburgh: Banner of Truth Trust, 1977), 100.

supremely demonstrates the Father's violent opposition to all that is unholy, then Christ's continuing and supreme purpose of our redemption is to present us holy, blameless, and blessed for all eternity (Eph 1:4; 5:26–27).

ANCIENT FOUNDATIONS

Understanding holiness begins by going back to the Old Testament. When the ancient people of Israel spoke of something as holy, they were expressing the idea of "separateness" or "otherness." The concept was simple: if someone or something was considered holy, it was set apart from that which is ordinary. In fact, the concept has a history that goes back to the creation of the universe itself. The very first use of the term *holy* is in Genesis 2:3 and refers to the seventh day being set apart from the other days. When the term is applied to God, an even richer picture emerges. To simplify it, *holy* describes what is intrinsic to God's nature (what He is), what is consecrated to God's service (what He requires), and what is reflective of God's character (what He imparts). Understanding all three of these aspects of the holiness of God is essential for a vibrant and consistent sanctification. For instance, if God were holy but had no solution to our unholiness, we would despair. At the same time, setting ourselves apart for service without a right view of God's holy nature leads to false standards and presumption. And longing to be holy without practicing the means of grace which God provides leads to powerlessness against temptation.

Pristine Purity

Since God *is* holy, all holiness springs from Him. He is the definition of holiness (Lev 19:2; Isa 6:3). Holiness permeates every one of His attributes and acts. R. C. Sproul richly describes this concept of holiness as it is contrasted from the created realm:

> When the Bible calls God holy, it means primarily that God is transcendentally separate. He is so far above and beyond us that He seems almost totally foreign to us. To be holy is to be "other,"

to be different in a special way. The same basic meaning is used when the word holy is applied to earthly things.[3]

God's "otherness" is at the heart of what it means for God to be holy, and yet the idea of separation does not exhaust the meaning. The holiness of God is an eternal perfection, which means God was holy before there was anything to be "separate from" or "other than." As the Westminster Shorter Catechism teaches, "God is a Spirit, infinite, eternal, and unchangeable, in his being, wisdom, power, holiness, justice, goodness, and truth."[4] Or, as Revelation 4:8 declares, "Holy, holy, holy, is the Lord God, the Almighty, who was and who is and who is to come." Such a bold assertion not only reminds us that God's holiness preexisted creation; it also goes right to the core of what God means when He declares that He is holy. His perfections are "infinite, eternal, and unchangeable" because He never violates, compromises, or dilutes His nature. He is holy, which means the perfections and purity of His nature can never be compromised.

We find this truth embedded in the very name God chose for Himself—Yahweh. When God said to Moses, "I am who I am" (Exod 3:14), He revealed part of what makes Him holy, namely, His eternality. His holiness is a perpetual and perfect holiness. But the essential quality of God's holiness is the purity of His nature. Sinclair Ferguson crisply declares it: "God's holiness is the searing purity of his eternal and infinite being."[5] It is God's pristine perfection that makes Him intrinsically holy. His being and His behavior transcend all creation, and His inherent perfection separates Him from the defilement of imperfection. God's holiness is the preeminent feature of Old Testament revelation and *the singular perfection* that governs the way we think about Him. First and foremost, when we speak of holiness, we are speaking of God!

[3] R. C. Sproul, *The Holiness of God*, rev. and exp. ed. (Wheaton, IL: Tyndale, 1998), 38.

[4] Westminster Shorter Catechism, Question 4.

[5] Sinclair B. Ferguson, *The Holy Spirit* (Downers Grove, IL: InterVarsity, 1997), 16.

Marked Out for Service

Not only is God said to be holy in Scripture, but also objects and people specifically dedicated to the service of God are said to be "consecrated" to Him. (The words *holy* and *consecrated* are usually translated from the same Hebrew root word.) In this sense, the Old Testament uses the word *holy* to describe buildings, days, land, offerings, sacrifices, garments, and even individuals—all of which have been set apart by God for the purpose of specific service to Him. These things do not possess *intrinsic* divine holiness or ethical holiness; they are holy because God marks them out for His purposes. For instance, Exodus 28:2 gives detailed specifications for the priest's "holy garments" to be used in temple service. These garments were consecrated by God for a special purpose and, in that sense, they were declared holy rather than common (Exod 40:13). To be consecrated to God was to be set apart (declared holy) as a service of worship.

Like the Holy One

God redeems His people so that we will ultimately reflect His moral purity. "Like the Holy One who called" us, we are to be holy in all our behavior (1 Pet 1:15). Man was created with the capacity for reflecting the holiness of God, which is part of what God meant when He said, "Let us make man in our image, after our likeness" (Gen 1:26). Because of this, His people are commanded to display His character by living according to His will. Leviticus 20:7–8 says, "Consecrate yourselves therefore and be holy, for I am the LORD your God. You shall keep My statutes and practice them; I am the LORD who sanctifies you." Since God's character and conduct are holy, His people are to be holy in all their character and conduct.

NEW EXPANSIONS

Amplifying those ancient foundations of holiness, the New Testament casts more redemptive light on its beauty, power, and practical blessings. In the New Covenant, we Christians have been set apart as a living sacrifice, holy and acceptable to God for worship (Rom 12:1). Our worship of the Father in spirit and truth (John 4:19–24) is not limited to holy places as in some ways it was for Israel in the Old Testament. We do not need to observe holy "days and months and seasons and years" (Gal 4:10). Nor do we need to ritually purify ourselves and our sacrifices for worship, for we have been cleansed in Christ (Col 2:10–17; Heb 10:1–10). Far beyond the everyday implements that were consecrated and used for worship in the tabernacle and temple, *we* are God's vessels set apart in holiness for His honor and glory.

Written on Our Hearts

Nor does the New Testament loosen or relax the righteous requirements of holiness for God's people as they were revealed in the Old Testament. If anything, it reveals an increased depth of holiness that penetrates all the way to the heart. Living by the Law of Christ—the royal Law (Jas 2:8)—does not free Christians from the obligation to pursue the holiness set forth in the Old Testament, but instead is the reflection of new holy desires written deep in our hearts. We are being made holy from the inside out by progressive sanctification. Amazingly, we are now able to live by the high and holy standard reflected in the Law of God (Rom 8:4). With a new Spirit-filled mind (Rom 8:6), with an unshakeable promise of resurrection life (Rom 8:11), and with the power to overcome sin (Rom 8:13), we can reflect the holiness of Christ in our thoughts, desires, words, and deeds. As Iain Murray says, "Holiness is the image of God visibly expressed."[6] This is a result of having God's Law written on our hearts (Jer 31:33; Heb 8:10)!

Conformed to His Image

The apostle Paul says that we have been "predestined to become conformed to the image" of Christ (Rom 8:29), who is infinitely

---

[6] Iain H. Murray, *Evangelical Holiness and Other Addresses* (Edinburgh: Banner of Truth Trust, 2013), 4.

holy. He "is the image of the invisible God" (Col 1:15) and there-fore manifests the fullness of God's perfections. As our high priest, Christ is intrinsically "holy, innocent, undefiled, separated from sinners" (Heb 7:26). Christ is the Holy One who possesses the intrinsic holiness of God. Hebrews 1:3 calls Him "the radiance of His glory and the exact representation of His nature … ." His miraculous works on earth proved to demons and disciples alike that He is the "Holy One of God" (Mark 1:24; Luke 4:34; John 6:69). When Christ spoke to the church in Philadelphia in Revelation 3:7, He declared His words to be the words of the one "who is holy," and the rest of the New Testament confirms that everything true about the intrinsic holiness of God is true of Christ. In His human nature, Jesus took on the exact same physical capacities as Adam, but through His divine nature He never ceased to be the impeccable "I am" (John 8:58; cf. Heb 13:8). Nothing could pollute the intrinsic holiness and human sinlessness of His divine nature, which is why His sacrifice was acceptable (Heb 10:11–14) and His resurrection was possible (Rom 1:4).

Every true child of God must "sanctify Christ as Lord" (1 Pet 3:15). As God incarnate, Christ perfectly met every requirement of God's holy character from His birth to His death on the cross (Matt 3:15; 5:17); thus, His righteous offering was eternally acceptable before the throne of God. The holiness of the Lord Jesus Christ is our benchmark in the New Covenant (1 Pet 1:15–16). We may bask in the wonders of gospel grace, but without a proper view of the holiness of Christ, we will inevitably cheapen grace by resisting the call to be conformed to His holiness.

Set Apart in the Same Way

Jesus is the standard of holiness that guides the church in sanctification. Everything taught about holiness in the Bible is found in the Person of Christ; therefore, there is no higher measure of holiness for a Christian than conformity to Christ. Holiness *is* Christlikeness, and the eternal design of salvation is to transform sinners into His holy and undefiled image. Christ is the Righteous One who perfectly reflected God's holiness by His righteous life on earth. The first Adam was made in the image of God to reflect the holiness of God, but failed. Through Adam's sin all of humanity became corrupted by nature, violated God's holiness, and fell short of His glory. Where the first Adam failed, the Second Adam did not. He is the only human being of whom it can be said that he "committed no sin, nor was any deceit found in his mouth" (1 Pet 2:22). As a man, Jesus perfectly reflected the holiness of God. His earthly existence was an exposition of heaven's holiness (Heb 1:1–3).

Christ was set apart by God for the purpose of salvation of sinners. The imagery of Old Testament consecration finds its fullest expression in the Person and work of Christ, which is why Jesus described Himself as the One "whom the Father sanctified and sent into the world" (John 10:36). Just as the Father ordained and consecrated the sacrifices of the Old Testament, Jesus was consecrated as a holy sacrifice unto God. It was not just the Father who set Christ apart: the entire Trinity participated in this consecrating work. Jesus set Himself apart (John 17:19), and He was anointed by the Spirit (Luke 4:18) for this purpose. He set Himself apart for His Father's redemptive plan, which includes the holiness and consecration of every redeemed sinner (John 17:19). We are set apart as "a royal priesthood, a holy nation, a people for God's own possession" that He might use us to "proclaim the excellencies of Him who has called … [us] out of darkness into His marvelous light" (1 Pet 2:9).

Taught by Grace to Be Holy

As Christians we strive—because of our justified standing—to "cleanse ourselves from all defilement of flesh and spirit, perfecting holiness in the fear of God" (2 Cor 7:1). In fact, the grace of the gospel becomes the believer's personal trainer in holiness, "instructing us to deny ungodliness and worldly desires and to live sensibly, righteously and godly in the present age" (Titus 2:12). Every biblical expression of holiness established in the Old Testament, amplified in the New Testament, and fulfilled in Christ is meant to put a burden in the heart of every Christian for the fervent pursuit of holy living. We are compelled to acknowledge God's holy character as the only criterion for sanctification (Lev 11:44–45; Matt 5:48; 1 Pet 1:15–16). Our union with Christ has consecrated us—set us apart—exclusively for God's service. We have been "sanctified in Christ Jesus" and are now "saints by calling [i.e., called for the purpose of holiness]" (1 Cor 1:2). We are the possession of God by sovereign grace. And every passage of Scripture that reveals the holiness of God explicitly or implicitly calls us to humbly believe and fervently strive in the Spirit. Sanctification—in the progressive sense—requires our personal effort to imitate and display God's character, because no one can have assurance that he will see God apart from the evidence of holiness. "Pursue … the sanctification without which no one will see the Lord" (Heb 12:14).

The more deeply we ponder it, the more we are left to wonder who could possibly accomplish the task of holiness in the work of sanctification? Who possesses the necessary perfection or power? We are not God, cannot set ourselves apart to God, and would not live righteously for God on our own. In ourselves and by ourselves, sanctification is impossible. So where can we look for our sanctification? We must look solely to Christ, who is not only the standard of holiness, but also its source. When we look to Christ in faith, a supernatural comfort rushes upon us in our weakness, knowing that where grace is operative human failure is never final.[7] With each new day we learn to entrust ourselves to Christ, "who became to us wisdom from God, and righteousness and *sanctification*, and redemption" (1 Cor 1:30). By faith we are brought into union with Christ so that we can be conformed to the holiness of Christ. It is no exaggeration when Joel Beeke asserts that "the primary secret of sanctification is a personal and vital union with Jesus Christ."[8] Through this vital union, we

[7] John MacArthur, Jr., *1 Corinthians*, *The MacArthur New Testament Commentary* (Chicago: Moody, 1984), 354.
[8] Joel Beeke, "Introduction to The Gospel Mystery of Sanctification," in Walter Marshall, *The Gospel Mystery of Sanctification* (Grand Rapids: Reformation Heritage Books, 2013), v.

believers enjoy the security of being His possession, the power to pursue holiness of life, and the anticipation of being perfected in holiness when we meet the Master.

In 1 Corinthians 6:9–11, Paul sharply contrasts the Corinthians' former life of unrighteousness and our present status as "saints" in the eyes of God: "Or do you not know that the unrighteous will not inherit the kingdom of God? Do not be deceived; neither fornicators, nor idolaters, nor adulterers, nor effeminate, nor homosexuals, nor thieves, nor the covetous, nor drunkards, nor revilers, nor swindlers, will inherit the kingdom of God. Such were some of you; but you were washed, but you were sanctified, but you were justified in the name of the Lord Jesus Christ and in the Spirit of our God." Despite the lowest level of Corinthian worldliness, Paul does not hesitate to speak of the converted as already washed, sanctified, and justified in the exact same manner.[9] The death of Christ not only secures our justification, it also makes sanctification, in some sense, a present reality (Eph 5:25–27). The full extent of sanctification has not yet been reached, but through the work of Christ we are holy—fully cleansed from our sin. Christians now live in the realm of God's holiness and not under the dominion of sin. The reality of this change is based on the reality of Christ's work and the believer's vital union with Christ. John Murray provides a helpful explanation of this aspect of sanctification: "The decisive and definitive breach with sin that occurs at the inception of Christian life is one necessitated by the fact that the death of Christ was decisive and definitive. It is just because we cannot allow for any reversal or repetition of Christ's death on the tree that we cannot allow for any compromise on the doctrine that every believer has died to sin and no longer lives under its dominion."[10]

The work of Christ has created a new reality in which we live. As Walter Marshall declares, "His resurrection was our resurrection

[9] Both terms translated "justified" and "sanctified" are aorist, passive, indicative verbs.
[10] John Murray, *Collected Writings of John Murray, Vol. 2: Systematic Theology*, (Edinburgh: Banner of Truth Trust, 1991) 293.

to the life of holiness, as Adam's sin was our fall into spiritual death."[11] We are not yet what we will be when our sanctification is completed at glorification, but our present position guarantees the future results. Through the finished work of Christ and the indwelling spiritual power of Christ, there is an eschatological reality that is already at work in the believer. This is great news because the positional reality of our sanctification frees us to pursue practical holiness. We are no longer bound by and to sin, but we have been liberated to pursue righteousness in the context of grace. God set us apart as holy (i.e., saints) so that we can glorify Him in every aspect of our lives.

CONFORMING TO CHRIST

As a result of being set apart in Christ (positional sanctification), believers are being conformed to the image of Christ (progressive sanctification). Positional sanctification is always for a purpose. We are totally consecrated, but not yet completely holy. Thus, there is a continuing need for progressive growth in holiness. The Holy Spirit set us apart through regeneration so that we would have the power to serve and follow Christ in increasing measure. Positional sanctification does not mean that we have already become as holy as we could be, but it does mean that every area of our life is now being transformed under the influence of the sanctifying Spirit.

Some contemporary scholars are expressing concern that the church is placing too much emphasis on the daily spiritual progress in our relationship with Christ. David Peterson writes:

> Sanctification is commonly regarded as a process of moral and spiritual transformation following conversion. In the New Testament, however, it primarily refers to God's way of taking possession of us in Christ, setting us apart to belong to him and to fulfill his purpose for us. Sanctification certainly has present and ongoing effects, but when the verb "to sanctify"

[11] Walter Marshall, *The Gospel Mystery of Sanctification* (Grand Rapids: Reformation Heritage Books, 2013), 36.

(Gk. *hagiazein*) and the noun "sanctification" (Gk. *hagiasmos*) are used, the emphasis is regularly on the saving work of God in Christ, applied to believers though the ministry of the Holy Spirit.[12]

Some, shortsightedly narrowing their study to passages with the term "sanctification," may assume a greater emphasis in Scripture on our position in Christ because, as Peterson noted, the word is often used to speak of our sanctified position. But the principles for spiritual growth are not limited to specific wording, and when we broaden our study to include everything the Bible has to say about maturity in Christ, the privileges and duties of daily sanctification become clear. Indeed, behind every command in the New Testament is the assumption that we are responsible to be pressing on toward Christlikeness. This is why G. C. Berkouwer had no problem saying that

> it is beyond dispute that the Bible itself treats of this progress. Many admonitions point to a required "movement." We are exhorted to perfect our holiness in the fear of God (2 Cor. 7:1), to following after the sanctification without which no man shall see the Lord (Heb. 12:14), to follow after that which is good (1 Thess. 5:15), after love (1 Cor. 14:1), after righteousness, godliness, faith, love, patience, and meekness (1 Tim. 6:11). Everything points to consistent and active endeavor.[13]

While Peterson puts a secondary emphasis on the progressive aspect of sanctification, many others go even further and relegate spiritual progress merely to an occasional by-product of our position in Christ. However, even Peterson admits that our "set apart" status in Christ is not the *only* emphasis in the New Testament. Progressive, measurable growth in the Christian life is a major theme throughout the Scriptures. It is commanded (2 Pet 3:18), it is assured by the indwelling power and presence of the

[12] David Peterson, *Possessed by God: A New Testament Theology of Sanctification and Holiness* (Downers Grove, IL: InterVarsity, 1995), 27.

[13] G. C. Berkouwer, *Faith and Sanctification* (Grand Rapids: Eerdmans, 1952), 101.

Spirit (Rom 6:11–20; Gal 5:16–25; Eph 4:12–24), and its neglect or absence is sternly warned against (Heb 12:14–17).

The New Testament affirms that we are positionally sanctified and, at the same time, that we have a responsibility to be striving for sanctification. These truths complement one another rather than compete with one another. "The Holy Spirit acts in sanctification to unite us to Christ, constitute us as God's saints, and begin the lifelong process of making us holy."[14] Progressive sanctification is nothing more than increasing conformity to Christ, the perfect man. Not only should we expect such a transforming dynamic in the Christian life, we are commanded to pursue it: "And do not be conformed to this world, but be transformed by the renewing of your mind, so that you may prove what the will of God is, that which is good and acceptable and perfect" (Rom 12:2).

Every Christian should be able to perceive this process in his own life. There are, of course, times when our growth is imperceptible or when we feel as though we are moving backwards. But when we examine the overall trajectory of our lives, there is—in every believer—evidence of the Spirit's renewing work (2 Cor 4:6). And the cumulative effect of all our Spirit-filled moments of faith and obedience is a growing spiritual maturity. Most of us can remember when we were new in the faith—spiritual babes surviving on milk. Looking back, we can see that is no longer the case. We've grown through the spiritual peaks and valleys on the journey toward Christlikeness. On the other hand, if you have been a Christian for many years and can digest only the milk of the faith, this is not as God desires. If you are not experiencing what the Scriptures describe as "the fruit of the Spirit" (Gal 5:22), it is likely that you have fallen short in what God calls every believer to do in the sanctification process. We are "duty bound to ... strive for ever-increasing sanctification by using the means which God has placed at ... [our] disposal."[15] To some,

---

[14] Robert A. Peterson, *Salvation Applied by the Spirit: Union with Christ* (Wheaton, IL: Crossway Books, 2015), 337.

[15] Louis Berkhof, *Systematic Theology* (Grand Rapids: Eerdmans, 1996), 534.

this might sound inconsistent with the concept of grace, but the authors of the New Testament had no problem speaking of our role in sanctification in these terms. Words like "run," "strive," "work," and similar imperatives abound in the pages of the New Testament (Rom 8:13; 1 Cor 9:24; 2 Cor 7:1; Phil 3:13–14; Col 1:10; Titus 2:7, 14; Heb 10:24; 12:4; 2 Pet 1:5; 3:17–18; 1 John 3:3). If the Holy Spirit did not hesitate to describe the Christian life in these terms, neither should we. The pursuit of holiness does not contradict grace; it celebrates it. In fact, Paul presents grace as that which teaches believers to pursue righteousness: "For the grace of God has appeared, bringing salvation to all men, instructing us to deny ungodliness and worldly desires and to live sensibly, righteously and godly in the present age" (Titus 2:11–12). By grace, we have a responsibility to put forth effort in the pursuit of holiness; it's what we've been saved for.

COMPLETED IN CHRIST

As we strive in the Spirit's power to grow in holiness, we stand firm on the promise that God will complete His sanctifying work in us. Our positional holiness and pursuit of holiness will one day culminate in the perfect realization of holiness in our glorification. We possess a secure position, we are being refined in our spiritual progress, and we will one day be completely transformed "into conformity with the body of His glory, by the exertion of the power that He has" (Phil 3:21) to complete our full sanctification. Known as glorification, this is the day we look forward to when we stand complete in Christ. It is the eschatological fulfillment of our sanctification (Rom 6:22).

Some have argued that the completion of our sanctification can take place on earth, that Christian perfection is possible. This certainly would have been a surprise to the apostle John, who said in 1 John 1:10, "If we say that we have not sinned, we make him a liar, and His word is not in us." John's words provide the death knell for this position. The possibility of perfection in this life is simply inconsistent with God's truth. As we earnestly anticipate the fullness of God's sanctifying work, we must recognize that our citizenship is in heaven with Christ. We will not experience perfect holiness in this age, but our perfection is guaranteed in the age to come. Faithfulness in this life will be graciously rewarded, not because it is worthy of God, but because God graciously promised to reward it. Moreover, all the human failure compiled by believers in this age will dissipate in the light of God's glorious grace. As 1 Corinthians 15:50–54 describes, in our glorification, we will be enveloped by our union with Christ:

> Now I say this, brethren, that flesh and blood cannot inherit the kingdom of God; nor does the perishable inherit the imperishable. Behold, I tell you a mystery; we will not all sleep, but we will all be changed, in a moment, in the twinkling of an eye, at the last trumpet; for the trumpet will sound, and the dead will be raised imperishable, and we will be changed. For this perishable must put on the imperishable, and this mortal must put on immortality. But when this perishable will have put on the imperishable, and this mortal will have put on immortality, then will come about the saying that is written, "Death is swallowed up in victory."

This is the great hope we have in our sanctification. How should we respond to this hope? What does an eternity of perfected sanctification mean for a Christian battling each day for progress in holiness? Should we simply sit back and ponder what has been done for us while we wait for that great day? Paul follows his celebration of what is to come with these sobering words about living in the meantime: "Therefore, my beloved brethren, be steadfast, immovable, always abounding in the work of the Lord, knowing that your toil is not in vain in the Lord" (1 Cor 15:58). Faithful effort in sanctification is never in vain because we have a sure hope that God will use every ordained means to perfect His work in us, including our effort. Our confident anticipation of the completion of our sanctification should greatly encourage us to continue moving forward on a biblical trajectory toward our ultimate hope. We can pursue change in Christ with the full expectation that He will one day completely conform us to His holy image.

God defines holiness in His Word and demands holiness from His people. Nowhere are these realities seen more clearly than in the gospel. The gospel is necessary because sinful man cannot withstand the consuming holiness of God. God had to save His people from their sin and set them apart unto holiness. He transferred His children from the domain of sin so that they can be transformed into the image of the sinless One, Jesus. His eternal purpose is for the holiness of Christ to have its full effect on the souls of His people. He has designed salvation not merely to grant forgiveness, but to make every believer a beneficiary of His holiness (Heb 12:10). From election to glorification, God's purpose is to make His people holy (Eph 1:4; 5:25–27). The work is not yet complete, but we can be confident that the same God who saved us to be holy will make us holy in Christ, like Christ.

CHAPTER 2

SAVED TO TRUST AND OBEY

Many of us have become sensuous Christians, living by our feelings rather than through our understanding of the Word of God. Sensuous Christians cannot be moved to service, prayer or study unless they "feel like it." ... But what happens when there is a conflict between what God says and what I feel? We must do what God says, like it or not. That is what Christianity is all about.[1]

I T was one of the most remarkable evangelistic encounters Pastor Ichabod Spencer had ever experienced. The year was 1875, and for months he had been interacting with a young man who was agitated by the gospel's call to simple faith. Like so many unbelievers, the frustrated inquirer craved some *justifiable motivation* for believing in God. He was seeking reasons by which he could be fully convinced that the promise of eternal life in Christ was worthy of his trust. Spencer's riveting conversation with him ultimately came to a head. With a shepherd's touch and surgeon's precision, Spencer exposed the real barrier to this young man's faith. The lengthy narrative is worth quoting in full:

> I finally said to him one evening: "I do not know, my dear sir, what more can be said to you. I have told you all that I know ... .

[1] R. C. Sproul, *Knowing Scripture*, 2nd ed. (Downers Grove, IL: InterVarsity, 2009), 31, 33.

I now put it to your own heart—if you are not a Christian, what hinders you?"

He thought a moment. Said he: "I can't feel!"

"Why didn't you tell me this before?"

"I never thought of it before, sir."

"How do you know this hinders you?"

"I can think of nothing else. But I am sure I shall never be converted to God, if I have no more feeling than I have now. But that is my own fault. I know you cannot help me."

"No, sir, I cannot; nor can you help yourself. Your heart will not feel at your bidding."

"What then can I do?" said he, with much anxiety.

"Come to Christ now. Trust him. Give up your darling world. Repent, so iniquity shall not be your ruin."

He seemed perplexed, annoyed ... and with an accent of impatience, such as I had never witnessed in him before, he replied, "That is impossible. I want the feeling to bring me to that, and I can't feel!"

"Hear me, sir," said I; "and heed well what I say. I have several points:

"1. The Bible never tells you that you must feel, but that you must repent and believe.

"2. Your complaint that you 'can't feel' is just an excuse by which your wicked heart would justify you for not coming to Christ now.

"3. This complaint that you 'can't feel' is the complaint of a self-righteous spirit."

"How is it?" said he.

"Because you look to the desired feeling to commend you to God, or to make you fit to come, or to enable you to come."

"Yes, to enable me," said he.

"Well, that is self-righteousness, in the shape of self-justification for not coming; or in the shape of self-reliance if you attempt to come. That is all legalism, and not the acceptance of a gracious Christianity. You cannot be saved by the law.

"4. Your complaint is the language of the most profound ignorance. To feel would do you no good. Devils feel—lost spirits feel.

"5. Your complaint that you 'can't feel' tends to lead you to a false religion—a religion of mere self-righteous feeling."

"But, sir," said he, "there is feeling in [the Christian life]."

"But, sir," said I, "there is duty in [the Christian life]; and which shall come first? You ought to feel; you ought to love God, and grieve that you are such a senseless sinner."

"I know I am a sinner, but I can't feel any confidence to turn to God, to draw me to him."

"You are like the prodigal in the fifteenth of Luke, when he thought of saying to his father, 'Make me as one of the hired servants.' Poor fool. Say that to his father! Why, the very idea is a libel on his father's heart .... Poor fool! He knew no better. And you are a greater fool than he. He went home. And where he met his father he found his heart. He could 'feel' when he found his father's arms around him, and felt the strong beatings of his father's heart. Do as he did. Go home, and you will feel, if you never felt before. You will starve where you are; your 'husks' will not save you."[2]

With compassion and extraordinary wisdom, Spencer showed this man that believing is seeing and not the other way around. The story illustrates man's sinful tendency to search for tangible signs *before* fully entrusting himself to the truth. We would rather see (and test!) something before we commit. To entrust our safety, our security, or our future to something or someone without a "test-drive" seems patently foolish. But in reality, genuine faith does the opposite. Grounded upon the God who cannot lie, faith is the act of entrusting ourselves to the truth He has spoken. It is to rest upon what God has promised *solely because of who He is.*

Faith is genuine when we entrust ourselves to what is "not seen" (Heb 11:1) or experienced. The remnants of our old life—old appetites of the flesh—prefer more tangible realities. Like the unbelieving man whom Spencer counseled who so badly wanted to "feel" before he trusted, Christians are often troubled by the same desire for tangible signs of emotion to ground our faith

[2] Ichabod Spencer, *A Pastor's Sketches* (Central, Hong Kong: Forgotten Books, 2010), Kindle Electronic Edition: Location 5226–76.

in the battle for spiritual growth. In fact, the church's ongoing confusion over the doctrine of progressive sanctification—how we grow in Christ—can be traced, in some measure, to misguided views of faith in our lives. To an alarming degree, a new generation of evangelicals is looking within themselves—to their emotions and personal experience—in order to evaluate truth claims, find meaning, and measure spiritual maturity. Today, people are emphasizing, not humble faith and obedience to Scripture, but emotions. In fact, the church is beginning to match our secular culture almost stride for stride.

For decades now, society's motivation for moral action or belief has been shifting from a rational basis to a sensual one. Before the postmodern era, the existence of universal truths worth knowing and believing was assumed by almost everyone. Truth-claims were foundational to life and were considered verifiable. Rational thinking and perception were believed to be rooted in universal principles worth seeking and knowing. People did not always agree on the ultimate authority behind their belief system (e.g., Bible, science, cultural consensus), but foundational and universal principles for life were deemed objective and worth discovering.

That framework has all but vanished. Postmodernity has abandoned the previous "foundationalism"[3] and has grounded truth-claims in the personal experiences of individuals. Each person's "truth" is equally valid, even if it contradicts someone else's. Objectivity is an illusion. Even irrational ideas are acceptable so long as they are fulfilling to the one who believes them. What matters today is the "truthiness"[4] of personal beliefs.

---

[3] Labeled "Foundationalism," these rational frameworks were believed to be universal for everyone. In other words, given enough self-actualization a society would be able to "justify and know" reality by that which is intuitive to every rational human being.

[4] "Truthiness" was coined by comedian and media icon Stephen Colbert, referring to the hyper-subjectivity of today's average Millennial. In a 2006 interview conducted by *Club* magazine, Colbert stated, "It used to be, everyone was entitled to their own opinion, but not their own facts. But that's not the case anymore. Facts matter not at all. Perception is everything. It's certainty. ... It's not only that I *feel* it to be true, but that *I* feel it to be true"; emphasis original.

All claims of absolute truth are suspect—the obvious attempt of one group to oppress another. In the search for reality today, skepticism is the new "spyware." Reality is what one thinks and believes in the moment. We are prone to look within ourselves *to find and verify* knowledge. Given this cultural tidal wave, it should not surprise us that many young Christians are being swept into the currents of uncertainty. Truth-claims that sound definitive or dogmatic are unattractive. Absolute declarations of what is true or false stifle personal autonomy, emotional expression, and artistic development. In a "not-your-grandma's-church" subculture, self-expression and emotional fulfillment are the new marks of "authentic" spirituality.

TURNING INWARD

In his capstone volume in a series of books on cultural morality and the state of the church, David Wells pinpoints the problem:

> Let me begin with a baseline truth of Scripture. It is that God stands before us. He summons us to come out of ourselves and to know him. This is the most profound truth that we ever encounter—or should I say, the most profound truth by which we are encountered?—and it is key to many other truths. And yet our culture is pushing us into exactly the opposite pattern. ...
>
> We are now thinking of ourselves in terms, not of human nature, but of the self. ... We are now inclined to see life, to understand what is true, to think of right and wrong, in uniquely individual ways ... and each perspective is as valid as any other. ...
>
> [A] person's own interior reality is all that counts, and it is untouched by any obligation to community, or understanding from the past, or even by the intrusions of God from the outside. ... And this self wants only to be pleased. It sees no reason to be saved. This is therapeutic deism, whose morals are self-focused and self-generated. ...
>
> The new therapeutic preoccupations of the Me Generation

Nathan Rabin, "Stephen Colbert," *The A. V. Club*, January 25, 2006, http://www.avclub.com/article/stephen-colbert-13970 (accessed June 2016).

would, of course, seep into the church, although in less glaring and more sanitized versions.[5]

One might humbly add that the "sanitized" versions of this inward focus are more subtle than their initial worldly versions, and therefore, more dangerous. Huge shifts are taking place in the way Christians view the evaluation of truth and spiritual growth. When discussing how to battle sin and grow in grace, many believers are no longer using common biblical phrases such as "walk by faith" or "deny yourself and take up your cross." On the topic of *justification*, faith terminology is generously used and, for the most part, rightly understood. There is no shortage of sermons and blogs on *sola fide*. However, dialogues on *sanctification* are filled with a different kind of language. It is trendy to speak of spiritual growth as animated and propelled by a "hunger for beauty,"[6] or "affectionate feelings for God." Rather than talk of "submission to Christ," many Christians prefer more aesthetic and emotion-laden concepts to describe what activates and motivates Christian obedience. Spiritual maturity is gained and measured by emotional affection rather than humble faith—trusting and obeying. And while not every emphasis on emotions today should be cautioned against, the church is increasingly aligning with the culture's paradigm shift toward the sensual.

Though perhaps sincerely desiring to serve Christ, many believers are now convinced that heightened emotions must be experienced for obedience to be genuine. Anything less is lifeless externalism. Rather than speaking of ways to grow "strong in faith" (Rom 4:20), the focus is now on "sensing" God's presence and His love. We are not asking, "What does *Scripture clearly say* about my heart and conduct?" but "How do I *feel* about my walk with the Lord?", and "Am I experiencing a joy and delight

[5] David F. Wells, *God in the Whirlwind* (Wheaton, IL: Crossway, 2013), 18, 25–27.
[6] Dane Ortland, "Increasingly Beautified: Jonathan Edwards' Theology of Sanctification," http://www.uniontheology.org/resources/doctrine/salvation/increasingly-beautified-jonathan-edwards-theology-of-sanctification (accessed May 2014).

in the Lord?" What many seem to fear is an obedience devoid of discernable emotion, a sense of merely following rules. Is this a legitimate concern? Should evangelicalism shift its focus from "trust and obey" to "feeling Christ's heart-filling glory?"[7] From one angle the argument seems reasonable. We are rightly alarmed when someone modifies his behavior without expressions of *true devotion* to Christ. Self-righteous externalism of any stripe is devilish. Robed in Christ's righteousness, we have peace with God and should never dream of offering our worthless deeds to gain His favor. There is no more deadly blindness than washing the outside of the cup while the inside remains filthy (Matt 23:25). Nor should we drift into a kind of moralism where we imagine that God's love is won or lost by our faithfulness or the lack of it.

To counteract these tendencies, many counsel that we should forsake talk of "duty" or "striving" and only emphasize what the grace of God has already accomplished. Without emotional passion, "trust and obey" sounds like externalism—as if we were faking it. Therefore, they maintain, we must liberate evangelicalism from her past years of "trying harder" to become better.[8] But should evangelicalism make such a seismic shift in emphasis? Has evangelicalism at large been suffering from decades of dead Pharisaism? Should we emphasize emotional affection as a corrective to years of militant legalism? Like Paul before his

---

[7] In a blog article, pastor Steve Fuller of Grace Church, Abu Dhabi attempts to make the case that Paul's use of the word "beholding" in 2 Corinthians 3:18 is equal to "feeling Christ's heart-filling glory." Steve Fuller, "In 2 Corinthians 3:18, Are We 'Reflecting' or 'Beholding' the Glory of the Lord?" http://livingbyfaithblog.com/2015/04/23/in-2-corinthians-318-are-we-reflecting-or-beholding-the-glory-of-the-lord/ (accessed April 2017).

[8] Steve Brown, *A Scandalous Freedom* (New York: Howard Books, 2004), 60. Brown asserts, "*The greatest cause for our not getting better is our obsession with not getting better. ... Sanctification becomes a reality in those believers who don't obsess over their own sanctification*"; emphasis original. While Brown may view personal effort as a primary culprit behind spiritual weakness, Scripture lays the blame at the feet of unbelief (Matt 14:26–31; Rom 4:20). Striving in faith always produces spiritual growth. Whereas faithless effort leads to self-righteousness or self-pity. Our problem is not trying too hard to be holy, but trusting in our own efforts rather than Christ to defeat temptation.

conversion, has the church boasted of spiritual pedigrees while trusting in her own righteousness? On the contrary, even a cursory glance at evangelicalism over the last forty years tells a different story.

Encountering God

The emotion-charged model of sanctification did not sprout suddenly, but can be traced to an extensive root system. In large measure, it is the fruit of the church's decades-long love affair with pragmatism and subjectivism. As explained above, post-modern culture rejected the idea of undergirding absolutes of Foundationalism and began looking to personal experience as the test of "truth." An individual's feelings became the new focus. And it didn't take long for the church to begin to mirror society's drift. We increasingly began putting a "sensual lens" on everything. The church opened itself up to every wave of mysticism. As far back as 1960, mainline churches were beginning to equate emotional experiences with true worship. The Charismatic Renewal Movement began boasting of a way to "experience" God beyond mere obedience to words in an ancient book.[9] Simple faith in the objective truth of Scripture was viewed as repulsively academic. Believers could "emotionally connect" with God through new revelations given to them personally. At the same time (the 1960s and 1970s), a turbulent youth culture—with its unrestrained self-expression, hedonism, and pursuit of mystical religious experience—began flooding into churches through the "Jesus Movement."[10] Young people inundated the church with raw emotionalism and pop cultural sentiment. They were fresh off the street, and they framed Christianity around

[9] For an outstanding critique of the movement birthed in Los Angeles among Episcopalians and Catholics, see John MacArthur, Jr., *Strange Fire* (Nashville: Nelson Books, 2013), 31–35. For a historical volume written by a Pentecostal, see Vinson Synan, *The Century of The Holy Spirit: 100 Years of Charismatic Renewal* (Nashville: Thomas Nelson, 2001).

[10] For a history and analysis of this movement and its influence on evangelicalism, I highly recommend Larry Eskridge's book, *God's Forever Family* (New York: Oxford University Press, 2013).

the entertainments and lifestyle habits most familiar to them. In order to "reach" the next generation for Christ, churches accommodated these seemingly innocent changes. What many leaders did not discern at the time was the subtle but significant shift in the way Christians viewed their relationship to God and His Word. It was not long before churches began capitulating to the demand for less doctrinal emphasis and more emotional expressions in corporate worship.

Emotional Payoff over Substance

Contemporary Christian Music was born during this era of tectonic shifts and then muscled its way, often defiantly, into the life of the church. Suddenly, ministries were deadlocked in battles over music styles. Dubbed "worship wars," the conflicts were a clash between the hymnology of previous generations and the songs and choruses being published by a new breed of musicians/artists. Young people, some of whom had grown up in the church, were critical of what they viewed as the passionless worship of their parents' generation. Traditional worship services were seen as lifeless and cold. But many Christians were becoming alarmed over these changes. The contemporary songs being introduced into Sunday services were often theologically shallow. Wave after wave of praise choruses, with insipid and sometimes heretical lyrics, were produced and sold by a now-standardized Christian music industry. Focused almost exclusively on the emotional payoff, the average young worshiper was uninterested in a song's doctrinal integrity. Music was being written for the purpose of *inciting an emotional response alone.* In many churches today, songs still mimic a maudlin style, expressing the Christian life in such emotional and romantic terms that it is unclear who is being adored: God or one's girlfriend. At the same time, the term "worship" has become synonymous with merely the part of the service when the church sings together. Furthermore, these trends opened the way for all previous traditional models of ministry—everything from Sunday school to preaching to music to evangelism—to be viewed with skepticism.

In fairness, some of the criticisms of the Jesus Movement generation may have been warranted and inevitable. A whole generation of church kids had become disillusioned. Their parents' generation expanded global missions, published an unprecedented number of Christian resources, initiated discipleship programs, etc. But despite these blessings, their children had front row seats to an ongoing drama of moral scandals in church leadership, rising divorce rates among their own parents, vicious church splits over preference issues, and worldly compromise. Raised in the church, these kids heard sermon after sermon about worship, gospel outreach, and power to live for Christ. But their parents' Christianity had not resulted in a passion for God or the power over temptation promised in the gospel. Gross hypocrisy in one generation always leads to exasperation, hostility, and yet more open rebellion in the next.

For some, disillusionment turned into an appetite for the world. Disguised as Christian liberty, they flaunted friendship with the base things of culture. Wanting church leaders who do the same, many have crowded into churches that celebrate edgy pastors who pander to pop culture. On the other hand, there are many others who genuinely desire a real walk with Christ that renews their mind and empowers their battle against sin. They desire to learn lessons from past mistakes and avoid repeating them. In other words, many of those who gravitate toward an emotion-driven Christianity do so, in large measure, as a reaction. They are convinced that "old" models of spirituality leave us passionless and powerless. On the minds of many is the question: "If our parents had all these spiritual privileges, why didn't it make a difference in their moral purity, marital fidelity, biblical clarity, spiritual maturity, and gospel audacity?"

Church Growth: Removing Emotional Barriers

The evangelical church's plunge into subjectivism was further advanced by its sellout to the pragmatic, megachurch movement. The church began to assume that the unchurched needed a way to "emotionally connect" with God without the trappings of the traditional way things had been done. New approaches to church gatherings were devised, and we witnessed the birth of the seeker service.[11] Years later, Rick Warren's bestseller, *The Purpose-Driven Church*, became the "how-to" manual of ministry. In that volume Warren writes, "It is my deep conviction that anybody can be won to Christ if you discover the key to his or her heart. ... The most likely place to start is with the person's felt needs."[12] A person's

[11] The term "seeker service" was coined by Bill Hybels, then pastor of Willow Creek Community Church, Chicago. It referred to the view that church services should be designed primarily by means of surveying what the unchurched desired most in a church. Before Hybels formalized the approach and gave it a name, famed self-esteem guru Robert Schuller had already pandered to cultural whims years earlier when he purchased a drive-in theater in Southern California, served popcorn, and gave an inspirational talk to unchurched families who were willing to visit a drive-in, but not a local church. The assumption was that the average person would likely "seek" God with genuine interest except that he or she finds traditional church aesthetics and format unattractive. Seeker services jettisoned the vestiges of the traditional church experience (pews, hymns, formality, etc.) and offered a "worship" service based on what the unchurched demanded. This, it was claimed, would break down the seekers' emotional barriers and open them to the gospel.

[12] Rick Warren, *The Purpose-Driven Life* (Grand Rapids: Zondervan, 1995), 219. In this book Warren merely reiterated the ideology of the late Dr. Harry Emerson Fosdick, a liberal pastor in New York City in the 1920s–40s. In an article in *Harper's Magazine* entitled "What Is the Matter with Preaching?" Fosdick famously wrote, "Who seriously supposes that, as a matter of fact, one in a hundred of the congregation cares, to start with, what Moses, Isaiah, Paul, or John meant in those special verses, or came to church deeply concerned about it? Nobody else who talks to the public so assumes that the vital interests of the people are located in the meaning of words spoken two thousand years ago. The advertisers of any goods ... plunge as directly as possible after contemporary wants, felt needs, actual interests and concerns. ... Only the preacher proceeds still upon the idea that folk come to church desperately anxious to discover what happened to the Jebusites" (Harry Emerson Fosdick, July 1928, 133–141, as reprinted in *What's the Matter with Preaching Today?* ed. Mike Graves (Louisville: Westminster John Knox Press, 2004), 9–10.

felt needs were specifically defined as whatever that person feels will make their life better. Services were designed to break down emotional barriers as the key to opening their heart to the gospel.

True biblical worship does involve the whole inner man (John 4:24), including our emotions, but worship is not the adoration of emotionalism. There is much to be commended in some of the fresh, new hymnology being written for the church today. But the desire to "experience God's presence"[13] emotionally during corporate times of praise has, sadly, turned believers further inward to define their spirituality. To be clear, Christianity is *not* opposed to emotional expression, and we should not imagine that our particular emotional makeup is the standard for everyone else. The body of Christ is gloriously diverse. We welcome all *sanctified* emotions. But visceral sensations are not, in and of themselves, a legitimate basis for defining or measuring true spirituality. Indeed, obsessing over the presence or absence of an emotional experience will lead to a faith grounded only in what is tangibly sensed at any given moment. In contrast, Jesus sternly warned Thomas about desiring to see before he believed (John 20:29).

Emotional Healing: The New Golden Calf

Another significant factor in the church's departure from a biblical model of sanctification has been the quest for "emotional wholeness." Decades ago, Christians began mingling Scriptural principles with the core assumptions of pop psychology. No longer was the church looking exclusively to the Bible to diagnose areas of unbelief.

Various psychological disciplines—with their assumptions about human goodness, "false guilt," victimhood, and

---

[13] During the early years of this trend, the corporate mission statement of a notable music publisher stated, "Helping people worldwide experience the manifest presence of God and develop a lifestyle of worship." The charter made no attempt to define "the manifest presence of God." I have to assume that people were free to equate their various emotional experiences with having been "visited" by God's presence during the music of a service. This is the very epitome of subjectivity.

environmental causes—were readily embraced by Christians looking for relief from the consequences of sin. Psychologists became the new "pastors" of the church, providing an endless list of causes (read: excuses) for the alarming rise of "mental and emotional disorders" among evangelicals. Christian counseling centers and clinics sprang up almost weekly. Church leaders were intimidated, being told that "disorders" were beyond the soul-care abilities of skilled pastors looking only to the Scriptures. "Professional" therapy became the path to restoring emotional wholeness.

At the same time, married couples were turning, not to pastors or mature Christian friends, but to psychotherapists to help them resolve conflict. And before seeking any biblical counsel from other experienced, godly families, parents were quick to diagnose their child's discipline problems as "chemical imbalances" in the brain. Medications were liberally prescribed by Christian doctors and enthusiastically administered by Christian patients. Biblical terms like "repentance" were replaced by words such as "healing" and "renewal." "Sin" was now called "dysfunction" and "disease." The Scripture's emphasis on mind renewal was replaced by "cognitive therapy." And behavioral tendencies God clearly attributed to "lusts which wage war against the soul" (1 Pet 2:11) were often wrongly recast as "disorders" for which other people and circumstances were to blame. The late Chuck Colson's analysis nearly twenty-five years ago unmasked the dangers of all these changes:

> The myth [that man is inherently good] deludes people into thinking that they're always victims, never villains; always deprived, never depraved. It dismisses responsibility as the teaching of a darker age. It can excuse any crime because it can always blame something else—a sickness of our society or a sickness of the mind. One writer called the modern age "the golden age of exoneration." When guilt is dismissed as the illusion of narrow minds, then no one is accountable, even to his conscience.[14]

---

[14] Charles W. Colson, "The Enduring Revolution: 1993 Templeton Address," (Pamphlet) "Sources, No. 4" (Washington: Wilberforce Forum, 1993), 4–5.

FREE TO BE HOLY

As a result of all this, churches embraced the assumption that aberrant behavior in both adults and children was likely the result of past emotional trauma yet to be resolved. More and more people were diagnosed as emotionally broken—victims of an unjust and ruthless environment. Soon, scores of Christians concluded that they simply could not turn to Scripture until they were emotionally "healed" enough to exercise faith in God's Word. Is it any wonder that the language of faith and humble obedience fell out of common use?

I DARE NOT TRUST THE SWEETEST FRAME

Years of pragmatism and emotionalism has not served our young people well. Fighting sin has become, not a battle to strengthen faith in God and His Word, but a search for "spiritual feelings." Few Millennials would rush to sign up for a conference called "Obedience," but advertise a gathering called "Passion" and 30,000 young people move heaven and earth to get there. Evangelical culture seems to thrive on feelings of astonishment. But no matter how many sermons, conferences, and praise services we fill our lives with, the emotional payoff is short lived. Apart from faith, the battle with besetting sins will always be a losing one. People today exhaust themselves trying to secure permanently the emotional high that overwhelmed them when they first learned of God's grace. Eventually, the guilt of frequent forays into sin puts out of reach the euphoria they had hoped to replicate, leading to serious doubt about their salvation and often despair. Instead of living by faith despite what they feel, many are seeking to stir emotional passion enough to carry them effortlessly past strong temptation. Genuinely searching for the "joy in God" they hear so much about, Christians are baffled as to why emotional fervor is not enough to defeat stubborn sins.

Let us admit it: emotional awe and a sense of wonder over our forgiveness in Christ "feels" better than guilt. We are attracted to these experiences because they are a welcome emotional relief from the intense pressures of daily life. Stirrings of passion often occur after humble reflection on the love of God displayed at the cross. We can be overtaken with pleasurable feelings as a theological reality captivates our mind and feeds our soul. Whether reading Scripture alone and crying out to the Lord from the depths of weakness, or belting out a hymn or midway through a sermon in a packed Sunday worship service, the Spirit of God pierces our heart with a new level of understanding and gratitude. Such spiritual mountain peaks are filled with emotional release, sensations of joyful exuberance, peaceful rest, and might be accompanied by a flood of tears, and also might lead to a deepened adoration for Christ.

It is easy to understand why people who experience such moments desire to perpetuate the euphoria. Being carried into the heavenlies on grateful feelings seems like a more attractive way to fight sin than merely trusting and obeying. We must acknowledge, however, that the Lord's work in us occurs quite often (perhaps most often) *without* heightened sensations of spiritual passion. Emotional signs are enticing, to be sure, but they are neither constant nor guaranteed—and as Martin Luther warned, neither are they reliable:

> Feelings come and feelings go and feelings are deceiving;
> My warrant is the Word of God, naught else is worth believing.
> Though all my heart should feel condemned for want of some
>   sweet token,
> There is One greater than my heart Whose Word cannot be
>   broken.
> I'll trust in God's unchanging Word till soul and body sever,
> For, though all things shall pass away, His Word shall stand
>   forever!

Unstable Ground

Scripture clearly and repeatedly teaches that our toughest-fought spiritual victories come, not when we rely on our senses, but when we entrust ourselves to God's promises. Believing God *when nothing else in life feels right or makes sense* is the very heart of spiritual maturity (Rom 4:18–21; Heb 11:1). It is thrilling when sanctified emotions align with theological conviction, but when our feelings collide with the truth, we must humbly entrust ourselves to the character of God and His promises. We must yield in obedient faith. Craving and expecting some inner sense or experience to charm away our sinful desires and to move our will brings serious trouble. In their pastoral work, the Puritans taught about the dangers of trusting in "sense" (emotions), rather than in the truth. Any ground outside of God's Word was, from their perspective, unstable and deadly. As Obadiah Sedgwick instructed centuries ago,

> Sense is not a fit judge of our condition …. We should be good and bad, found and lost, cheerful and sorrowful, many times in one day, nay, in one hour, if [emotion] gave sentence on our condition. Beloved, think well on this. How can sense reach unto the times of desertion, unto the times of want, unto the times … where faith expresses no acts but such as are pure and clear, and only grounded upon the promises? In these … times, [emotion] finds nothing to speak to us, … and we have nothing but a word of promise (all other things seem to fail and forsake) to sustain and retain us.[15]

Some are teaching today that emotional sensations of gladness must accompany our faith and obedience as a test of authenticity. But the Scriptures teach that faith is genuine when grounded and verified exclusively in God's revelation (Heb 11:1ff). When we rely on our awareness of emotions, we turn inward, making ourselves and our feelings the ground of our faith. Any ground of faith besides God's Word is a false hope or shifting sand.

Reading Scripture and pondering the work of Christ in salvation are essential disciplines of the Christian life, but without faith they have no impact beyond the accumulation of facts. Please do not mistake my concern: it is *not* that a deepened grasp of Scripture accomplishes nothing or is unimportant. In

---

[15] Obadiah Sedgwick, *The Doubting Believer* (Pittsburgh: Soli Deo Gloria, 1993), 65.

fact, without the frequent intake of divine truth there will be no spiritual sail for the Spirit to fill in order to thrust along the ship of our spiritual maturity. However, beyond what we read and ponder, it is what we *humbly believe* that empowers us in the Spirit. No matter what we may be experiencing in our circumstances or emotional responses, it is faith in God's Word that gives us immediate access to the gracious empowerment freely supplied by His Spirit. What is alarming about the current emotional and contemplative emphasis found among the "young, restless, and Reformed" is the absence of Scripture's most crucial component of sanctification: faith grounded solely in divine promises. Perhaps some are smuggling faith into concepts like "beholding" and "affection for Christ." But if beholding Christ means something other than knowing, believing, and obeying Christ in love, then it cannot be a legitimate ground of faith.

Meditation on the gospel changes nothing if we do not entrust ourselves wholly to the Word of Christ. Praying for the Holy Spirit to work through our cross-thoughts cannot enlist His power if we are not believing the truth and humbly yielding to it. Again, Obadiah Sedgwick shapes our understanding on this crucial nuance:

> We are, oftentimes, troubled by our own pride and folly. God ... gives unto us His word of promise to ground our believing, and we will have our [emotion] to be the ground. ... "If they hear not Moses and the prophets, neither will they be persuaded though one rose [sic] from the dead," Luke 16:31. So say I, if men will not believe because God has promised, neither will they believe if sense should stand up and speak. ... Know that {you must first put to your seal and hand of faith} before He delivers over to you the assuring evidences ... for though it is the favor of God which properly comforts, nevertheless it does not actually comfort unless faith has taken in that favor.
>
> "But are not former experiences ... grounds to future belief? Did not David remember the days of old?" I answer, "True." Experiences are good encouragements to the future acts of faith, but the Word of God is still the ground of faith. ... You have had

God's favor; you have had an answer, but how did you obtain them? Was it not by believing? Was it not by waiting upon some good word of promise? Your enjoying of them did not prevent your believing the word of promise, but believing that the word of promise let in and brought unto your soul that sweet and gracious experience; and, therefore, your experience was not the ground.[16]

Spiritual growth does not occur without our active involvement by the exercise of faith. To teach otherwise is to implicate God for the absence of fruit. When painful trials traumatize and rattle us, we must trust and obey God's character and promises. When feelings are flatlined and indifferent, we are called to entrust ourselves to our faithful Creator who knows our feeble frame. As with Abraham, these are "hope against hope" moments when circumstances do not make sense, earthly securities unravel, and nothing feels right (Rom 4:18–20). Such faith-filled humility has the makings of serious spiritual growth—when we simply believe, yield to, and obey the Word of Christ.

There is a very real danger in reducing spiritual change primarily to talk of the presence or absence of emotional "affections." All of us must ferociously guard against a heartless orthodoxy—a prime weapon of hell. But obsessing over what we "sense" and "feel" is not a clear way forward. It leads to a problem as equally hellish as legalism: people who "feel" close to God but do not believe Him! Jesus told the woman at the well: "You worship what you do not know" (John 4:22). The Samaritans produced generations of passionate worshipers (John 4:20), but they were ignorant of the truth. We should reject the deadness of self-righteous legalism, but neither should we be fooled by the pseudo-vitality of mere enthusiasm. The Father seeks those who worship Him in "in spirit and truth" (John 4:24) Truth is utterly objective. It comes from God—from outside of us—and is revealed to us by His special grace. We are called to believe it and to respond to its inherent objectivity, clarity, and authority. It is exceedingly dangerous to

[16] Ibid., 67–68.

pursue or to measure a relationship with God by means of sense and experience. The Word of God alone grants us "everything pertaining to life and godliness (2 Pet 1:3). When we entrust ourselves wholly to divine truth, we are never on unstable ground. In fact, humble faith—not feelings—is how the believer walks in the power of the Spirit and grows strong against temptation (Gal 5:16).

CHAPTER 3

SAVED TO WALK BY FAITH

FAITH is the foundational responsibility of God's people. By faith we receive sovereign grace. By faith we submit to divine truth. By faith we persevere. By faith we enjoy the saving and sanctifying grace of God. By faith we grasp and embrace the living and active Word of God. By faith we engage in genuine and spiritual worship of God. "Faith is the pivot on which everything revolves"[1] and is the primary means by which we participate in our spiritual growth. As it says in Romans 1:17, "For in it [the gospel] the righteousness of God is revealed from faith to faith; as it is written, 'But the righteous man shall live by faith.'" In other words, as believers in Jesus Christ, we have been saved to walk *by faith*.

There are other responsibilities and realities in the Christian life, but none are as crucial as faith. We *should* concern ourselves with loving, obeying, desiring, finding joy in, and beholding God. These are indispensable obligations and are helpful ways to think about our relationship with the Lord. However, we *cannot* perform any of these works apart from believing. How can we love Christ if we do not first accept what the Bible says about Him? How can we obey Him if we don't trust His commands? How can we desire Him if we are not fully persuaded of His eternal beauty? How can we find joy in Him without entrusting ourselves to His

[1] G. C. Berkouwer, *Faith and Sanctification* (Grand Rapids: Eerdmans, 1952), 93.

sovereign care? How can we behold Him apart from the eyes of faith? Without faith we cannot fulfill a single duty—let alone enjoy the many blessings—of spiritual growth.

Perhaps it is helpful to reaffirm on the one hand that conquering sin *will not happen apart from the Spirit's power* working in us (Eph 2:10; Phil 1:6; 2:13). He must illumine our minds, convict us of sin, increase our discernment, grant us power, produce gratitude, bring comfort, nurture faith, and lead us to maturity. We should equally affirm, on the other hand, that conquering sin *will not happen apart from our faith-empowered effort*. We must pour biblical truth into our minds, entrust ourselves to that truth, be alert, flee from sin, persevere, be prayerful and grateful in everything, and make God's glory our highest aim. Through the Spirit, we have been given the mind of Christ (1 Cor 2:16). When we entrust ourselves to the truth (i.e., exercise faith) and take every thought captive to Christ (2 Cor 10:5), then sinful perspectives give way to righteous ones.

The result is the spiritual renewal of our affections, motives, emotions, and will. We discern truth from lies (Heb 4:12; 5:14); we experience power over the flesh (Rom 8:4–13; Gal 5:16); we grow strong in faith (Rom 4:18–21; 2 Pet 3:18); we know a deeper love and intimacy with the Lord (Eph 3:16–19); our pride is subdued (1 Pet 5:6–10); and we are drawn upward in richer worship (Rom 12:1–3). Every fruit and every failure in the Christian life is a barometer of our trust in God. Indeed, we will not see a harvest of mature fruit in our lives without hearts made fertile through faith. There are no methods or motifs that can replace the necessity of faith in our walk with the Lord. In short, when it comes to how we think about our task in the Christian life, we must prioritize faith.

THE PRIORITY OF FAITH: ENJOYING GRACE

Faith Receives Grace

Faith is vital because grace is vital. We never outgrow our need for both (2 Pet 3:18). The unmerited favor of God found in Christ is the fountain from which all spiritual blessings flow. Any talk of progress, growth, or maturity in sanctification occurs in the context of grace, which is where faith comes to life. We have been given the gift of faith so that we can benefit from God's gift of grace. Through faith we are justified by God's grace, and through faith we rely on God's grace for sanctification. Without grace there is no power for spiritual growth, but without faith we cannot benefit from the grace that leads to spiritual growth. Like an infant's umbilical cord, faith channels to us the supernatural nourishment supplied by divine grace. Therefore, to "walk by faith" is to rely on grace. The two are inseparable.

Just as we have been gloriously saved "by grace … through faith" (Eph 2:8), we have also been saved to "walk by faith" (2 Cor 5:7). Acts 26:18 records that Jesus told the apostle Paul that believers are "sanctified by faith in Me." In Christ we are *eternally* set apart as His own possession and *progressively* set apart for greater spiritual fruitfulness. As one churchman observed, "Faith does not become unemployed after justification."[2] Paul affirms this truth in Galatians 2:20–21: "I have been crucified with Christ; and it is no longer I who live, but Christ lives in me; and the life which I now live in the flesh I live by faith in the Son of God, who loved me and gave Himself up for me. I do not nullify the grace of God, for if righteousness comes through the Law, then Christ died needlessly." Based on Paul's logic, when we fail to grow in our faith, we "nullify," as it were, the grace provided in the gospel. We need grace to be faithful each day, and this means a *moment-by-moment* walk of faith. To put it another way, through faith we are brought into union with Christ, and through faith we experience our communion with Christ.

Faith Pleases the Lord

Nowhere is the priority of faith seen more clearly than in Hebrews 11:6, where we are told that "without faith it is impossible to

---

[2] George J. Zemek, *A Biblical Theology of the Doctrines of Sovereign Grace* (Eugene, OR: Wipf & Stock, 2005), 182.

please Him, for he who comes to God must believe that He is and that He is a rewarder of those who seek Him." In order to please God, we "must believe that He is." But to believe in God in any meaningful sense means that we must wholeheartedly believe His self-revelation. The author of Hebrews is drawing from the language of the Old Testament, where God disclosed Himself as the great "I am." He is the eternal, self-existent, and all-glorious Creator of the universe. Genuine faith seeks after God *as He has revealed Himself to be.* Anything less is akin to the faith of demons, who affirm God's existence but refuse to worship Him (Jas 2:19).

Hebrews 11:6 also declares that God is the "rewarder of those who seek Him." Grace is at the center of the entire principle, and our reward is the fulfillment of what He has promised. The concept of reward was introduced earlier in Hebrews 10:35–36: "Therefore, do not throw away your confidence, which has a great reward. For you have need of endurance, so that when you have done the will of God, you may receive what was promised." The reward of faith mentioned here is not a "trophy" earned by believing, but the reality that you will receive what was promised if you believed—grace. *Thus, we are pleasing to God only when we humbly confess His sovereign existence and entrust ourselves to His gracious presence.* This is what makes faith so important: it yields to God's authority ("He is") and rests in God's grace ("He is a rewarder").

Without faith, good works are not good, and strong affections are not worshipful—at least not from God's perspective. God is pleased with humble faith, not bare human effort. Therefore, if for no other motivation than the pleasure of God, we must make faith a priority in our lives. In fact, "if we are not living a life of faith, we cannot be pleasing to God. We cannot have God's smile on our lives without faith."[3] Faith is important not only because it receives God's grace, but also because it pleases God.

---

[3] R. Kent Hughes, *Hebrews: An Anchor for the Soul,* vol. 2 in *Preaching the Word* (Wheaton, IL: Crossway Books, 1993), 79.

Faith Protects from Sin

In addition to receiving grace and pleasing God, faith also plays a vital role in protecting us from sin. It functions as a "shield" to protect us from "the flaming arrows of the evil one" (Eph 6:16). If we neglect to use our shield, we leave ourselves unprotected from the allurement to sin that comes from Satan's attack. Romans 14:23 reveals the principle that "whatever is not from faith is sin." Paul is not teaching some kind of subjective morality whereby, if you believe a practice is acceptable then it is okay for you to do it. On the contrary, Paul is using the issue of conscience to reinforce the principle of Hebrews 11:6—faith pleases God—from a different angle. If you think that something is sinful, but you do it anyway, you are not acting in faith. Something other than the pleasure and presence of God is driving your actions. God is displeased when we trust in anything and anyone apart from Him. Anything we might do or feel apart from faith will be polluted by self-reliance or self-righteousness. Religious acts and emotional stirrings may satisfy our personal quest for a deeper sense of spirituality, but God will not be satisfied unless they arise from genuine faith. Thus, in order to truly worship and please God, our actions and affections must rise from our trust in Him alone.

While there are many helpful spiritual disciplines and vital responsibilities in the Christian life, none of them eclipse the need to walk by faith; in fact, all are fueled by faith. The battle for growth and maturity is a battle to believe God. To borrow the language of Sinclair Ferguson, "Strong faith in Christ draws on the resources of his grace and sets us free from many inhibitions that bind our lives."[4]

THE NATURE OF FAITH: EMBRACING TRUTH

The Biblical Language of Faith

Formulating a full-bodied explanation of the nature of faith can be a daunting task. However, when we turn to the Bible, the

---

[4] Sinclair B. Ferguson, *The Christian Life: A Doctrinal Introduction* (Edinburgh: Banner of Truth Trust, 2001), 67.

language used to describe faith is surprisingly straightforward. For instance, in Genesis 15:6 Abraham "*believed* in the LORD; and He [the LORD] reckoned it to him as righteousness." Here, the Old Testament term for "believed" describes Abraham's confidence in the promise and the promise Giver. Similarly, Proverbs 3:5 commands us to "*trust* in the LORD with all your heart and do not lean on your own understanding." The Old Testament term for "trust" highlights the contrast between reliance on self and reliance on the Lord.

The New Testament uses similar terms to describe faith: the Greek words *pístis* and *peíthō*. The *pístis* word group is the most significant New Testament term for faith. In its passive uses *pístis* signifies that which is believed (i.e., "the faith") or that which evokes trust. Thus, in Galatians 1:23 Paul speaks of "preaching the *faith* which he once tried to destroy." In this verse, "the faith" is the objective body of truth which elicits the trust of God's people. In its active sense, *pístis* signifies active believing, trusting, relying upon, or depending upon someone or something. Romans 3:26 illustrates the active use of *pístis*: "for the demonstration, I say, of His righteousness at the present time, so that He would be just and the justifier of the one who *has faith* in Jesus." The one who has faith is the one who actively and dependently looks to Christ.

Turning to *peíthō*, this term signifies a firm persuasion, a certainty, or an assurance about its object. Paul uses this term in Romans 8:38–39 when he says, "For *I am convinced* that neither death, nor life, nor angels, nor principalities, nor things present, nor things to come, nor powers, nor height, nor depth, nor any other created thing, will be able to separate us from the love of God, which is in Christ Jesus our Lord." Paul's assurance was rooted in his persuasion of the certainty of God's love. This kind of persuasion is the essence of faith.

The Theological Descriptions of Faith

In addition to the language of faith found in the Bible, Hebrews 11:1 provides a biblical baseline for our understanding of the nature of faith. In the previous chapter, the author of Hebrews presents Christ as the only sufficient source of true life, and thus faith in Christ as the only hope of "preserving … the soul" (Heb 10:39). Chapter 11 proceeds to describe what this soul-preserving faith looks like in the context of real-life situations. A host of saints lines the pages of this chapter as a great cloud of witnesses, testifying to the vitality of their faith and to the trustworthiness of God in every conceivable situation. Each example of faith set forth in this chapter can be described as "the assurance of things hoped for, the conviction of things not seen" (Heb 11:1). This brings us back to the essence of faith. You can say more about faith than what is found in this verse, but you must not say less. Faith grounds our hope in the promises of God (Heb 10:1–18) and guides our lives according to the instruction of God (Heb 10:19–39), even when we cannot see any external evidence to substantiate the trustworthiness of God. Faith, without seeing, finds resolute assurance in the hope of the gospel and is firmly convinced of the worthiness of Christ. To borrow the words of Herman Bavinck, "Only by faith does a promise become our possession."[5]

Admittedly, the Bible's teaching on faith could never be reduced to a few brief word studies or a couple cross-references. However, we've seen that even a cursory look at the Bible's vocabulary for faith reveals its nature. The language of the biblical authors across the sweep of redemptive history includes the concepts of humble recognition, dependent response, and committed reliance upon the gracious revelation of God. Faith humbly embraces God as He has graciously revealed Himself. In other words, faith, when biblically understood, is a holistic commitment to the truthfulness, authority, and graciousness of God. In the words of the Westminster Confession of Faith,

> By this faith, a Christian believes to be true whatsoever is revealed in the Word, for the authority of God Himself speaking therein; and acts differently upon that which each particular

---

[5] Herman Bavinck, *Reformed Dogmatics: Abridged in One Volume*, ed. John Bolt (Grand Rapids: Baker Academic, 2011), 127.

passage thereof contains; yielding obedience to the commands, trembling at the threatenings, and embracing the promises of God for this life, and that which is to come. But the principal acts of saving faith are accepting, receiving, and resting upon Christ alone for justification, sanctification, and eternal life.[6]

Or, to put it more succinctly, "saving faith … is the whole of my being embracing all of Christ."[7]

Historically, the nature of saving faith has been explained by theologians with the Latin words *notitia, assensus,* and *fiducia.* Faith *understands* the truth to be believed (*notitia*); it is *persuaded* by the truth as it is revealed (*assensus*); and it *trusts* in the truth when it is received (*fiducia*). This explanation of faith was not intended to dissect the psychology of faith; it originated to demonstrate the nature of faith as a response to objective truth. Clearly, there is a subtle danger in examining faith as a psychological phenomenon. By its very nature, faith looks outside of itself, not deeper within self. In fact, the moment a person orients his faith inward, it ceases to be faith. The pleasing power of a life of faith is not found in the faith itself, it is found in the object of the faith. God is pleased by faith and promises to reward faith, but there is nothing meritorious about faith that deserves such a response.

The Objective Mooring of Faith

The efficacy of faith lies in the worthiness of the object, not in the sensations of the subject. For example, I might have complete confidence in someone who is, in fact, a liar. In that case, the vigor of my trust in him makes no difference in the situation, since the liar (unlike God) has no intention of fulfilling his promise. Faith, for it to be of any value, must be understood in relation to the objectivity of truth. This is why the church has historically formulated its understanding of faith in relation to the truth. Without truth there is no faith, because if you don't know what you believe,

[6] WCF, 14.2.
[7] John MacArthur, Jr., *Faith Works: The Gospel According to the Apostles* (Dallas: Word, 1993), 45.

then you don't believe. In order for faith to be genuine, it must know, accept, and trust in the truth revealed by God in the Scriptures. Faith receives grace by believing and surrendering to truth.

If it seems impersonal to emphasize truth to this degree, remember that God made His truth personal when He sent His Son into this world. Jesus came into this world "full of grace and *truth*" (John 1:14; cf. v. 17), and He continues to be "the way, and the *truth*, and the life" (John 14:6). Emphasizing the role of truth in the formation of faith isn't impersonal because Jesus is the truth, and the truth of the Bible is where we find Him. In this present age we do not have sight of spiritual realities; we have truth that must be believed. The truth of Scripture teaches us to trust and rest in the God of Scripture. The clearer we see the Person and promises of God on the pages of Scripture, the more confident we will be in Him. This is why we must inform our faith with the deep truths of the Bible if we want to see it increase. As Calvin put it, "Faith is a knowledge of the divine benevolence toward us and a sure persuasion of its truth."[8] In order to believe in what we cannot see, we must hear about it from the Bible. Romans 10:17 confirms that "faith comes from hearing, and hearing by the word of Christ." Put simply, the truth produces faith, and faith responds to truth.

THE FRUIT OF FAITH: ENGAGING WORSHIP

A faith that receives divine grace and responds to biblical truth will produce spiritual fruit. Maturity comes as we believe what God says more than we believe what we "see." If we want to intensify our worship, we need to increasingly respond to our circumstances in faith. More and more we need to accept and appropriate His promises and precepts in our lives. This is not always easy; in fact, many times it is a struggle to believe in the midst of the day-to-day grind and the overwhelming trials of life.

---

[8] John Calvin, *Institutes of the Christian Religion*, trans. Ford Lewis Battles, ed. John T. McNeill, 2 vols. (Louisville: Westminster John Knox Press, 1960), 3.2.12.

All Christians can see a reflection of their own spiritual life in the man who cries out in Mark 9:24, "I do believe; help my unbelief." This is one of the truest and purest confessions in the entire Bible, and it describes every individual in the process of sanctification. It also demonstrates the need for increasing faith as we seek to glorify God in the throes of everyday life.

Fake Faith

When we walk by faith rather than sight, we will see God-glorifying growth in our lives. In fact, "Faith is to be the foundation of good works. And it follows from the nature of faith which clings to divine grace that it cannot possibly be unfruitful."[9] The radical change in belief that both initiates and sustains the Christian life will result in a radical change in behavior. This was certainly James' expectation when he said, "faith, if it has no works, is dead, being by itself" (Jas 2:17). James wasn't undermining the principle of salvation by faith alone; he was challenging the idea that saving faith could stay alone. He recognized that genuine faith leads to genuine change, and where there is no change, there is no faith. On this side of heaven, our faith will never be perfect, nor will it lead to perfection. However, true faith is not fruitless. God's sanctifying grace flows freely through the culvert of faith so that the stronger the faith is, the steadier the growth will be.

Because faith is our first responsibility in the Christian life, it is the first place we must examine when fruit is lacking. "Supplies from Christ do not fail. But our faith fails in receiving them."[10] If you are not seeing spiritual growth and fruit in your life, the root problem can be traced back to some form of unbelief in your heart. When you don't desire the all-surpassing worth of Christ above the fleeting pleasure of sin, the Bible diagnoses your problem as weak faith (Heb 11:24–28). When the joy of the Lord feels like a trite superficiality, rather than a deep-seated comfort,

[9] Berkouwer, *Faith and Sanctification*, 41.
[10] John Owen, *Communion with the Triune God*, ed. Kelly M. Kapic and Justin Taylor (Wheaton, IL: Crossway, 2007), 269.

you need to seek a deeper faith—not new emotional sensations (Rom 15:13). You simply cannot drum up deep and lasting spiritual fruit in your life; you must dependently rely upon the Spirit and His prescribed means to do this work. In this way, "faith is man's response to God's initiative and enablements."[11]

Futile Works

Fruitless faith is a dead faith, yet at the same time, works without faith are futile. Genuine trust in God opposes self and worshipfully looks to Him in reverence and humility. Think of it this way: if faith orients us toward God and His grace, then anything we do apart from faith will be self-oriented effort. "Good works in the strict sense are those done out of true faith, in conformity with God's law, and to his glory."[12] If we are not clear on this point, we run the risk of divorcing our responsibility to the law from the promise of grace. We risk prioritizing human effort over simple faith. This is particularly true when it comes to love. Our relationship with God rests on the eternal foundation of His love (Eph 1:4), and our duty before God is summarized by the command to love (Matt 22:37–40). Love is the greatest good work and the essence of law keeping. However, we cannot love apart from faith, at least not in this present age. There will come a time when perfect love will spring forth from pure hearts, but that will not happen until we are transformed into the glorified image of Christ. When we see Christ we will be made like Him and love like Him. In the meantime, however, we need faith in Christ to produce a love for Christ. In order to obediently love Christ, we must genuinely believe what He has revealed to us about Himself.

---

[11] Zemek, *A Biblical Theology*, 183.

[12] Herman Bavinck, *Holy Spirit, Church, and New Creation*, vol. 4 of *Reformed Dogmatics* (Grand Rapids: Baker Academic, 2008), 231. Bavinck's language reflects the teaching of the *Heidelberg Catechism*, Lord's Day 33: "Q. But what are good works? A. Only those which are done out of true faith, in accordance with the law of God, and to his glory, and not those based on our own opinion or on precepts of men."

Fruitful Worship

The objectivity of truth-informed faith is the only way to guarantee that our subjective affections are actually directed toward Christ and not some idol of the heart. I might experience all the inward sensations in the world, but if I am not believing in what the Bible says about Christ, then those emotions are idolatrous, not worshipful. True worship only takes place when the spirit is engaged with truth by faith (John 4:24).

We are sanctified when we look to Christ as the author and perfecter of our faith, but the only way to behold the transformational glory of the Lord is to believe what we find about Him in the Bible (2 Cor 3:18). Christ's glory cannot be seen or experienced apart from the truth found in the Bible. Additionally, the sanctifying beauty of Christ will have no effect on those who do not entrust themselves to Him. No one can love Christ and find joy in Him unless they first believe what He has said about Himself and trust in what He has promised to do for them. As 1 Peter 1:8–9 reminds us, "Though you have not seen him, you love him, and though you do not now see Him now, but believe in Him, you greatly rejoice with joy inexpressible and full of glory, obtaining as the outcome of your faith the salvation of your souls."

Genuine love for Christ stems from genuine faith in Christ. In Galatians 5:6 Paul writes, "For in Christ Jesus neither circumcision nor uncircumcision means anything, but faith working through love." Paul is not arguing that the need for affectionate love overshadows the role of simple belief. In fact, the grammar of the passage clearly communicates that love is what faith *does*.[13] The principle embedded in Paul's logic is that faith, not rituals of self-righteousness like circumcision, is what produces fruits like "waiting for the hope" (v. 5) and "love" (v. 6). Thus, the more we trust God, the more we will love Him and will be freed to love those around us. This makes sense when we recognize that this entire section of Galatians emphasizes the priority of faith over works (vv. 4–5). For the Galatians, a reversion to the Old

[13] The sentence reads literally, "but faith, through love, is working."

Covenant laws of circumcision would have severed them from Christ (v. 4) and prevented them from truly keeping the law of love (vv. 13–15). From a broader theological perspective, it is crucial to recognize this distinction, because if we place love for Christ before faith in Christ then we have placed a work of the Law (v. 14) before believing. Human efforts to produce justification always prove powerless to save and powerless to produce fruit.

By contrast, simple faith in Christ possesses the God-ordained efficacy to bring us into a right relationship with God and produce fruits consistent with His Law (e.g., love). Rather than trusting works of the Law to gain entrance into the faith, we can trust that simple faith will result in our justification, and it will produce the fruits of justification in our lives (vv. 5, 22–24). Thus, love does not generate faith; it is the outworking of faith.

This in no way demeans the role of love in the Christian life; it merely demonstrates how the Spirit produces the fruit of love in our lives. "Faith is not a competitor of love and good works but rather a sponsor, and gives foundation to them because it acknowledges the grace of God."[14] Love for God consists of obedience to His Word proceeding from faith. Any so-called love without the root of faith is human effort, and any so-called faith without the fruit of love is dead (1 Cor 13:2). As Walter Marshall explained, "That love which is the end of the law, must flow from faith unfeigned."[15] We must walk by faith in order to walk in love. Sovereign grace flows through the channel of faith to produce joy, love, and every spiritual fruit. Thus, as a result of God's grace in the process of sanctification, our love and all other forms of law-keeping become faith-driven acts of worship. This is how God glorifies Himself and makes us worshipers.

---

[14] Berkouwer, *Faith and Sanctification*, 32.
[15] Walter Marshall, *The Gospel Mystery of Sanctification* (Grand Rapids: Reformation Heritage Books, 2013), 94.

FREE TO BE HOLY

THE LIFE OF FAITH: WALKING BY FAITH

A Life of Entrustment

Faith is the priority of the Christian life because it allows us to enjoy the grace of God by embracing His truth and engaging in true worship. Faith is both the first responsibility of the Christian life and the continuing imperative of Christian living. But what does it mean to walk by faith? What does this kind of faith look like in the course of everyday life? The word *entrustment* provides a helpful explanation of the life of faith. It goes far beyond gaining knowledge or mental assent. To entrust yourself to someone involves placing yourself at the complete disposal of his promises and character. The apostle Peter said that Jesus offered Himself as our supreme model for this kind of faith: "For you have been called for this purpose, since Christ also suffered for you, leaving you an example for you to follow in His steps, who committed no sin, nor was any deceit found in His mouth; and while being reviled, He did not revile in return; while suffering, He uttered no threats, but kept entrusting Himself to Him who judges righteously" (1 Pet 2:21–23). Our Savior "entrusted" Himself to God on the basis of His Father's righteous justice in all things. The result was a willingness to "hand Himself over" to the sovereign purposes of God. That's the essence of genuine faith.

Not long ago a young man mentioned that he was shocked to hear that true faith isn't verified by whatever we're sensing at the time. He always assumed that faith—if it was real—had to be somehow "felt" or "emotionally experienced." He went on to explain that he didn't think he could truly obey until certain emotional sensations accompanied his submission to Christ. It's a common but unnecessary confusion. As we have already seen from Hebrews 11:1, "Faith is the assurance of things hoped for, the conviction of things not seen." The writer defines faith without any reference to how we feel. It's rooted in spiritual "hope" and "conviction," regardless of what we are experiencing. When we entrust our lives to the character of Christ in spite of what's

66

happening on the outside or what's being "felt" on the inside, the fruit is obedience to His will. It's not that we're totally unmoved by our surroundings and emotions. But real faith is the "assurance of things hoped for"—not of things sensed. Real faith says: "Christ is worthy no matter how I feel." For many today their failure to have victory over sin isn't rooted in a lack of emotions, but the neglect of true faith in the face of temptation.

Genuine faith in God produces, not a fragile wish or inward focus on experience, but an unshakeable hope, anvil-hard convictions, and Spirit-empowered strength over the world, the flesh, and Satan's schemes (Heb 11:3–40). Trusting God despite our fears and subjective assessments is the essence of entrustment. Faith is grounded in God's Word alone and expressed in unflinching conviction. The Scriptures teach that believing is seeing, and not the other way around (John 20:29; Rom 8:24–25; Gal 2:20; 2 Cor 5:7). Faith is real entrustment to Christ and loving submission to His commands. In this case, it is the conviction of things "not felt."

A Life of Self-Denial

In addition to entrustment, a walk of faith will include self-denial. Jesus said that the Christian life is all about denying ourselves in order to follow Him (Matt 16:24). Each moment of genuine faith is an act of self-denial. To believe the Word of Christ is to starve our old appetites which are demanding to be fed. Our permanent union with Christ gives us new spiritual inclinations and power (Rom 8:2–14), but we sometimes want to satisfy ourselves more than we want to honor the Master who bought us.

When our flesh entices us to grab temporary pleasures, courageous faith should go into action. This is what Moses did! Hebrews 11:24–26 says, "By faith Moses ... refused to be called the son of Pharoah's daughter, choosing rather to endure ill-treatment with the people of God than to enjoy the passing pleasures of sin, considering the reproach of Christ greater riches than the treasures of Egypt; for he was looking to the reward." By faith he

FREE TO BE HOLY

chose God's will rather than the "passing pleasures of sin" because heavenly riches were greater than what is found on earth. How did he know God's promises were better? Instead of believing the lies propagated by his pagan culture, the flesh, or Satan's temptations, he believed the character of the One who promised the reward.

In a word, Moses died to himself. If he had looked inward for an emotional sense of affection, he would have been turning toward himself rather than entrusting his entire existence to God's promise. And it wasn't an easy choice. He was enticed with everything most people only dream about. With a simple nod to his flesh, Moses could have enjoyed power, riches, round-the-clock sensual pleasure, and insulation from many of life's afflictions. In fact, Hebrews 11:27 says, "By faith he left Egypt, not fearing the wrath of the king; for he endured, as seeing Him who is unseen." To the unbeliever, that is a strange way to describe someone's motives. How does anyone "see" what can't be seen? But that is precisely what drives the self-denial of Christian obedience. Taking up our cross means believing God regardless of the lying promises of outward or inward enticements. The hymn writer declares, "I dare not trust the sweetest frame, but wholly lean on Jesus' name." Indeed, that is the very definition of self-denying faith—it simply rests on the knowledge of God. The Puritans seemed to understand this issue clearly. Richard Sibbes writes:

> Obedience is most direct when there is nothing else to sweeten the action. Although the sacrifice is imperfect, yet the obedience with which it is offered is accepted. Feeling and freeness of spirit are often reserved until duty is discharged ... . This does not hinder the Spirit's freedom in blowing upon our souls when He pleases ... . As in sailing, the hand must be to the helm and the eye to the star, so here we must put forth that little strength we have to duty and look up for assistance, which the Spirit, as freely as seasonably, will afford.[16]

---

[16] Richard Sibbes, *The Bruised Reed*, originally published 1658 (n.p., Fig Pub: 2013), 57.

A Life of Submission

Along with entrustment and self-denial, faith includes submission. Some today are teaching that our will is passive in sanctification—as if faith consists merely of right thoughts with no relationship to self-denial or yielding the will. But according to Scripture, an unyielded will betrays a dead faith (Jas 2:17). Divine power is behind our ability to turn from sin and to prefer Christ, to be sure. But although God is the ultimate cause of our sanctification, the means of grace He has provided include more than merely "going back to our secured pardon." Preferring Christ above vices does not simply happen as we bask in the "shock and awe" of God's amazing grace! God could have designed progressive sanctification that way. He could have ordained that as we revisit the theme of scandalous grace over and over, our pride is melted away, sin no longer entices, fleshly desires take flight, and our will seamlessly melds into delightful conformity to Christ. No real battle, and no moment when "by the Spirit" we must "[put] to death the deeds of the body" (Rom 8:13). There are times when our obedience to Christ seems to happen in just that way! Reflecting on a victory over a particular sin, it is as though we experienced the delight of saying "yes" to God without the pain of saying "no" to the flesh. Biblically speaking, however, true obedience happens only when both things occur. Whatever we "feel" in the battle, Sinclair Ferguson is correct: "You cannot 'mortify' sin without the pain of the kill. There is no other way!"[17]

We're all familiar with the profound words of Jesus in the Garden on the night of His betrayal. Under the terrifying prospect of having His righteous life counted as sinful and condemned, in His humanity Jesus strained for hours to yield His will to that dark moment. It was not that He did not fully delight in obedience or that He did not truly desire eternal rewards over earthly comfort. His mind and affections were always truth-filled,

[17] Sinclair B. Ferguson, "The Practice of Mortification," *Tabletalk* Magazine, Ligonier Ministries, last revised January 1, 2007, http://www.ligonier.org/learn/articles/practice-mortification/ (accessed March 2016).

humble, and wholly submissive. The intense struggle in the Garden was caused by a combination of the fierce temptation to flee, our Lord's revulsion at having a foreign guilt counted against Him, and the frailty of His human will. He was troubled in His soul as the divine will collided with the temptation to run for His life! He knew His Father's character was unimpeachable. He fully understood that drinking the cup of the Father's wrath would be rewarded by "the joy set before Him" (Heb 12:2). But our Lord needed to act on what He knew. His humble submission in the Garden was an act of obedient faith and a yielded will. The two always go together. Especially in the darkest emotional upheavals, it is humble faith in the truth that ignites passion for Christ's worthiness and moves the will in righteousness.

Let's be clear. Faith is not some passive "yielding," where we try to deactivate our will and drift on the currents of sense and whim. That's an old and disastrous trick of the Keswick Movement.[18] Inevitably, some of them went so far as to teach that obedience is not us behaving like Christ, but Christ behaving through us. In other words, the Keswick Movement taught that Christians' obedience is not directly willing and active, but instead that believers should passively expect God to do everything for them. If that sounds eerily similar to what many are claiming today, that is because it is. There is no denying that the contemporary emphasis on what Christ has done for us in the past is leaving many confused about submitting to His will in the present. But, according to Scripture, spiritual transformation and withstanding temptation involve both believing in Christ's finished work and obeying His enduring commands.

We have been saved by grace through faith (Eph 2:8–9). In Christ, we are no longer condemned nor under the dominating power of sin (Rom 6:4–11; 8:12). Our eternity is secure (Rom 8:28–30); God is willing and working in us for His pleasure

---

[18] I.e., a theological movement that started in Great Britain in the 1800s which thought that by deep contemplation on Christ, God would do everything in regard to their progressive sanctification, without any complementary effort on man's part.

(Phil 2:13), and He most certainly will complete the work He began in us (Phil 1:6). After having given in to sin, donned the old grave clothes, and experienced the Spirit's conviction and displeasure—God's forgiveness in such cases reminds us of our no-condemnation status. Hallelujah! But with each failure also comes a piercing conviction of our need to trust God and to obey His will more aggressively. God is working in us, but He promises to accomplish that work by means of commands we are called to obey willingly.

Trying to silence our conscience simply because our sin was paid for is to miss the point. Saving faith frees us from the pangs of condemnation, and we are now filled with a longing to be conformed to the image of Christ. A guilty conscience does not make a mature Christian cower in fear of judgment (1 John 4:18). Instead, it sends us to the Word of God for repentance and renewed faith. The Spirit convicts our conscience in order to clarify God's holy desires, prompt a godly sorrow, cultivate greater hatred for sin, lead us to true repentance, and call us to more humble faith and self-denial. These are all divine works of growth in grace and are promised in the gospel. This is the heart and soul of the faith-centered life. I fear that some today are pursuing a temporarily relieved conscience through emotional stimulation rather than a daily clean one. To walk by faith is to trust the power of the gospel and to live by Christ's resolve, "Not my will, but Yours be done" (Luke 22:42).

Here is the good news about the battle for spiritual growth: we can know for certain, even temptation by temptation, whether we are walking with God by evaluating our heart and conduct by the Word of God. Where it speaks, we are called to believe it, entrust ourselves to it, and yield to the Spirit in obedience (Gal 5:16, 25; Eph 5:18). If we constantly obsess with our feelings, we are left to human assessments of our spiritual condition—an inconclusive enterprise, as the apostle Paul observed in 1 Corinthians 4:4. Sin and disobedience are not rooted ultimately in a lack of joy or in the absence of affectionate emotions toward Christ; they are rooted in a lack of faith. Consequently, waiting to obey in faith until we can crank up enough internal passion for Christ is a spiritual dead end. Humble, obedient faith is the essence of loving Christ. True faith does not wait for anything that can be seen or felt. It simply believes.

Faith, not sight, summarizes the entire Christian life (2 Cor 5:7). Walking by sight is natural and easy. It takes little work to live without faith. Man intuitively lives according to his senses rather than God's promises. It is hard not to let feelings, experiences, and circumstances determine your perspective of reality when you can see them so clearly. Sight naturally becomes our guide when we are passive about our faith. But when we actively pursue faith, the truth regulates our lives. By faith we hold onto the certainty that God, who transcends our feelings, experiences, and circumstances, is the One who determines reality. *His truth is true, even when it doesn't feel right. His will is ultimate, even when our experiences seem determinative. His hand is mighty, even when our circumstances seem omnipotent. His character is holy, even when our emotions betray us. His promises are final, even when despair seems permanent.* Realities such as these can be grasped only by faith—a certainty in the truth of God despite our natural wisdom. When we walk by this kind of faith, the sanctifying grace of God's truth is unleashed in our hearts to conform us to the image of Christ.

CHAPTER 4

SAVED FROM SIN'S TYRANNY

NOT long ago, as I was sitting in my study working through the text I was to preach on Sunday, I remember being struck by the thought that every day I wake up to meet the new day, and my affections and convictions are still centered on the honor and glory of my Savior, Jesus Christ. Despite the previous day's battles and spiritual weariness, despite the passing of another night of sleep, I wake each morning still loving the Lord, still desiring to be like Him, and still longing to see Him face to face. My old wicked self has not driven out the Holy Spirit and overthrown the reign of new life in my heart. Similarly, if I go to sleep with a burdened conscience, by morning it's yet burdened even more to be in unhindered fellowship with my Savior. That's the wonder of God's grace and power. He not only redeems us but also sustains our faith, continues the work He began at our conversion, and promises to make us "stand in the presence of His glory blameless with great joy" (Jude 24). The morning-and-evening cycle of every day continues to demonstrate that even though—as the apostle Paul said—I haven't yet become fully mature (Phil 3:12), I've been justified and placed permanently into the family of God. I cannot be lost.

To be justified is to be faultless and without guilt. In justification, God's attitude toward the sinner is utterly reversed.[1] Being formerly condemned, the redeemed now enjoy full vindication

---

[1] John MacArthur, Jr., *Faith Works: The Gospel According to the Apostles* (Dallas: Word, 1993), 89.

from God.[2] But how can a sinner be faultless before a holy God? On the basis of man's own nature and intrinsic character, it's impossible. Every thought, word, and deed of fallen human beings is worthless in the sight of God. Even the most noble expression of human "righteousness" is a vile garment discarded by God (Isa 64:6). Until conversion we were "by nature children of wrath" (Eph 2:3), dead in sin and headed for "the day of wrath and revelation of the righteous judgment of God" (Rom 2:5). Justification occurs when, by the sovereign grace of God, we turn (repent) from self-worship and the pursuit of sin, and we entrust (exercise faith) our life and eternity to the Person and work of Jesus Christ. Having repented and believed, God *declares* us righteous in His sight, not on the basis of our own deeds, but on the basis of the perfect righteousness and atoning death of Christ put to our eternal account (Rom 4:2–5; 2 Cor 5:21; Gal 3:11; Phil 3:9; Col 2:13–14).

And being declared righteous by God, our status changes from condemned to fully pardoned. Explaining this divine transaction, John MacArthur writes:

> In its theological sense, justification is a forensic, or purely legal, term. It describes what God declares about the believer. In fact, justification effects no actual change whatsoever in the sinner's nature or character. Justification is a divine judicial edict. It changes our status only, but it carries ramifications that guarantee other changes will follow.[3]

We're still sinners through and through, but no longer guilty before the bar of divine justice. Our fallen nature and fleshly appetites are still present, but they are no longer held against us (Ps 32:1–2). We are treated by God as entirely righteous in His sight—free from the penalty of sin! The "reckoning" of right-eousness to the believer is an act of divine grace whereby God credits His righteousness to our moral account. Just as the Father placed (imputed) our guilt upon the innocent Son of glory, so

[2] Ibid.
[3] Ibid.

74

He imputes to us—the guilty—His righteousness, that we might be declared innocent (2 Cor 5:21). Romans 4:3 states, "Abraham believed God, and it was credited to him as righteousness." And verse 5 states that "to the one who ... believes in Him who justifies the ungodly, his faith is credited as righteousness."

It may seem at first glance that Abraham's act of faith made him personally righteous, compelling a divine pardon. Verses 4 and 5, however, soundly refute that error. Verse 4 indicates that if Abraham's obedient faith were a justifying "work," then God's righteousness would be given as a "wage"—as "what is due." But the object of Abraham's faith was not himself, his deeds, or his own righteousness, but God, who alone "justifies the ungodly." Therefore, God imputed righteousness to Abraham as *a favoring grace* (Rom 4:4–5). Abraham's faith sprang from the knowledge of his own ungodliness and resulted in his confession that God's righteousness alone, imputed to his wretched moral account, can render him acceptable.

VITAL UNION WITH CHRIST

But freedom from guilt at conversion is not where our liberation ends! Our vital union with Christ (John 14:20–21, 23; Rom 6:5; 1 Cor 6:17) sets us free, not only from the penalty of sin, but also from the grip of it. Sin's dominion—its mastery over our heart, soul, mind, and strength—has ended. The power of our former bondage has been utterly shattered, and the implications are massive and glorious. In Christ, we've made a very real break with the way our hearts naturally recoil at truth. Our spiritual constitution has changed. Union with Christ's death and resurrection actually crucifies our old life and ignites the resurrection power of our new one (Rom 6:4–7). We don't have to let sin reign (Rom 6:12). We are no longer slaves of unrighteousness, chained to sin and serving our lusts by compulsion (Rom 6:16–19). There are certainly times, however, when we behave as though we're still imprisoned. Instead of believing the truth and yielding to the Spirit's power, we walk right back into our former cell and shackle ourselves to the old ways. But our union with Christ has unlocked those old chains. We may foolishly wear them on occasion, but they have no hold on us. Hallelujah!

Because of our union with Christ, we are alive to God. The apostle Paul tells us to "consider [ourselves] to be dead to sin, but alive to God" (Rom 6:11). To be alive to God is to live in the power of Christ's resurrection. Our faith is grounded in the reality of new life and the future certainty of our final glory. How can we know? Paul says, "If we have died with Christ, we believe that we shall also live with Him, knowing that Christ, having been raised from the dead, is never to die again; death no longer is master over Him" (Rom 6:8–9). Jesus Christ took on human flesh and willingly came under the "reign of sin." Though He was sinless, He experienced sin's guilt and penalty. Since death and the grave were not able to hold Jesus, He proved that sin's mastery has been conquered. He never succumbed to its reign, its dominion, its bondage. The Lord Jesus Christ simply cannot die again (Rom 6:9). It occurred once and was done (Rom 6:10; Heb 1:3; 10:12). Sin, death, and the father of both—the devil—have all been rendered impotent through the resurrection (Heb 2:14).

NO PLACE FOR SIN

If we're honest about the Christian life, we have to admit that the battle with unredeemed appetites of the flesh can cause serious questions about where we stand with the Lord:

If I'm a new creature in Christ, why do I fall into some of the same destructive sin patterns?

I possess the power of God's Spirit; shouldn't I expect a more accelerated growth?

If I still battle so much sin in my life, how can I be sure I've been truly converted?

If I fail the Lord so often, will His love for me diminish?

If questions like these have ever invaded your mind, you're

normal. All believers wrestle with these questions from time to time. In Christ we are truly free from sin's tyranny, but the unredeemed appetites of our old life still wake each morning with a declaration of all-out war against the Holy Spirit who dwells in us. Sin's penalty and its bondage have been shattered, but the echo of our "old self" has not stopped reverberating. When seasons of sin and weakness have left us exhausted, defeated, and despairing, we must take our broken heart to Christ immediately. What marvelous grace we enjoy, knowing that the tyrannical reign of sin over us has forever come to an end! Its destructive regime has been permanently toppled. It may break through our defenses here and there, even cause serious damage to our faithfulness for a time. But it can never shackle and imprison us in our former cell of bondage. Our new man is alive in Christ (Rom 6:6–11)! These great realities are the spiritual current of our lives, enlightening our minds and hearts with the hope of ultimate victory in Jesus. They are a supernatural anchor, granted by grace, keeping us from the deadly reefs of faithlessness.

While we're basking in our no-condemnation status, however, we must guard against the notion that sanctification is merely a new status and not something to strive for. In Romans 6:1, Paul anticipates the gross error that inevitably hatches when sinners learn of the supreme power of grace over sin's curse: "What shall we say then? Are we to continue in sin so that grace may increase?" The question is a very simple one: if a true Christian has experienced the abounding grace of God, should they willfully live in a lifestyle of sin[4] so that God's grace will keep pouring out upon them? Paul knows that someone could twist the superabundant grace of Romans 5:12–20 into an excuse for neglecting their new power over the flesh or worse, as warrant for inciting it. In fact, multiple problems arise from not understanding grace properly:

- Some are defeated by sin through poor discipline and

---

[4] The verb and singular noun combination here (*epiménomen tē hamartía*) indicates a lifestyle pattern of sin, obviously for the purpose of increasing iniquities to trigger greater displays of grace.

patterns of weakness so that they become despondent and simply "give in" to temptation more frequently. In order to minimize guilt, they begin to downplay the seriousness of sin, railing against "rules" and turning grace into the freedom to indulge. "God is gracious," they say. "He'll forgive me," or "God knows my weakness, and He accepts the way I live because He's big enough to handle my messy Christianity."

- Then there are others who conclude that being under grace means they have no morally binding demands on their conduct. They claim to "follow the law of Christ," giving them freedom from the work of having to strive for practical holiness. This is the deadly error of antinomianism (see chapter 5).

- And at various times in church history, some have flipped the grace of God on its head, turning God's mercy into *the primary catalyst* to pursue a life of sin. One such fool lived a little over a century ago, appointed as the chief monk and religious advisor to the Romanov family in Russia. Kent Hughes writes: "[Rasputin] argued that because those who sin more require more forgiveness, those who sin with abandon will as they repent experience greater joy; therefore, it is the believer's duty to sin."[5] He took antinomianism to its outer reaches and taught the ruling monarchy "that salvation came through repeated experiences of sin and repentance."[6] Mangling Romans 5:20, he believed that since God's grace abounded toward sinners in response to sin's increase, therefore they can bring greater glory to God by increasing sin and thereby magnifying His grace.

People may wonder how anyone can go that far, but the perspective isn't very different from the garden variety, practical antinomian today who excuses sin because he "prayed

---

[5] R. Kent Hughes, *Romans: Righteousness from Heaven* (Wheaton, IL: Crossway, 1991), 121–22.

[6] Ibid., 121.

a prayer" or "grew up in church" or "went forward during an invitation." Grace is twisted into license when believers rationalize carnal ideologies and lifestyles in the name of freedom. "We are reaching the culture for Christ," many claim. Yet, their attitudes, speech, and conduct appeal to the flesh rather than the biblical call to be separate from the world (2 Cor 6:14–7:1). The Scriptures warn us about the self-deception of using "[our] freedom as a covering for evil" (1 Pet 2:16; cf. Gal 5:13). And not only is grace often twisted to accommodate worldliness, but the power of grace is insulted by those who've concluded that Scripture's commands are not binding on believers. In their zeal for the doctrine of justification they are ignoring, redefining, or outright denying the necessity of the disciplines of the Christian life for growing in grace (1 Cor 9:26–27; Heb 12:12–17; 2 Pet 3:18).

All of these errors are the result of swinging the theological pendulum beyond Scripture's guardrails. And admittedly, maintaining a biblical balance is anything but simple. If we're in Christ and have truly died to sin's rule over us, then we cannot ignore the implications. Paul declares the idea absurd that someone who has died to the power of sin could "still live in it" (Rom 6:2). I like J. B. Phillips' rendering: "What a ghastly thought!" (Rom 6:1). How can anyone whose "old self" has actually died be the same sinful person they were before? Dead is dead! New life has come in the power of God.

Romans 6:4 says, "So that as Christ was raised from the dead through the glory of the Father, so we too might walk in newness of life." Grace has saved us in order to live in a new quality of existence. We are "new creature[s]" (2 Cor 5:17), and have "put on the new self" (Eph 4:24). Our fruit is inevitable, even if at times difficult to see consistently. H. C. G. Moule wrote, "The grapes upon a vine are not merely a living token that the tree … is alive; they are the product for which the vine exists. It is a thing not to be thought of that the sinner should accept justification—and live to himself."[7]

[7] H. C. G. Moule, *The Epistle to the Romans* (London: Pickering & Inglis,

STOP OBEYING SIN AS IF IT WERE SOVEREIGN

In Romans 6:12–13 Paul declares the heart of his instructions: "Therefore do not let sin reign in your mortal body so that you obey its lusts, and do not go on presenting the members of your body to sin as instruments of unrighteousness; but present yourselves to God as those alive from the dead, and your members as instruments of righteousness to God." Because we know that God has made us alive in Christ, we must live in the light of that truth! This is where we see the importance of the indicative/imperative motif of Scripture: *Here's the reality given to us by the grace of God (the indicative); now go live the rest of your life in the power of that reality until Jesus returns and makes you completely perfect (imperative)!* We sometimes say it like this: "Become on a daily basis what you already are in reality."

We must stay biblically balanced in the indicatives and imperatives of Scripture, lest we fall into error on either side. If we emphasize only the imperatives—the fact that we must strive for holiness, staying away from sin and obeying the Lord in everything—then we will drift into a kind of legalism or moralism, convinced that holiness can be attained by willpower or spiritual determination:

> If by the Spirit *you are putting to death the deeds of the body* ... (Rom 8:13).

> We are His workmanship, created in Christ Jesus for good works, which God prepared beforehand that *we should walk in them* (Eph 2:10).

> Work out your salvation with fear and trembling (Phil 2:12).

On the other hand, if we emphasize only the *indicatives*—that we're already complete in Christ—then we will begin to neglect the fact that our new life is worked out through our active striving against sin on a daily basis:

---

n.d.), 161, as quoted by John MacArthur, Jr., in *Romans 1–8, The MacArthur New Testament Commentary* (Chicago: Moody, 1991), 323.

If *by the Spirit* you are putting to death the deeds of the body … (Rom 8:13).

Good works, which *God prepared beforehand* that we should walk in them (Eph 2:10).

It is God who is at work in you, both to will and to work for His good pleasure (Phil 2:13).

Conquering sin will not happen apart from the Spirit's power working in us to:

- see sin rightly;

- grasp biblical truth as our counter-offensive;

- develop discernment and avoid deception;

- cultivate endurance;

- produce gratitude and the peace that passes understanding; and

- bring about victory and maturity.

At the same time, conquering sin will not happen apart from our efforts to:

- flee sin;

- pour biblical truth into our minds;

- think soberly about life, morality, and eternity;

- press on in faith;

- be prayerful and express gratitude in everything; and

- desire God's glory through spiritual victory and maturity.

Master Your Passions

We naturally want things to be easy, comfortable, without a struggle, and completed this weekend! But sanctification doesn't work this way. God doesn't offer a secret formula or previously hidden insights that will now somehow make sanctification a breeze. We're tempted to think, "Well, I just want to be holy right now so I can please the Lord in everything." But if you think that God gets more glory from making your sanctification quick and easy, then you haven't understood how sanctification works! It's true: God could take us all home right now and there wouldn't be another sin committed by any of us. And in God's perfect timing, that will happen when all is accomplished and all sin has finally ended. But for now, He saves us and leaves us here to serve Him in faith for whatever purpose He calls us. Every time you believe His truth, desire His will above your own, resist the flesh, stand against temptation—and obey Jesus Christ—you put on display His perfections (power, mercy, grace, love, etc.) and bring Him glory, which will be made known throughout all eternity!

I love the fact that Paul simply states the command in Romans 6:12: "Do not let sin reign," or literally, "Stop letting sin reign." And the imperative is not impossible. That's why Paul can be so straightforward. If he gave us a command that we had no power to bring about, it would be like telling a drowning person to simply swim to shore. But on the basis of the indicative, "For sin shall not be master over you" (Rom 6:14), we don't have to "let sin reign" (Rom 6:12)!

The rest of verse 12 is critical: "Do not let sin reign in your mortal body so that you obey its lusts." What does Paul refer to when he speaks of "lusts"? The word for lusts (*epithumía*) here means *passions* or *cravings*. Essentially, Paul is commanding that we stop letting the old desires of "our old self" (v. 6) rule us: wanting our own way, coveting what others have, exalting self, dominating others, desiring self-pleasure above all, etc. The battle with sin is a battle with all that remains of the old life—the natural man's "leftovers."

But notice that all this battle is with reference to "your mortal body" (v. 12). This points us to some encouraging truths as we fight sin. First, we know that this battle with sin is not going to continue forever. "The world is passing away, and also its lusts"

(1 John 2:17). Also, this life is not where our salvation ends: we are eagerly waiting for the return of our Savior (1 Thess 1:10; Titus 2:13), when "we will be like Him" (1 John 3:2). And when this struggle with the old "body of sin" (Rom 6:6) is over, we will receive our new body, fashioned for glory (1 Cor 15:12–26)!

Master Your Usefulness

The first imperative, then, is a call to stop obeying sinful passions and desires when they tempt you. Paul goes further with the imperatives in Romans 6:13: "And do not go on presenting the members of your body to sin as instruments of unrighteousness; but present yourselves to God as those alive from the dead, and your members as instruments of righteousness to God." The term here for "the members [*mélos*] of your body" doesn't refer to arms and legs per se, but simply the way a person lives his life. Such features involve our bodies, but Paul's meaning here is not only that we must stop using our abilities and skills in the service of sin, but also that we must enlist them in the service of God "as those alive from the dead" (v. 13)!

The text doesn't get specific in terms of application, but it would no doubt include how we use our natural abilities and the skills we've developed. Our natural abilities include our mental acumen, physical strengths, emotional makeup, personality "wiring," etc. Stop using your thought life as a playground for sinful imaginations and reasonings. Rather, present your thought life (Rom 12:2; Eph 4:23; Phil 4:8) to God as His instrument to use! Stop using your physical capacities as instruments for acting out sinful deeds. Whatever physical strengths you have, use them to serve Jesus Christ as a testimony to His grace and favor! Stop using your emotional makeup and personality "wiring" as instruments of sin. If you're outgoing, stop stepping all over people in order in order to exalt yourself and be noticed. Instead, use your extroversion to put Christ on display. If you're quiet and timid, stop coddling yourself in a corner somewhere and use your less conversational disposition to pay close attention to needs, and then pray fervently and work behind the scenes to meet those needs. If you're emotionally expressive, stop wishing that the rest of the world was as sensitive and weepy as you, and instead pour out your tender heart in the name of Christ and let the Spirit direct your emotions according to truth. Yield your personality traits and emotional tendencies to the Spirit's control and seek to put the Lord Jesus Christ on display!

Your skills are the special abilities that time, experience, and training have produced. Stop using your education, experience, and accomplishments for self-interest. For those who are highly educated: if you aren't using your training to exalt Christ as the giver of all ability to learn, it is being adulterated. For those who are highly skilled: if you aren't using your honed skills to exalt Christ as the giver of all ability to develop and achieve, they are being adulterated. And for those who are highly decorated: if your trophies aren't used to exalt Christ as the giver of all ability to reach milestones of accomplishment, they are being adulterated. "Present yourselves to God as those alive from the dead, and your members as instruments of righteousness to God" (Rom 6:13). "Whether, then, you eat or drink or whatever you do, do all to the glory of God" (1 Cor 10:31; cf. Col 3:17).

When God redeems a sinner, it is a work of the Spirit to transform the whole person. The "old man" is dead, but his old grave clothes and appetites are not completely gone. When Christ returns, we will be given a new redeemed body—all the old appetites and fleshly tendencies will be swallowed up in the perfect holiness of Christ. But until then, we have been given the Spirit of God within us to fight against the sins of the flesh and of the mind to walk in obedience, being slowly conformed into the holy character of Jesus day by day.

CHAPTER 5

SAVED TO LOVE GOD'S LAW

T HE contemporary and sometimes heated debate over the relationship between justification and sanctification is becoming familiar ground within evangelical churches. One side is concerned that churches are drifting from the freedom of grace by emphasizing the spiritual disciplines for holy living. We hear statements like, "Christians are not under a moral obligation to obey God," "You can't kill sin with duty, but only by faith," and "Obedience from a sense of obligation is not grace but Law." To cross-centered ears these declarations initially have the ring of truth. Terms like "moral obligation" too closely echo pre-Christian guilt under the Law—so they jettison the idea completely. To suggest motives of duty and obligation seems antithetical to the Bible's gospel grace themes, and therefore a return to legalism.

Conversely, the other side strongly believes that the Law of God has a role in the Christian life as a guide for holy living, and that all true believers "love [God's] law" (Ps 119:97). They believe that today's emphasis on grace is out of balance, tending to minimize or ignore the imperatives of Scripture and falling into the old heresy of antinomianism. There is likely some imbalance on both sides of the issue, as with similar debates throughout church history. Overemphasizing our duty to obey God can cause some to miss the eternal refuge of our union with

Christ in the gospel. They may forget the foundation of Christ's finished work and begin to obey for fear of losing God's favor. That can lead only to ingratitude and a begrudged obedience. But it is also out of balance to overemphasize our standing in Christ while downplaying His commands. The power of the gospel is more than mere indicatives—it assures us of the daily power to overcome sin and be conformed to the image of our Savior. And though both sides admit that Christians *should be obedient to Christ*, the language used to explain what motivates our obedience has been dramatically changing.

This new emphasis speaks of obedience as rising spontaneously from gratitude, unrequired, driven only by love or by "a hunger for beauty." Duty or moral responsibility is cast as treason against grace and a return to the Galatian heresy. "We are not under law," comes the challenge. I wholeheartedly agree that we're free from the Law's condemnation, but does that stunning reality liberate us from obligation or duty to Christ? Not at all. Scripture is clear that Law and gospel are distinct but not mutually exclusive. As R. C. Sproul warns, "If you do not delight in the law of God, don't deceive yourself into thinking that you are a regenerate person. Don't think that the gospel which frees you from the curse of the law is a license for you to despise the law or ignore the law."[1] On the contrary, the Bible teaches that God's sovereign grace excites a sinner's heart and mind toward submission to God's commands, will, and warnings.

OLD PROBLEMS

In seventeenth-century New England, several very astute preachers began to teach that because the Law's condemnation and dominion are rendered powerless against those in Christ, Christians are no longer under any sense of obligation or duty to God.[2] To allow the Law of God to be a motivating influence on our

[1] R. C. Sproul, "Oh, How I Love Thy Law!," in *Trust and Obey, Obedience and the Christian*, ed. Don Kistler (Morgan, PA: Soli Deo Gloria, 1996), 6.

[2] Ernest F. Kevan, *The Grace of Law* (Ligonier, PA: Soli Deo Gloria, 1993), 167–69.

hearts and minds was viewed as turning "Christ into Moses, and Moses into Christ."[3] Leaders of this teaching were quickly labeled "antinomians" by their Puritan contemporaries. They came to be known as those who were "against Law" as it relates to the New Covenant believer. These bygone preachers were much like those who push against all sense of moral obligation today. They had trouble synthesizing freedom from the condemnation of the Law with Scripture's plain commands to obey God. The antinomians took our no-condemnation status to mean that we cannot be obligated, in any sense, to obey the Law. Therefore, our obedience to Christ must never be motivated by an inner sense of duty to a binding standard. To feel a moral obligation to obey would be to go backward, fearing God's condemnation and obeying without faith.

Is this true? Does our freedom from moral culpability under the Law ultimately eliminate our moral obligation to it? And what if my desire to obey God is sometimes—so far as I can tell—rooted in reverence for Him as the Lawgiver? Would that be a return to legalism? How could we spend our lives "as children of light" "trying to learn what is pleasing to the Lord" (Eph 5:8, 10) and not love His Law, which "reveals to us what is pleasing"[4] to Him? What has changed to render God's perfections as expressed in His Law something we no longer love or delight in?

THE END OF THE LAW?

To answer these questions we must deal with Romans 10:4, where Paul declares that "Christ is the end of the law for righteousness to everyone who believes." Paul uses the term "law" in the way it is often used in the Old Testament. He's not referring merely to the commandments given to Moses at Sinai, but it's a more general designation for God's Word—His revealed will. In Psalm 119:97, when the psalmist's passion explodes with "Oh, how I love

---

[3] John Eaton, *The Honey-combe of Free Justification by Christ Alone* (EEBO Editions: ProQuest, 2011), 381, quoted in Kevan, *The Grace of Law*, 167.

[4] Sproul, "Oh, How I Love Thy Law!," 12.

Your law," he's not thinking only of rules for the nation of Israel delivered by Moses. He's expressing his love for the entire revelation of God. The Scriptures reveal God's character, His works, and His will for us. The psalmist loves the Law because he loves the Lawgiver.[5] The law is his "delight," which keeps him from perishing (Ps 119:77, 92). If the power and freedom of God's truth are enjoyed by those whose "delight is in the law of the Lord" (Ps 1:2), then all believers for all time ought to love God's Law. Being free from its condemnation does not sever us from the Law but rather causes us to delight in it.

Some have taken the clause, "Christ is the end of the law," to mean that we have no ongoing *obligation* to respond to a law or command in Scripture. It is supposed, then, that obedience is not a requirement, but only the delighted response of a grateful heart. But this is an overreach that misses the point of Paul's statement. The Jews were zealous for a right relationship with God, but since they did not acknowledge the chasm between His holiness and their sinfulness, they tried to use the Mosaic Law as a path to their own righteousness. Paul counters by teaching that Christ is our only access to God's righteousness. When he says "Christ is the end of the law," he means that Jesus is the fulfillment of the Law's righteous demands—and by implication, it is the "end" of the Law's consequences for all who put their faith in Him. His incarnation, His obedient fulfillment of "all righteousness" (Matt 3:15), His death to pay for the Law's righteous judgment on sinners, and His embodiment of the Law's holiness, all make Him the epicenter of the sinner's hope. And that hope can come to the sinner *by faith alone*. Christ is the end of the law indeed— "for righteousness to everyone who believes" (Rom 10:4).

A Natural Obligation

When we entrust ourselves to Christ we are no longer condemned. However, being under grace does not liberate us from God's Law/ Word. And that's because God's Word is inseparable from His

[5] Ibid., 14.

Person. In the gospel we're free from the condemnation incurred by our failure to live up to the Law perfectly, but we are never free from our obligation to God. In fact, no human being, let alone a Christian, is ever out from under an obligation to their Creator and His character. The whole world is in a constant state of accountability to God—to His character and His will (Rom 3:19). Even before Adam sinned, while in a perfect sinless relationship with God, having nothing but love as his highest motivation for obedience, he was given a prohibition, a law to obey. Why would God obligate His child with a law when a heart of love was at the center of Adam's walk with God? It is because aside from being a moral test of faith and devotion, the forbidden tree reflected man's inherent moral duty to his Creator. Therefore, it is incorrect to say that we are under no obligation to God's Law. That would be the same as saying we are under no obligation to our Creator. In fact, being in Christ means we have the power to "walk ... according to the Spirit" and become like Him, thus fulfilling "the righteous requirement of the law" (Rom 8:4).

In the New Covenant, love for God fills our hearts in Christ by the power of the Holy Spirit, but this doesn't erase our moral obligation to Him as His creatures. Our submission to Him is our immediate moral duty. He has a right to command us because "from Him and through Him and to Him are all things" (Rom 11:36). We are obligated to God by nature. Therefore, it is unbiblical to declare that the grace of the gospel frees us from all moral obligation to God. As His redeemed people, we certainly obey Him from a heart of love, but our submission should also always reflect a heart bound and accountable to God's will.

A Glorious Obligation

In addition to our natural obligation, we are bound to God's Law because it is the manifestation of His majestic glory and eternal perfections. Ernest Kevan once wrote, "The authority of God lies in His glorious Godhead and Creatorhood. God's personal majesty and His relation to His creatures give a quality of permanence to His Law which is inseparable from His personal glory."[6] The Law/Word of God is "holy and righteous and good" (Rom 7:12). His laws are the "expressions of his holy perfect Will and Nature."[7] Therefore, to claim that we have "no relationship to God's Law" is, ironically, to declare a separation from the holiness of God reflected in the Law. If the goal of the gospel is to make us holy as He is holy (1 Pet 1:16), then we can never truly have *no relationship* to the Law. When we talk of not being "under law, but under grace" (Rom 6:14), we mean that we're no longer under its condemnation, its inevitable death trajectory. But the Law itself "is a source of wonder (Ps. 119:18) and grace (Ps. 119:29) and is something precious (Ps. 119:72) and true (Ps. 119:142). It is not only to be obeyed, but loved (Ps. 119:97, 113, 163, 165)."[8]

A Gracious Obligation

Not only does the Law reflect God's majesty and beauty, it is also an expression of His boundless grace. So much emphasis today is on grace as the antithesis of Law. But while we declare that salvation is by grace alone and not through the works of the Law, we also declare that the Law is a necessary expression of God's grace, without which the sinner cannot see their need for a Savior. The Puritans focused on this reality in all of their soul care. William Perkins, for example, described his personal evangelism as centered around four necessities: "First of all a man must have knowledge of … the law of God, of sin against the law, of the guilt of sin, and of the judgment of God against sin, which is the eternal wrath of God."[9] Being the ultimate standard of righteousness, the Law of God is the divine halogen that blazes upon humanity's fallen condition and exposes everything that comes short of God's glory.

---

[6] Kevan, *The Grace of Law*, 47.

[7] Richard Baxter, *Catholick Theologie*, Book 2, 30, quoted in ibid., 63.

[8] Paul Lamey, "Preaching the Law" (Expositors Forum, Seminar Four, Grace Community Church, Huntsville, AL, 2017), 1.

[9] William Perkins, "Two Treatises" in *Works*, 541, quoted in Kevan, *The Grace of Law*, 91 (spelling modernized).

LAW AND GOSPEL?

Similar to the confusion of seventeenth-century antinomianism, some today make a sharp distinction between the Law and the gospel so that they preach only grace and consider the preaching of the Law as a gospel of works. Since the Law has no power to save and can only condemn, then, they reason, preaching the demands of the Law implies that the sinner can obey the Law and justify themselves before God—the Pharisees' deadly error. But this is an oversimplification. The apostles preached more than just the grace of redemption in Christ. They also called sinners to repent and believe! Repent of what? Repent of the sin which the knowledge of the Law exposes (Rom 7:7–11). As Ernest Kevan remarked, "Antecedently to faith, it is presupposed that there has been the work of the Law in the conviction of sin, and the order, relation and use of the Law and the Gospel evince this."[10] In that sense the Law is given to sinners *as a grace* that they might see what their hearts spend so much time trying to deny. Not only does our flesh want a God who is less holy than He is, but it also wants a heaven that is accessible by our own "righteousness." Without the Law we will continue inventing attainable moral standards and continue fashioning a God of lesser holiness who is okay with that.

The Law as a Tutor

A parent once told me that they never call their children to know the Law of God or worry about its ethical demands. I (Jerry) asked: "Then how do you suppose they will ever see their need for Christ?" To be saved, we must see our sin in light of the unbending righteousness of God (John 16:8). These parents were afraid of raising a Pharisee, but I explained that our children are born Pharisees, and the more we bring the lofty, unreachable standard of truth the more they are compelled to see their true condition. "Therefore the Law has become our tutor to lead us to Christ, so that we may be justified by faith" (Gal 3:24). To be honest, my wife and I were

[10] Kevan, *The Grace of Law*, 89.

relentless in giving the Law of God (moral and ethical) to our kids and they still battled with unbelief, minimizing sin, and the desire to self-atone. The Law is "our tutor to lead us to Christ," but many spend their entire lives chafing at God's Law and never go to school on its heart lectures. And just for clarity, once a sinner begins to experience the misery of never measuring up to the Scriptures, they should be urged to run to Christ immediately in faith and repentance. Too often we coddle the sinner in their self-pity over "not being worthy enough for Christ." We try and convince them that they have intrinsic worth so valuable that Christ was willing to die to redeem them. It's the wrong message to send. Discouragement for failing to meet the Law's demands is exactly what God intended His Law to produce. It's at that moment of hopelessness that the gospel finds its most fertile soil.

Our self-esteem-saturated culture has a bad habit of correcting people's discouragement with lavish doses of "Don't you know how wonderful you are" sentiments, as if God loved us so much because of our inherent worthiness that He sent His Son to die for such a prize. It's a popular idea that is thoroughly unbiblical. John 3:16 describes a love so profound and magnificent that God gave His only Son, not because we were worthy of such a cost, but *precisely because we were unworthy* of it! B. B. Warfield brought piercing clarity when he insightfully said, "[That God loves the world is] not to suggest that it takes a great deal of love to embrace it all, but that the world is so bad that it takes a great kind of love to love it at all."[11]

The Law as a Covenant

Such has been the wonderful grace and mercy wrapped up in the giving of the Law. Sometimes the Bible refers to Law and it means the commandments given to Israel by God through Moses—the Mosaic Covenant. At other times Scripture speaks of God's Law in reference to the overall moral code of ethics applicable to all

[11] B. B. Warfield, *The Saviour of the World* (Edinburgh: Banner of Truth Trust, 1991), 114.

human beings. The Ten Commandments may have formed the nucleus around which all of the laws for Israel in the Old Covenant have revolved, but they represent so much more than that. When God gave the Law to Israel under the Old Covenant, it was a gracious ministry to His people in several ways:

1. It revealed the exceeding sinfulness of man's depraved heart (Rom 3:19–20). Of course, guilt was still a reality in fallen man (Rom 5:13–14) even before anyone was aware of the Law's moral high ground, but its arrival in Israel exposed just how dark and dead our corruption is (Rom 7:13).

2. It revealed sin's aggressive, enslaving nature (Rom 7:8–13). Paul said it is the corruption within us, not the Law, which rails at God's holy standard (John 3:20) only to bring further condemnation against the sinner (Rom 7:8–13).

3. It was given as a custodian/teacher to bring its subjects to the end of themselves that they might see their need for a Savior (Gal 3:24).

4. It restrained outward anarchy to protect the moral, social, and religious institutions of Israel.

5. It hemmed the nation in with promises of blessings and cursings to keep them from running violently away from its unbending standard (Lev 26; Deut 28).

Do the above purposes for the Law still stand? Are they applicable in any way to us today? So long as the spiritual principles in the Law have not changed, then these five ministries of the Law still apply in some way to every believer, Old and New Covenants.

Reading and studying Scripture sets forth the moral standard by which all of us are measured. The Old Covenant was given to God's people as the standard of His holiness, which they were required to obey perfectly or else pay the consequences. It made demands and expected them to conform. The problem was that Israel had no power to obey, so the Law only continued to expose them as slaves to sin. The content of the Law was good, holy, and righteous, but it could not save. It was a "teacher" designed to help Israel become desperate for a Savior (Gal 3:24). Tragically, over and over Israel missed the entire gracious design of the Law. Not only were they blind to the moral inability it exposed in them, they went one disastrous step further and presumed to make the Law their own personal stairway to justification. Instead of Scripture's moral principles being unattainable, they became Israel's self-atonement manual (Rom 9:31–32; 10:3). It's not hard to understand why the era of the Sinaitic Covenant was one of slavery. In the New Covenant, believers have "died to the law" (Rom 7:6), and have been given the Spirit of God so that we can actually obey God's standard (Law) "from the heart" (Rom 6:17).

The Law as a Freedom

In Romans 6:14 Paul says, "For sin shall not be master over you, for you are not under law but under grace." As stated earlier, when Paul declares that we are "not under law but under grace," he means that we are not under the Law's penalty, nor are we under the power of sin's bondage—we are not shackled to our old chains. Our hearts now rejoice in the Law of God rather than rising up against its every "Thou Shalt Not" to our own destruction. Before conversion, "Life under the law leads to death because sin has free reign."[12] But sin's absolute mastery has been shattered in Christ, and life reigns in us rather than death. Now that's freedom! Someone will likely say, *Well then, if I'm not under Law but under grace, then I shouldn't have to worry about being obligated to some standard of holiness. I can simply bask in the freedom of being justified in Christ and set aside all those Old Testament requirements, all of which are a return to legalism.*

Not so fast. How do we relate to the standards of the Old Testament? Does the New Covenant supersede or even eliminate the moral standards of the Old Covenant? Has the era of Jesus Christ and the Spirit simply "run the Law out of town"? If true,

---

[12] Thomas R. Schreiner, *New Testament Theology* (Grand Rapids: Baker Academic, 2008), 649.

how are we to understand a massive number of New Testament passages that bind us to commands straight out of the Old Covenant? And what about direct statements by Paul, such as Romans 3:31, which says, "Do we then nullify the Law through faith? May it never be! On the contrary, *we establish the Law*." If we're supposed to view the Law as something set aside, how is it that Paul can say that we are proof that the Law is holy, and that we "establish" it by coming through Christ in faith?

In Romans 8:3–4 Paul declares that God "condemned sin in the flesh, *so that the requirement of the Law might be fulfilled in us*, who do not walk according to the flesh, but according to the Spirit." Our salvation does not sever our relationship to the holiness reflected in the Law. Everything about the Old Testament Law and the Sinaitic Covenant mediated through Moses pointed ultimately to Jesus Christ. Therefore how we relate to Old Covenant restrictions, moral principles, and implications must be understood in light of the coming of Jesus Christ to fulfill it. Jesus came to fulfill the Law (Matt 5:17) and He did just that. Every divine promise is fulfilled in Christ (2 Cor 1:20). God's unbending, righteous demands were all met perfectly by the Lord Jesus (Rom 10:4), and the penalty for sin required by the Law was poured out on Christ, fully satisfying the holy justice of God (Isa 53:4–10).

A REMAINING LAW?

Many claim that since Christ has come we are under only "His royal law" which renders all past laws non-binding. We are indeed under "the law of Christ" (Gal 6:2), under His "law of liberty" (Jas 1:25), "the royal law" (Jas 2:8), the law of love (Rom 13:8–10). But does Christ's royal law exclude the moral framework and all specific commands given to Israel at Sinai? The debate throughout church history often hinged on the basic difference between Law as covenant and Law in the form of commands.[13] The Law of God as a covenant could only condemn us since we could never perfectly obey and fulfill the requirements. But the commands given as part

[13] Kevan, *The Grace of Law*, 148.

of the Old Covenant still reflect God's baseline moral standard for all of humanity. The Law of God as the standard of morality did not pass away when humanity fell. Moral inability does not erase our obligation.[14] And so, if the moral Law is not canceled by man's inability, neither is it canceled by the grace of redemption.[15] In Christ, the Law is fulfilled and its demands were "abolished" in the covenantal sense. We are no longer held accountable to keep the whole Law (which of course we have no moral capability of doing), and therefore are no longer condemned by failing to do so. But on the other hand, in Christ we now love the Law of God, expressed in His commands which reflect His eternal moral perfections—His majestic holiness. This is why some of the commands given to Moses are given in the New Covenant as the ultimate ethic for all of God's people (Rom 13:9; Gal 5:14). This is what we often call the Third Use of the Law.

Remaining as a Standard

As indicated earlier, all of God's Law (including its unique expression in the Sinaitic Covenant) served a primary purpose of exposing sin for the high moral treason that it is. This same use (the so-called First Use) of God's Law continues through all of redemptive history. God's righteous standard is always exposing sin and filling the conscience with guilt. As Augustine stated, "The law orders, that we, after attempting to do what is ordered and so feeling our weakness under the law, may learn to implore the help of grace."[16] The Second Use of the Law was for the governing of civil life. Again, its use today continues as the structure of civil societies ground their laws in the basic framework of the Ten Commandments. In general, evil is punished and good is rewarded on this basis. Finally, the Law still serves as a moral standard and guide to believers in the New Covenant. It no longer stands over us in condemnation, but resides favorably in our

---

[14] Ibid., 151.

[15] Ibid., 155.

[16] John Calvin, *Institutes of the Christian Religion* (Bellingham, WA: Logos Bible Software, 1997), 2.7.9.

hearts as that which we've come to believe in, love, and submit joyfully to.

Remaining as an Ethic

That is why Paul grounds our ultimate Christian ethic—love—in the moral standards of the Ten Commandments. Romans 13:8 tells us to "owe nothing to anyone except to love one another." In the New Covenant, genuine love toward others is, Paul says, "the fulfillment of the law" (Rom 13:10). But what "law" is the apostle referring to? He goes on to explain in verses 9 and 10 how love for God and others fulfills the law. "For this, 'You shall not commit adultery, you shall not murder, you shall not steal, you shall not covet,' and if there is any other commandment, it is summed up in this saying, 'You shall love your neighbor as yourself.' Love does no wrong to a neighbor; therefore love is the fulfillment of the law" (Rom 13:9–10). Notice how the moral requirements of the Law given to Israel at Sinai speak of how we are to treat one another. And there's no need to wonder whether Paul is being consistent with what he said in Romans 6:14: We "are not under law but under grace." He said the same thing in Galatians 5:18: "If you are led by the Spirit, you are not under the Law." It is obvious that Paul sees the holy morality reflected in the Law as a self-evident ethic for all of God's people.

- *You shall not commit adultery*—Why? Because it is not loving to either your spouse and children or to the others involved when you betray vows instead of building trust and honor in relationships.

- *You shall not murder*—Why? Because it is not loving to unlawfully end someone's life instead of protecting and preserving their life which God gave to them.

- *You shall not steal*—Why? Because it is not loving when you take for your own what belongs to others instead of being content.

- *You shall not covet*—Why? Because it is not loving when you lust after what others possess instead of rejoicing in their prosperity.

Paul sees love and Law as moral companions in any area where we have the opportunity to do good to others. To be bound to the "law of Christ," "the royal law," the law of love, is to be rooted and grounded in His perfect obedience to the whole Law. He is the law of love personified, and when we obey His commands we are fulfilling the entire Law—a reflection of His holy love.

So, should we look to some or all of the Law given at Sinai for standards on how to live? In the overall sense, we already do! Of course, we are not under the penalty of the Law, or its relentless bondage (i.e., the flesh railing against the Law), or its inevitable death trajectory. But we are fulfilling the Law when we obey the will of Christ. The holy morality reflected in the Law has not passed away for Christians. It is also profound that the "law of Christ" in the New Covenant includes some of the commands originally given at Sinai. We saw how Paul refers to the Ten Commandments as the root of the law of love. In Hebrews 10:16, the writer quotes Jeremiah 31:33, indicating that once forgiven in Christ, believers have God's laws within us, written there by God Himself: "This is the covenant that I will make with them after those days, says the Lord: I will put My laws upon their heart, and on their mind I will write them." The Lord gives us the power in His grace to love His commands, as well as the power to bring our hearts, minds, and wills under them.

Remaining as a Guide

When Christ came and finished the sacrifice for sin—granting pardon for all who have faith in Him—the Old Covenant schoolmaster gave way to the New Covenant power within every believer. Now our obedience not only reflects the two greatest commandments (Mark 12:30–31) but also *sums up the expression of the Law in all of its moral and ethical intention.* Laws reflecting exclusive devotion to God and sacrificial love toward others do not change; they are mirrored in the New Covenant. All laws foreshadowing redemptive realities to be fulfilled in Christ are no longer ethically binding now that He is the fullest expression of those truths:

- *No more civil and national separation from other nations*—because we are now set apart in Christ and sent into the world for the gospel.

- *No more circumcision*—because circumcision is now "of the heart" (Rom 2:29).

- *No more clean/unclean things*—because "God has cleansed" (Acts 10:15).

- *No more holy days*—because redemption and rest are gained in Christ (Heb 4:11).

- *No more sacrifices*—because Christ was sacrificed "once for all" (Heb 7:27)

- *No more central temple*—because believers are now the temple of the Holy Spirit (1 Cor 3:17)

Yet, the love ethic inherent in God's Law *crosses over* into the New Covenant since God's love is not merely a foreshadowing of Christ's saving purpose but the supreme expression of His Person.

Evangelicalism's current one-sidedness with the doctrine of sanctification has produced serious confusion about the role of God's Law, and even nurtured in some a rash disregard for the Ten Commandments specifically and all biblical commands in general. All of this is not only unnecessary, it is unhelpful. Just like the psalmist, we can delight in the Law of God because it reflects Who He is, it defines our obligation before Him, and it guides our life toward Him. The Law is not a burden from God, it is a grace. Just as sure as we love God, we must love His Law.

CHAPTER 6

SAVED FOR LIFE IN THE SPIRIT

IN his autobiography, Charles Spurgeon recalled the profound spiritual turmoil he experienced before he was saved:

> When I was for many a month in this state, I used to read the Bible through, and the threatenings were all printed in capitals, but the promises were in such small type I could not for a long time make them out; and when I did read them, I did not believe they were mine; but the threatenings were all my own. "There," said I, "when it says, 'He that believeth not shall be damned,' that means me!" But when it said, "He is able also to save them to the uttermost that come unto God by Him," then I thought I was shut out. When I read, "He found no place of repentance, though he sought it carefully with tears;" I thought, "Ah! that is myself again." And when I read, "That which beareth thorns and briers is rejected, and is nigh unto cursing; whose end is to be burned;" "Ah!" I said, "that describes me to the very letter." [1]

Spurgeon knew this tumult for some time, summarizing it in this way: "Whatever staggering doubt, or hideous blasphemy, or ghastly insinuations, even of suicide itself, may assail my feeble heart, they cannot outdo the horror of great darkness through which my spirit passed when I was struggling after a Saviour." [2] In such a condition Spurgeon "happened" into a chapel one Sunday

---

[1] Charles Haddon Spurgeon, *The Early Years 1834–1859*, vol. 1 of *C. H. Spurgeon Autobiography* (London: Banner of Truth Trust, 1962), 64–65.
[2] Ibid., 67–68.

during a snowstorm. The message he heard that day was given by a fill-in preacher whom Spurgeon supposed to be a shoemaker or tailor. His text was Isaiah 45:22: "Look unto me, and be ye saved, all the ends of the earth." That very day Spurgeon believed and obeyed that text and was born again. Reflecting on his conversion, he wrote, "Between half-past ten o'clock, when I entered that chapel, and half-past twelve o'clock, when I was back again at home, what a change had taken place in me! I had passed from darkness into marvelous light, from death to life. Simply by looking to Jesus, I had been delivered from despair, and I was brought into such a joyous state of mind that, when they saw me at home, they said to me, 'Something wonderful has happened to you.'"[3]

One of the realities you must keep in mind when you consider the doctrine of sanctification is that if you have believed in Jesus, something wonderful *has* happened to you. People desperately seek supernatural experiences and miracles that would manifest the finger of God. But there really is no need to run around looking for God to suspend the laws of nature to convince us that He is involved with His people. We witness the most miraculous display of divine power every time a condemned sinner's darkened soul is engulfed by the saving light of truth in Jesus Christ.

The conversion of a single sinner is a miracle of staggering proportions. To be "rescued ... from the domain of darkness, and transferred ... to the kingdom of His beloved Son" (Col 1:13) required an invasion of this world by God so profound that no other work of God even touches it. God had to become one of us; Jesus Christ had to take our sin upon Himself; He had to be rejected by His Father; He had to die in agony and spiritual humiliation under the curse of sin; and He had to conquer death through the resurrection so that we could be given life. Pondering the magnitude of the miracle that transforms sinners from the old life to a new spiritual reality causes deeply grateful worship. Facing what we were gives profound meaning to what we are now in Christ, which is the same line of reasoning the apostle Paul has

[3] Ibid., 89–90.

as he transitions in Romans from chapter 7 to chapter 8. After describing the impossible scenario of trying to be a "good moral person" without submitting to the Spirit's power, he erupts with a spontaneous word of gratitude: "Thanks be to God through Jesus Christ our Lord!" (Rom 7:25). Why? Because God has rescued His people from the old life of destruction and death, and has given them new life in the Spirit. Paul will go on in Romans 8 to highlight four miraculous privileges of a new life under the Spirit's control.

A MIRACULOUS NEW IDENTITY

The first miraculous privilege of a new life under the Spirit's control is the new identity every believer possesses. Paul's opening declaration in Romans 8:1 is loaded with amazing truth: "Therefore there is now no condemnation for those who are in Christ Jesus." This is the first word concerning our new identity. "Condemnation" here conveys not only the guilty verdict due us, but also the penalty to be paid. It was the sheer liability against us because of our unreconciled position before God. Our new identity means having a completely different standing before God. Absolutely no divine thought, word, or action of accusation or retribution can ever be leveled against us, for all eternity, for any sin of the past, any sin in the present, or any sin we may commit in the future! "Those who are in Christ Jesus" have been *completely* pardoned.

Released by the Spirit's Life

What kind of power, or on what principle can condemned sinners be declared not condemned? It takes nothing less than divine power. Paul explains: "For the law of the Spirit of life in Christ Jesus has set you free from the law of sin and of death" (Rom 8:2). By using this term "law" in this context, Paul signifies the idea of *dominance* or *ruling principle* (cf. Rom 7:21, 23). So while sinners used to be under the dominating influence of sin and death, those who are in Christ Jesus are now under a new dominating influence—namely, "the law of the Spirit of life in Christ Jesus." This "law," or dominating life principle, is the irrevocable *grounds* of our new identity. Christians have been set free—permanently—from sin's relentless dominance and sin's ruinous end, which is death. We've been completely liberated from sin's ability to imprison us, fill us with more rebellion against truth, compel us to further lawlessness, and turn us headlong into spiritual death.

Redeemed by the Father's Love

Paul gets more specific on what it took to release sinners from condemnation. It was the wondrous love of God that sent His beloved Son to bear our guilt. "For what the Law could not do, weak as it was through the flesh, God did: sending His own Son in the likeness of sinful flesh and as an offering for sin, He condemned sin in the flesh" (Rom 8:3). Jesus was sent "in the likeness of sinful flesh." Paul emphasizes the fact that the Son entered the world of sinful men, as a man, in order to have the full experience of humanity—frailty, dependence, limitations, suffering, and the humiliation of sin's consequences (Gal 4:4; Phil 2:7). The word "likeness" is Paul's careful description of one who could take on the infirmities of human existence, yet without being ruined by a sinful nature. Christ was not tainted by sin; otherwise, He could not be the worthy sacrifice to free us from sin's bondage.

In order to be given this new identity in Christ, our due punishment had to be satisfied. Because of His love for us, God sent His Son "as an offering for sin" and poured out His wrath upon Him on the cross. This is how God chose to resolve the problem of sin's dominion over sinners. "He condemned sin in the flesh" of the God-Man, sent to be the pleasing sacrifice. And in so doing, God reconciled us to the Law, the revelation of God's perfect standard. All the Law could do was give the standard and be used by our sinful flesh as an instrument for stirring up further rebellion, thus becoming a greater source of condemnation (Rom 2:12). But through Christ's sacrifice, those who are in Him are reconciled to the Law (Col 2:13–14).

The redeeming love of God not only satisfies the punishment due us, but also covers us in His holiness. The stunning result of Christ receiving the condemnation for sin is "that the requirement of the Law might be fulfilled in us" (Rom 8:4). The Law's just demand has been provided for us. We couldn't satisfy the demands of God's holy standard because the sin of our flesh would only continue to rebel against God. But Jesus Christ, in His perfect life and obedient death, provided for us a "covering" of His holiness that gives us a new identity. In our new position we are treated by God as holy in Christ. God sees us as having fulfilled the holy demand of His Law because we are found *in the One who fulfilled it all for us.* And now that God views us as having fulfilled the demand of the Law, we receive everything that was procured by Christ at the cross (Eph 1:3, 11, 14).

A MIRACULOUS NEW INCLINATION

A second miraculous privilege of a new life under the Spirit's control is the new inclination every believer possesses. Holiness is the greatest and highest treasure of life in Christ. It is the great goal *toward* which God ordains everything for believers (Eph 1:4), *through* which the ministry affects souls (Matt 5:16), *for* which the cross conveys all grace (Heb 2:9–11), and *against* which all sin is violently opposed (Rom 1:18–32). We've been saved to be holy and blameless (Eph 1:4; 5:26–27; 1 Pet 1:1–2, 14–16; 1 Cor 1:2; 1 John 3:3), to make disciples, teaching them to obey all of Christ's commands (Mat 28:19–20), and to be perfected in the holiness of Christ at His coming (John 17:22–23; 1 John 3:2). Our old inclinations were opposed to holiness at every turn—always worldly, always of fleshly things, and without the divine influence of God's Spirit. But now everyone who is in Christ has a miraculous new inclination that leads us toward holy desires and godly fruit.

New Life Patterns

The contrast between those who are unredeemed and those who are in Christ may be summarized simply by what Paul wrote at the end of Romans 8:4. There, he refers to those "who do not walk according to the flesh, but according to the Spirit." When Paul is talking about the "flesh" in Romans 7–8, he includes not only

the frailty and limitations of our humanness, but more particularly the part of us that is by nature filled with "sinful passions"
(Rom 7:5). These passions are cravings for satisfaction through
worldly things with no understanding of, nor desire for, finding
gratification in the realm of the Spirit of God. The flesh refers to
the morally corrupt counsels of the heart and resolves of the will
that work themselves out through our bodies (in our choices and
behavior patterns). Simply put, the flesh is the vehicle through
which sinful passions work.

People who "walk according to the flesh" are those whose
patterns are controlled by all that is of the flesh, and nothing
of the Spirit of God. They have never submitted to God's will
or lived for His glory. We know that Paul is talking about life
patterns because he uses a term, "walk" (*peripateō*), commonly
used in the New Testament. This word depicts a life that adheres
to a standard of conduct:

> He who follows Me will not walk in the darkness (John 8:12).

> If we say that we have fellowship with Him and yet walk in the
> darkness, we lie and do not practice the truth; but if we walk in
> the light as He Himself is in the light, we have fellowship with
> one another, and the blood of Jesus His Son cleanses us from
> all sin (1 John 1:6–7).

> The one who says he abides in Him ought himself to walk in the
> same manner as He walked (1 John 2:6).

> And this is love, that we walk according to His commandments
> (2 John 1:6).

A person's "walk," therefore, manifests the beliefs, desires, affections, and motivations that drive him. This explains Paul's contrast
between walking according to the flesh and walking according
to the Spirit. Christians no longer pattern their lives after fleshly
motivations, but now pattern their lives after the controlling
influence of the Spirit's holy motivations, affections, and will.

New Reasoning

Part of believers' new life patterns is the way we reason. Paul says in Romans 8:5: "For those who are according to the flesh set their minds on the things of the flesh, but those who are according to the Spirit, the things of the Spirit." The term translated "set their minds on" (*phroneō*) refers to one's orientation, bent, or pattern of reasoning. It conveys the comprehensive range of reasonings and convictions by which a person makes choices. It's the term used by Christ when He told Peter he was not "setting [his] mind on God's interests, but man's" (Matt 16:23; cf. Phil 3:19).

Setting one's mind on the things of the flesh is a succinct description of a thought life without the influence of the Spirit. Before the Spirit's indwelling power, our pattern of thinking was all about whatever earthly interest captivated our eyes and satisfied our natural lusts. Our reasoning faculties were always bent toward self-preservation, self-exaltation, and self-justification. Our emotional expression tended toward sinful fear (driving self-preservation and trusting in earthly things), sinful anger (driving self-exaltation and attempts at self-determination), and sinful despair (driving self-justification and denial of guilt). All of these synergized in a cycle of further carnal reasonings, visceral responses, and self-will. The result is death—not only in the temporal sense of Romans 8:6 (no spiritual power over sin and its consequences; no relationship with the Creator), but also death in the ultimate sense (cf. Rom 6:21, 23; 7:5).

The unbeliever's entire reasoning pattern produces nothing but fleshly things followed by earthly dissatisfaction, resulting in compounded guilt and increasing bouts of misery, despair, loneliness, and an empty heart. But those who are in Christ Jesus have a totally new—and miraculous—life pattern of reasoning. The Spirit's power changes everything: we set our minds on the things of the Spirit (v. 5). We are no longer dominated by the things of the flesh and the death they produce. We are now under the power of the Spirit and the "life and peace" (v. 6), which He produces, both in our transformed character here and in our secured holiness and glory with Christ in eternity.

So what's begun to change on a tangible level since we've come to know our Savior through faith? Our reasoning faculties (mind, motivations, affections/desires) have been transformed to be conformed to the mind of Christ. Self-preservation gives way to trusting in God's preserving work on our behalf:

- Hedonism turns to finding fulfillment in Christ and obedience to His will.

- Deceit turns to honesty before God and men.

- Hiding weakness turns to being teachable with a desire to grow.

- Blameshifting turns to confession and repentance.

Self-exaltation gives way to humility and self-sacrifice:

- Boasting turns to praising others.

- Condescension turns to serving others.

- Prejudice and hatred turns to unconditionally loving others.

Self-justification gives way to brokenness and gratitude for redemption:

- Minimizing sin turns to hating what God hates.

- Unforgiveness turns to free mercy for all.

- Religious pretense turns to genuine worship in spirit and truth.

Following our renewed reasoning, even our emotional expression begins to change:

- Sinful fear turns to trusting God, acknowledging His perfect love.

- Sinful anger turns to submission to God's will with a gentle spirit.

- Sinful despair turns to supernatural exulting in even the severest of trials, knowing that our guilt is gone.

As a result, the will (choices acted out in behavior) is renewed, producing a cycle of further-renewed reasoning, controlled emotions, and increasing love for God's glory.

New Morality

Here's what's at the root of this grand transformation that has taken place in believers: our moral nature and capacity *has been changed*. Paul gives us the clearest picture of our previous moral disposition apart from Christ: "The mind set on the flesh is hostile toward God; for it does not subject itself to the law of God, for it is not even able to do so" (Rom 8:7). We were naturally hostile toward God because we desired to rule ourselves, honor ourselves, and live for ourselves, all for the ultimate satisfaction of ourselves. Even the strongest human effort to please God, without faith and apart from the Spirit of God, has impure motives and cannot please Him (Heb 11:6). The unbeliever is incapable, on his own, of reversing his desire for autonomy and bringing himself by faith under the holy standards of God's truth and loving them:

> Can the Ethiopian change his skin or the leopard his spots? Then you also can do good who are accustomed to doing evil (Jer 13:23).

> A good tree cannot produce bad fruit, nor can a bad tree produce good fruit (Matt 7:18).

> But a natural man does not accept the things of the Spirit of God, for they are foolishness to him; and he cannot understand them, because they are spiritually appraised (1 Cor 2:14).

This bent within our nature had to be utterly transformed. Just how did that happen?

> But God, being rich in mercy, because of His great love with which He loved us, even when we were dead in our transgressions, made us alive together with Christ (Eph 2:4–5).

> He saved us, not on the basis of deeds which we have done in righteousness, but according to His mercy, by the washing of regeneration and renewing by the Holy Spirit (Titus 3:5).

This divine, regenerating, saving work is what makes the difference between what we were in the eyes of God and what we are now.

As we walk according to the Spirit (pouring truth into our minds, throwing off old thoughts, desires, and affections while subjecting our wills to God's will), the Spirit of the living God empowers us from within. And the result is new, godly ways of thinking, which produce godly convictions, which begin to transform our life patterns of behavior. Our response to this new power in our lives is simply to worship God with thanksgiving and with a new passion to honor Him in obedience.

A MIRACULOUS NEW INFLUENCE

A third miraculous privilege of a new life under the Spirit's control is the new influence every believer possesses. Having been given a new identity in Christ and a new inclination in life, we are not left alone in our striving: we also have a miraculous new influence, the Spirit's indwelling work. As believers, we want to come under the maximum influence of the Spirit of God in all our attitudes, perspectives, and actions. We want to tap into everything that is already given to us in Him to bring our mind and heart under the direct and constant control of the indwelling Spirit.

All those regenerated by the Spirit of God also have the abiding presence of the Spirit of God. Paul wrote to the believers, "However, you are not in the flesh but in the Spirit, if indeed the Spirit of God dwells in you. But if anyone does not have the Spirit of Christ, he does not belong to Him" (Rom 8:9). Here Paul comes right back to a fundamental difference between Christians and non-Christians—namely, that believers are indwelt by the Spirit of God. In fact, the new influence in believers is a trinitarian influence. Christians have "the Spirit of God," "the Spirit of Christ," and John 14:23 adds that the Father and the Son "will come to him, and make our abode with him." Having God's Spirit within us provides us with the power and influence of the entire Godhead.

So now, through the indwelling Holy Spirit, we have Jesus Christ and God the Father taking up residence within us, in the empowering sense. Because of this new influence, Christians are no longer "hostile toward God" (Rom 8:7)—they can submit to God's standard, and they can actually please God (cf. Rom 8:8). How is it possible to be able to please God, when, before, every part of me was opposed to God? The difference now is that we have the very life of God, His Spirit, personally indwelling (*oikeō*—to reside and be at home) us and providing the divine power needed to conform to the image of Christ. To be "in the Spirit" is to be in the realm of, and under the controlling influence of, the Spirit so that we can be empowered for spiritual victory.

At conversion the Spirit of Christ not only regenerated our nature, but He also began transforming us into the likeness of Christ. It is He who provides the new inclination toward holy things, and He who provides the power to gain victory over sin. The indwelling Spirit of God produces:

- increasing love for Jesus Christ;

- increasing desires to know Him through His Word;

- increasing understanding of, and hatred for, sin; and

- increasing love for God's people.

The Holy Spirit is working in every believer to produce fruit. Specifically, according to Galatians 5:22, "The fruit of the Spirit is love, joy, peace, patience, kindness, goodness, faithfulness, gentleness, self-control." In every true Christian, there is some evidence of the desire for and movement toward these things. Such evidence will, at times, get obscured by weakness and yielding to temptation, but they cannot be totally absent from a true believer.

How do we know that evidence of this fruit shows up in every true Christian? In Romans 8:9 Paul points out the inescapable reality: "But if anyone does not have the Spirit of Christ, he does not belong to Him." If there is no evidence of the Spirit's power anywhere in a person's life in dealing with any sinful desire, that person does not belong to Christ—he is not a Christian.

The Spirit not only produces a new influence for fruit in this life but also pledges believers a new body for the life to come: "If Christ is in you, though the body is dead because of sin, yet the spirit is alive because of righteousness" (Rom 8:10). The deadness of the body speaks of the effects of sin on our "unrenewed" part— our "outer man" (2 Cor 4:16). Sin's consequence is spiritual and physical death. But when we come to Christ, our "inner man" becomes alive by the regenerating power of the Spirit, while our outer man waits to be "redeemed" when Christ returns (Rom 8:23).

While this is true, a bit of a technical observation must be made in Romans 8:10 to understand exactly what Paul means by "yet the spirit is alive because of righteousness." The NASB and NIV take this as a reference to the inner spirit of man, largely because of the contrast with "the body." But there are two problems with this interpretation. First, the word *pneuma* (rendered either *Spirit* or *spirit*) refers to the Holy Spirit throughout the immediate context of Romans 8. The only exception where the word is used in this sense is verse 16 where the Holy Spirit and the human spirit are explicitly distinguished. The word *zōē* should be translated "life" rather than "alive." The Greek literally reads, "But the Spirit is life because of righteousness." The idea here is that because we are now seen as righteous before God (justification), the Spirit dwells within us and is "life" to the believer, from the inside out. In the next verse Paul explains the meaning a bit further: "But if the Spirit of Him who raised Jesus from the dead dwells in you, He who raised Christ Jesus from the dead will also give life to your mortal bodies through His Spirit who dwells in you" (v. 11). What's the simple conclusion of all this? Romans 8:10–11 is a guarantee of our bodily resurrection.

A MIRACULOUS NEW OBLIGATION

A fourth miraculous privilege of a new life under the Spirit's control is the new obligation every believer possesses. Believers, having a new nature by the regenerating power of the Holy Spirit, are no longer bound by sin and death. With a no-condemnation status, we have a new identity in Christ and fruit-producing influence by the Spirit. Being saved for life in the Spirit means that our old obligation is totally gone.

We Owe the Flesh Nothing

We owe nothing to the flesh, which means we must give nothing to the flesh. As unbelievers we fed the flesh, made provisions for the flesh, and strengthened its influence over our lives. We were keeping the flesh alive and it was killing us. But now, in Romans 8:12, the roles have been reversed: "So then, brethren, we are under obligation, not to the flesh, to live according to the flesh." To be "under obligation" (*opheilétēs*) means to be a debtor who is obligated by the right of the creditor. Used in this context, it means *living by the dictates of the old fleshly desires as though we owed them our unquestioned allegiance.*

But now, we've been set "free from the law of sin," (v. 2), and the Holy Spirit has taken up permanent residence within us. He provides us with new, holy affections, and His power is readily at our disposal to see sin rightly. So now, *we owe the flesh nothing.* It is a fact of our justification: we have no obligation to the flesh. Although temporary defeats, various setbacks, seasonal patterns of weakness and failure still occur, none of these things change our status before our Heavenly Father. And as we engage in the battle for sanctification, none of these things can demand our total allegiance as their slave.

We Starve the Flesh with Divine Lethal Force

The apostle Paul goes on to make yet another distinction between the life pattern of unbelievers and believers: "For if you are living according to the flesh, you must die; but if by the Spirit you are putting to death the deeds of the body, you will live" (Rom 8:13). Those who "are living according to the flesh" refers to unbelievers (cf. vv. 4–5), who will face their ultimate end, death. Believers, by contrast, are those who "are putting to death the deeds of the body."

There are three assumptions in verse 13. First, it is assumed that believers can "put to death the deeds of the body." In other words, *the power is there* for those who are in Christ. When we sin it is not because God has somehow left us without the spiritual resources to gain victory. Sometimes we just want to make excuses:

- *The trial was too hard.*

- *The temptation is more powerful than I can run away from.*

- *I need God to take away my sinful desires.*

- *I need someone to push me or I just can't do it.*

Second, it is assumed that it is *the Spirit's power* that ultimately gives us victory. As we strive and yield our will to His truth rather than to the lies told by the world, the flesh, and the devil, it is the Spirit of God who is giving us the power to flee temptation—and He never loses in that equation! Third, it is also assumed that we must *identify* "the deeds of the body" and then put them to death. The Spirit's power is there and is available all the time, but He will not see us through to holiness without our actual striving against sin and humbly yielding our will to His. This is the great paradox of spiritual growth.

Paul would likewise write the Philippians, "Work out your salvation with fear and trembling; for it is God who is at work in you, both to will and to work for His good pleasure" (Phil 2:12–13). Similarly in 2 Timothy 2:1 Paul tells Timothy, "You therefore, my son, be strong"—and then he adds, "in the grace that is in Christ Jesus." We "[put] to death the deeds of the body" by striving in the truth and yielding our will to God's will, and in all our efforts the Spirit is supernaturally dispensing His power so that our flesh is literally overrun by divine influence—and we obey. The power to obey is always through the Spirit's indwelling presence. But we don't always tap into divine resources to defeat these weaknesses. Troubleshooting our sins takes time and careful thought. Knowing the triggers which pave the way for our sinful tendencies is essential in putting them to death. We could put some of our weaknesses in a category called sins of *ignorance*:

- Superficial exposure to truth (shallow teaching, infrequency of hearing, distractedness)

- Superficial view of truth (generalities, pragmatism, simplistic grasp of the Word, eisegesis of Scripture)

- Superficial use of truth (trite applications, fad-driven ministry, earthly strength)

If that weren't enough, we also struggle against sins of *resistance*—idolatries, comfort, reputation, vain pleasure, self-atonement, shallow repentance, etc. Given such wicked, fleshly perils, it is evident that life and sanctification require nothing less than "by the Spirit ... putting to death the deeds of the body" (Rom 8:13; cf. Ps 34:11–14). This is how we starve the flesh with lethal divine force.

It is not commonly used in the same sense today, but the term *mortify* was previously used to refer to "putting to death." Older translations put it this way, using this adept and succinct expression. John Owen, the seventeenth-century English Puritan, recognized the gravity of such a command. Commenting on Colossians 3:5 and Roman 8:13, he soberly warned, "Do you mortify; do you make it your daily work; be always at it whilst you live; cease not a day from this work; be killing sin or it will be killing you."[4] Because a miraculous work has been done to us, we can work to kill the remaining sin in us. As Spurgeon put it, we passed from darkness into marvelous light, from death to life.

---

[4] John Owen, *Of the Mortification of Sin in Believers, Works of John Owen*, vol. 6, ed. William H. Goold (n.p., Johnstone & Hunter, 1850–53; reprint, London: Banner of Truth Trust, 1967), 9.

PART 2: GRACE FOR HOLINESS

CHAPTER 7

ENSLAVED BY GRACE

COMING home from the hospital with your first child is the kind of experience that embeds itself in your memory, especially the way it happened for my (Paul's) family. The birth of our oldest came with complications that kept mom and baby in the hospital longer than we had expected. Finally, after living on hospital beds and NICU couches, the doctors gave us the all clear to go home. I vividly remember that it was a warmer than usual October day in Florida—actually, it was hot. The reason I recall this detail is because when we walked in the door of our home, the power was out, and it had been that way for some time. We had been so engrossed in the birth of our first child that we had no idea all the food in our freezer and fridge had long since spoiled. More importantly, we were coming home to a dangerously hot and humid house, at least for the fragile daughter we were bringing home from the hospital.

As soon as we put down our bags, I started investigating. Once I determined that all our neighbors had power and none of the breakers had been tripped, I had exhausted my expertise. So I got on the phone with a representative of our power company who confidently told me I needed to call an electrician to solve the problem. When I spoke with the electrician he insisted there was nothing he could do; I needed to take up the problem with the power company. Meanwhile, I had a recovering mom and a delicate baby waiting in the heat. Figuratively and literally, I had no power to do anything about the situation, and I was making no headway in discovering the culprit behind the problem.

A frustrating lack of power, an unidentified cause, and contradictory answers: this accurately describes what many Christians experience in their spiritual lives. Frequently, believers find themselves battling swells of trials and temptations accompanied by sets of failure and exasperation. They see a lack of power over sin that characterizes their lives and they feel the constant weight of a guilty conscience, and they wonder what the problem is. Frustrated, they desperately search for a key to victory, or least an answer that might quiet their conscience, but increased spiritual power just doesn't seem possible. And the counsel often given seems quick to blame a person's weakness and guilt, not on a lack of faith, but on the moral standards they've been taught to obey.

Worse, some are being told that striving to obey commands is either unimportant or works-based righteousness. In other words, the culprit isn't a lack of spiritual power; it is Christians looking to the Law instead of grace to direct their spiritual lives. The reality of justification and union with Christ is undeniable, and empowering when truly believed (Rom 6:11). But what do we do when it seems that the standard for obedience is too high? Should we put a dimmer switch on the commands of Scripture and bask in the grace of Christ's forgiveness? As appealing as this solution may sound, it is no real solution at all! *Too much* effort is the wrong diagnosis when *faithless* effort is the real problem.

SIN'S THE CULPRIT, NOT THE LAW

Too much Law instead of grace is a false dichotomy, not a solution (Heb 4:2). The battle with sin cannot be won apart from grace, but neither can it be won without the guidance of the Law or the diligence of repentance. Some may want to emphasize grace and downplay holy striving, but we all must admit what every one of us experiences on a daily basis: overcoming sin isn't simply achieved by "thinking deeply about grace." *Indicatives always inevitably lead to imperatives*, but not apart from proactive faith and grace-filled effort. There has been so much muddled teaching over the past few years on progressive sanctification. Many today have decided that an emphasis on holy living and obedience are *what ultimately led* to their failure and weakness in the first place. Perhaps they grew up chaffing at authority and rules, or maybe they simply nurtured a growing contempt for Scripture's high standards because they loved the world's passing pleasures. Whatever the circumstances, they now place the blame for years of guilt and weakness on the oppression of rules—moral obligation itself. They hold God's Law responsible for their heart's tendency to rail against it.

Paul was crystal clear on this issue, exonerating the holiness of the Law while indicting the principle of sin within himself as *the cause* of his failures (Rom 7:7–13). This is what makes it so strange that language about grace is laced with animosity toward God's holy Law. Paul's theological understanding of grace was unmatched, yet he always vindicated the Law. He boldly taught it and frequently warned against its violation. Yet for countless people the commands of the Bible are attractive only if they are redefined as "delightful invitations," couched as the "fruit of grace contemplation," and *never* followed by threats of chastening for disobedience. They fear an emphasis on duty and obedience, convinced it will lead others away from the joy of knowing that Jesus "paid it all," and will plunge them back into a so-called false guilt caused by striving and failing.

Yet, we shouldn't mistake real guilt for "false guilt." The notion of false guilt spawned by the pop psychology movement of the '70s has resurfaced in evangelicalism. Today's amplified stress on the grace of the gospel has caused many people to assume that the guilt they experience is *likely, if not always*, the result of a false sense of obligation to obey God. A sense of obligation is a betrayal of grace—a slide into self-atoning legalism. Dangerously, some are shouting down their consciences, nurturing contempt for God's Law, separating from healthy ministries, and flirting with worldly lifestyle choices.

SLAVES OF RIGHTEOUSNESS

I love the biblical concept of sinners being purchased from the slave market of sin to be owned by a new Master. We are "bought with a price," and so we belong to Christ; we are not our own (1 Cor 6:19–20). There can be no sweeter Master than King Jesus, but with the contemporary disdain for being obligated to Him, you would think the Lord cared nothing about our practical devotion and only about our affectionate feelings for Him. We're supposed to follow Him only because He longs to give us the personal sense of satisfaction we all crave. But this is to pit one truth against another. As John MacArthur has keenly argued:

> The New Testament reflects this perspective, commanding believers to submit to Christ completely, and not just as hired servants or spiritual employees—but as those who belong wholly to Him. We are told to obey Him without question and follow Him without complaint. Jesus Christ is our Master—a fact we acknowledge every time we call Him "Lord." We are His slaves, called to humbly and wholeheartedly obey and honor Him.
>
> We don't hear about that concept much in churches today. ... Instead of teaching the New Testament gospel—where sinners are called to submit to Christ—the contemporary message is exactly the opposite: Jesus is here to fulfill all *your* wishes. Likening Him to a personal assistant or a personal trainer, many churchgoers speak of a *personal* Savior who is eager to do their bidding and help them in their quest for self-satisfaction or individual accomplishment.
>
> The New Testament understanding of the believer's relationship to Christ could not be more opposite. He is the Master and Owner. We are His possession. He is the King, the Lord, and the Son of God. We are His subjects and His subordinates.
>
> In a word, we are His *slaves*.[1]

God does completely satisfy our longings (Ps 37:4), but this is born from a robust faith in Him and submission to His will regardless

[1] John MacArthur, Jr., *Slave* (Nashville: Thomas Nelson, 2010), 14–15; emphases original.

of whether we feel satisfied or not. The apostle Paul dealt with this issue in a very straightforward way, and he didn't shy away from using the language of slavery to make his case. Paul clarifies that there are only two possible paths in this life: willful slavery to sin, resulting in death, or willful slavery to obedience, resulting in righteousness. "Do you not know that when you present yourselves to someone as slaves for obedience, you are slaves of the one whom you obey, either of sin resulting in death, or of obedience resulting in righteousness?" (Rom 6:16).

The way Paul equates slavery with a commitment to righteousness could have been misunderstood. Some may conclude that Paul speaks of human degradation as the image of serving Christ. But by using the slavery imagery, he is picking up the themes of *ownership, complete mastery,* and *unquestioned obedience.* In this way the language of slavery does not violate grace, since slaves do not earn their place, determine their status, or pay for their position. Slaves are at the mercy of their master, which, in the case of Christ, is a lavish grace.

In our ongoing battle with sin, we can be encouraged that there is only one possible solution to slavery to sin. It is not "making a decision for Jesus," "hungering for beauty," or cranking up passion. It is nothing less than becoming "slaves of righteousness" (Rom 6:18)! Using the terminology of slavery again, Paul commands us to set ourselves apart for righteousness: "For just as you presented your members as slaves to impurity and to lawlessness, resulting in further lawlessness, so now present your members as slaves to righteousness, resulting in sanctification" (Rom 6:19). Slaves of righteousness have only one possible outcome—sanctification. To put it simply, we're enslaved to God, so we will prevail in Him. So the only response which slaves of righteousness have is to get busy living in holiness!

SECURE IN ETERNAL BENEFITS

Slaves of righteousness can know and enjoy several benefits, chief among which is eternal life. "But now having been freed from sin and enslaved to God, you derive your benefit, resulting in sanctification, and the outcome, eternal life. For the wages of sin is death, but the free gift of God is eternal life in Christ Jesus our Lord" (Rom 6:22–23). The whole picture can be summarized like this: *striving leads to sanctification and sanctification leads to eternal life.* But there are a host of other benefits which slaves of righteousness can enjoy. Having the gift of eternal life, we can also enjoy the *assurance* of eternal life. This grows with our faithfulness and is manifested by increasing holiness. It can be shaken by a ravaged conscience, and it fades with patterns of neglect and rebellion. (Eternal security and assurance are further discussed in chapter 11.)

Closely related to personal assurance is *encouragement*. Lapses in spiritual fortitude and moral integrity are common in the spiritual warfare we wage against the flesh. The severity and length of such compromises decrease as holiness and obedience increase (2 Pet 1:9–11). During times of confusion, when doubts rage because of sin, we have the encouragement of inward conviction, godly sorrow, and new hope from God, who "is greater than our heart" (1 John 3:20).

Another wonderful benefit of perseverance is *clarity*. Over time it becomes clear that there will be those who profess to know Jesus Christ, but who are not being saved. The most graphic illustration is given by Jesus in the parable of the soils from Matthew 13:3–8, 18–23. Three of the soils represent times when the gospel is graciously offered, but where no final fruit of conversion remains. Two of the three experience some temporarily visible change, but for the lack of firm convictions they fall away.

Slaves of righteousness can also know true *humility*. The reality of God's electing love and guaranteed preservation crushes pride and causes the believer to tremble in His presence. With each act of obedience comes the realization that God is willing and working according to His good pleasure so that we might be caused to revere Him (Phil 2:12–13). It is an underserved privilege to be given the grace of sanctification, and in light of such mercy we are called to "conduct [ourselves] in fear during the time of [our] stay on earth; knowing that [we] were … redeemed … with precious blood, as of a lamb unblemished and spotless, the blood of Christ" (1 Pet 1:17b–19).

Diligence, likewise, is a God-given benefit to His slaves. Paul declares in Romans 6:4 that we were saved to "walk in newness of life." God did not secure Christians in a continuum of preservation so that they would be free to dishonor Him on the way there. Part of the genius of our Savior is the assignment of persevering obedience so that we would display His manifold glory through our daily sanctification (1 Thess 5:21–24). He supplies the grace and power to serve Him (1 Pet 4:11); He guards us from total failure (1 Cor 10:13); He gives special strength in times of weakness (Isa 40:29); He conforms us to the image of Christ (Phil 1:6); He has promised to keep our hope secure (1 Pet 1:3–5); and He is working all things "to the praise of His glory" (Eph 1:12). Our final salvation is not the result of our faithfulness; rather, our perseverance is the proof that God is preserving our redemption.

Finally, slaves of righteousness enjoy the benefit of *accountability*. The command to obey Christ and follow Him as the Lord of our lives is a gracious provision from God to help us remain focused. Even though we have confidence that God is working out His redemptive purpose in our lives with unfailing certainty, we also are protected from self-deception, enslavement to sin, pride, laziness, and idolatry as we dependently strive in perseverance. Our faith is strengthened, prayers refined, minds alerted, affections checked, choices scrutinized, and hearts enlarged! Persevering duties *are* the delight of the Christian as we keep "fixing our eyes on Jesus, the author and perfecter of faith" (Heb 12:2).

* * *

After what seemed like dozens of phone calls, I finally convinced the power company they needed to come out and investigate the reason why my house was powerless. Within five minutes the technician who came out identified the problem. The meter at my house had been mislabeled, so when my neighbor failed to pay his electric bill they turned my power off instead of his. Once we determined the culprit, I had power again, and the same thing is so often true in our spiritual lives.

Blaming the Law, the pursuit of righteousness, or the desire of greater assurance is not the cause of our spiritual powerlessness—no matter how much our flesh would love for that to be the answer. Weakness and weariness are caused by the same culprit, unbelief. The heart of legalism isn't striving too hard; it is striving without a faith solely in Christ. In other words, the problem is not your level of effort; it is the object of your faith. So long as you are trusting in yourself, you will never experience the promised power of grace. If, however, you have entrusted yourself to Christ, the comforts of grace will be available to you even in the midst of the most strenuous service.

CHAPTER 8

MEANS OF GRACE (PART 1)

WHILE reading the Gospels, have you ever noticed that Jesus didn't always heal diseases in exactly the same way? On one occasion He merely spoke the words from across town and a centurion's prize servant was made well. Another time He gave back sight to a blind man by spreading dirt and saliva on his eyelids. Sometimes Jesus healed with words alone and other times by using some physical expression or means. Onlookers were shocked when a crippled man began to jump around at merely a healing command from the Lord. But in another dramatic moment He gently touched a woman's hand, and her deadly fever left her. He spoke and Lazarus "came forth" from the dead, but during a funeral processional in a small village He touched the coffin to give new life. Why was Jesus' power so often mediated to men and women through various means? Isn't God able to display His power without involving His creation? Of course He is. Yet, marvelously He receives glory through the use of means. God most often mediates His rule through earthly instruments. Herman Bavinck described this reality in simple terms:

> He illuminates and warms the earth with the sun. He waters the plowed fields with the rain that he causes to fall from the clouds. He builds the house by means of the workmen ... . He nourishes by means of food. He quenches by means of

FREE TO BE HOLY

water … . Always and everywhere the Lord binds outcomes to pathways, ends to means.[1]

LORD OF THE ENDS AND THE MEANS

The means of grace are the lifeblood of sanctification and the believer's chief resource in the pursuit of holiness. God has chosen these instruments through which we are conformed to Christ. Yet, some believers remain unaware of these gifts, or they've been taught that we grow in grace by the Spirit's power without any involvement on our part at all. So, if the means of grace are essential to our walk with Christ and growth in sanctification, what are they? Louis Berkhof provides a helpful starting point:

> Fallen man receives all the blessings of salvation out of the eternal fountain of the grace of God, in virtue of the merits of Jesus Christ and through the operation of the Holy Spirit. While the Spirit can and does in some respects operate immediately on the soul of the sinner, He has seen fit to bind Himself largely to the use of certain means in the communication of divine grace. The term "means of grace" is not found in the Bible, but is nevertheless a proper designation of the means that are indicated in the Bible.[2]

In other words, the means of grace are divine instruments given by God to equip us "for good works, which God prepared beforehand, so that we would walk in them" (Eph 2:10). They are the tools used by God to chisel away our hard hearts and conform us to the image of Christ. And though God is always actively working in our lives through His Spirit, we are never passive in our growth. If we are maturing in our walk with Christ, it's because we are actively trusting Him and humbly obeying His commands. God does not somehow infuse us with spiritual growth apart from our faith and submission. He has chosen ordinary means to help us in our Christian life.

[1] Herman Bavinck, *Saved by Grace* (Grand Rapids: Reformation Heritage Books, 2008), 134.
[2] Louis Berkhof, *Systematic Theology*, combined ed. (Grand Rapids: Eerdmans, 1996), 604.

128

For example, He uses preaching, prayer, corporate worship, the ordinances of the church, discipleship, as well as various other implements to bring us to Christ and help us live the Christian life. It is this way, at least in part, so that we will know where to look for His grace. We do not need to browse aimlessly through strategies and innovative methods for spiritual growth when God has revealed His plan already. He wisely chose to use these *means of grace* over time so that the longer we experience this work the deeper our faith in divine grace grows.

If you're passively waiting to be "overwhelmed" by the grace of God, your soul will shrivel up long before it is ever strengthened. God's grace is poured out through means, and maturity comes as we actively submit ourselves to these means of grace. People who sporadically attend worship services, chafe at hearing sermons, rarely pray, never give, and whose Bible collects dust should not be confused about why they keep falling into sin. It's not difficult to identify the problem. They have separated themselves from the spiritual disciplines—the means—God uses to grow His people, and as a result, they are seeking victory in the Christian life by their own strength rather than by the grace of God.

As vital as these tools for growth are for God's people, many struggling believers have been taught that spiritual disciplines are an unnecessary burden, that putting forth human effort is to try to please God by works. The idea is that real growth happens when we relax and enjoy the grace of God, so that new motivations to obey can eventually rise up again in our hearts. What an attractive message! You don't have to put forth any effort for your sanctification, and you don't have to feel bad about it either. It is an emotional prosperity gospel that promises the visceral benefits of sanctification without the strenuous effort of "taking up the shield of faith" and wielding His "sword of the Spirit" in the battle against temptation (Eph 6:13–17). A passive approach to spirituality may offer a sense of personal affirmation, but it cannot truly sanctify. God designed our growth to involve our full personal conviction, devotion, and striving to believe the truth and flee from lies.

Practicing spiritual disciplines for personal growth does not violate grace. When we cling to the practical disciplines given in Scripture, we are growing "in the grace" of Christ (2 Pet 3:18). God promised to strengthen us "in the grace that is in Christ Jesus" (2 Tim 2:1), and the tools given to us for growth are a vital fulfillment of that promise. When we strive in the disciplines of His grace, it is an act of faith and humble obedience. Remember, the same God who despises legalism also commands diligent effort to experience growth (2 Pet 1:5). If we seek to grow apart from the means God has given, *we will be striving in our own efforts*, despite labeling it grace. You can't claim to revel in the glorious grace of God and reject the means by which He bestows that grace. When we detach ourselves from the disciplines God commanded and promised to bless, we are seeking sanctification on our terms. This, of course, will never work. Growth in grace happens only on God's terms.

Even though it is virtually impossible to list all the means of grace God uses in our lives, we can identify the instruments He ordinarily and most effectually uses. At the top of this list is biblical truth—actually, it permeates every item on the list. Sanctifying change occurs as our faith is informed with the truth (John 17:17), our minds are transformed by truth (Rom 12:1–2), and our convictions about life are established in the truth (2 Tim 1:12; Heb 11:1). This is why, in John 17:17, Jesus prayed to the Father, "Sanctify them in the truth; your word is truth." Jesus not only interceded for our sanctification, He expected it to happen as a result of God's truth.

Any suppression of the truth, therefore, stunts growth while the clear proclamation of it stimulates growth. This simple principle acts as a linchpin for practically applying the means of grace to our lives. There is no such thing as a spiritual discipline that is detached from biblical truth. For instance, prayer must be rooted in the promises and priorities of the Bible in order to be spiritually profitable. The Lord's Table and believer's baptism must proclaim and adorn divine truth to have a sanctifying effect.

Trials will serve as a means of grace in our lives only when they deepen our enduring faith in the precepts of Scripture. The means of grace are designed as aids in the process to explain, confirm, remind, and apply sanctifying truth. As we study God's ordinary, practical means of grace, it will become evident that there is no such thing as spiritual growth without faith-filled effort in the regular use of these tools. They are at the very heart of what it means to be conformed to the image of our Savior, Jesus Christ.

PREACHING

Of all the ordinary means of grace God has designed for our growth, none has proven more powerful than preaching. It is certainly not impossible for a Christian to experience some level of maturity without preaching, since preaching is not the only practical discipline for the Christian life. However, growth apart from preaching is neither the rule nor without risk. When unique circumstances prevent believers from regularly sitting under the faithful preaching of Scripture (e.g., if there is no good church available, or one is shut in due to a long illness), they should not settle in comfortably with the situation. God's abundant grace will be necessary in extra measure for such unique circumstances, to be sure, but we're vulnerable to greater temptation and deception without being reproved, corrected, and exhorted by preaching (1 Tim 4:6).

From a historical perspective, preaching has always played a major role in making and maturing disciples. This began when Jesus prioritized preaching in his earthly ministry (Mark 1:15, 35–39). Jesus' conviction about the sanctifying power of His truth (John 17:17) formed the basis of His commitment to preach it. The apostles championed Jesus' high view of preaching by devoting themselves "to prayer and to the ministry of the word" (Acts 6:4). And every subsequent generation has been bound by this same priority, most notably when Paul commanded Timothy to "preach the word" (2 Timothy 4:2). As A. E. Garvie eloquently asserts, the Church Fathers followed suit: "Probably there had never been in human history a period in which preaching had been so widely and keenly appreciated, as when the Christian Church went forth to conquer the world by 'the foolishness of preaching.'"[3]

The Reformation also demonstrated the spiritual potency of preaching. Luther wrote his *Ninety-Five Theses*, but it was his preaching that breathed spiritual life into the church. Calvin's *Institutes of the Christian Religion* became the theological standard for future generations, but it was his preaching that transformed the city of Geneva. And it was Zwingli's exposition of Matthew that compelled city leaders to mandate expository preaching in all of Zurich's pulpits. The spirit of the Reformation was delivered, nurtured, and matured from the pulpit. For the next several centuries, preaching would be the catalyst for dramatic reformation. Puritan pulpits propelled the gospel forward, the evangelistic pulpits of the Great Awakening woke up the sleeping church, and the expository resurgence of modern decades refocused a distracted church.

The clear and consistent pattern of church history is spiritual growth through preaching. *In fact, for nearly two thousand years Christians had to grow through preaching because they didn't have their own copy of the Bible.* For the majority of church history preaching has been the most ordinary instrument God uses for spiritual growth, and it still is today. The doctrinal truth standing behind the role of preaching in the history of the church is that preaching is a primary means of grace. As Romans 10:17 reminds us, "faith comes from hearing, and hearing through the word of Christ."

God loves to glorify Himself by conforming us to Christ through preaching. The preaching ministry of promised shepherds is how God pours out His grace on His people and propels His kingdom work forward (Jer 3:15; Eph 4:11–12). This is why the maturity and ministry of the church rises and falls on the strength of its pulpit. Faithfulness in the church requires faithfulness in preaching—it

[3] A. E. Garvie, *The Christian Preacher* (New York: Charles Scribner's Sons, 1921), 59.

does not stop there, but it always begins there. This is not true of merely the church corporately; it is true of you individually. You need to recognize that your maturity depends on the maturity of the preaching you are exposed to on a regular basis.

Preaching brings the Word of God to bear in your life in a way that you cannot otherwise experience. Truth must be understood in order to be sanctifying, and preaching brings understanding through instruction. Additionally, preaching brings the authority of Scripture to bear in the life of a believer with unmatched power. John Owen recognized this uniquely sanctifying impact of preaching:

> Sometimes in the reading of the Word, God opens a passage that cuts him to the heart, and shakes him as to his present condition. More frequently, in the hearing of the Word preached, His great ordinance for conviction, conversion, and edification, God strikes with the sword of His Word at the heart of cherished lust.[4]

Preachers explain the meaning of Scripture, they draw out the implications for our heart and conduct, they illustrate, and they exhort our wills, calling us to obedience. The Chief Shepherd Himself has given grace-gifts—preachers—to the church for our spiritual growth (Eph 4:7, 11). Corporate worship in the church is a unique dynamic whereby the Spirit ministers grace to the body through the preaching of His truth. He makes our hearts pliable so that the Word dwells richly among us (Col 3:16). He unifies us around the truth so that we're mutually built up in love (Eph 4:13–16). Together we are protected from subtle errors (Eph 4:14). Through the Spirit's power we are edified by the expressions of praise from those around us (Eph 5:19), we are humbled and encouraged to pray as the word burdens our hearts. And our sins are exposed in a congregation full of those with like weakness. All of this is accomplished through the faithful exposition of Scripture.

---

[4] John Owen, *The Mortification of Sin*, Richard Rushing ed. (Edinburgh: Banner of Truth Trust, 2004), 62–63.

FREE TO BE HOLY

You and I need preaching for sanctification if for no other reason than to make sure that we are understanding and submitting to the authority of Scripture. In Romans 16:25–27 the apostle Paul recognized preaching as the primary means of grace to bring about the obedience of faith and strengthen us in this faith: "Now to Him who is able to establish you according to my gospel and the preaching of Jesus Christ, according to the revelation of the mystery which has been kept secret for long ages past, but now is manifested, and by the Scriptures of the prophets, according to the commandment of the eternal God, has been made known to all the nations, leading to obedience of faith; to the only wise God, through Jesus Christ, be the glory forever. Amen."

Paul was absolutely committed to preaching as a chief means of grace, and we should be too. In the seventeenth century the assembly of pastoral leaders at Westminster made a similar declaration when they wrote the Westminster Shorter Catechism. They recognized the vital role preaching plays in the spiritual maturity of God's people, and they confirmed this reality in question #89 of the catechism:

Q. How is the Word made effectual to salvation?

A. The Spirit of God maketh the reading, but *especially the preaching*, of the Word, an effectual means of convincing and converting sinners, and of building them up in holiness and comfort, through faith, unto salvation.[5]

"Especially the preaching." That is how you should think about preaching in your own life. Yes, God uses multiple means of grace to grow His people, but He has chosen to use the preaching of His Word in a unique and special way. Personal study, regular prayer, and the church ordinances all play a role in your spiritual growth; however, any strategy for spiritual growth that does not include submission to biblical preaching will be less than what God has designed for you. We simply cannot progress in the Christian life apart from the benefits of God's kind disposition toward us—and

[5] Westminster Shorter Catechism, Question 89; emphasis added.

the fresh breeze of God's sanctifying grace blows most consistently through the channel of the pulpit. *Preaching is a time-tested,
truth-saturated, divinely-authorized source of sanctifying grace.*

THE ORDINANCES

In addition to preaching, God uses the ordinances of baptism
and the Lord's Table as means of uniquely explaining, confirming, reminding, and applying sanctifying truth to the life of the
church. And the primary truth permeating baptism and the
Lord's Table is the truth of Christ's Person and redeeming work.
Baptism is a prescription of Christ. With all the contemporary
talk about being Christ-centered, we often forget that Jesus is
just as much the law-giving Lord as He is the suffering Savior
(Jas 4:12). As Lord, He requires that all believers be baptized
(Matt 28:19; Acts 2:37–38; 10:47–48) as a public declaration of
their faith in Him and allegiance to His Lordship (Matt 6:24;
Rom 10:9–10; Col 1:13).

But not only is baptism a command of Christ, it is also a
picture of the work of Christ. We are not permitted to make our
own images of Christ for worship, but He has provided us with
spiritual images to deepen our faith. Baptism is a graphic portrayal
of the death and burial of Christ, which resulted in the believer's
cleansing and forgiveness (Rom 6:3–4a). It pictures the death
of the old bondage to sin, the cleansing of our conscience from
dead works, and the resurrection life now belonging to us. Being
justified by faith alone, baptism also pictures the righteousness
of Christ, which is imputed to the Christian through faith (Rom
6:4; Col 2:12). Just as the bread and wine point to the body and
death of Christ, the immersion and emersion of baptism point to
the death and resurrection of Christ.

And yet the ordinance of baptism is much more than just
identifying with Christ and picturing His work of redemption.
Baptism represents an abiding promise from Christ, and
graciously reminds the church of the power we possess through
our new vital union with Christ. It is a visual reminder of the

forgiveness and power we have through this union (Gal 3:25–27). Just as you were immersed in the waters of baptism, through faith you are immersed into Christ by the Holy Spirit. Baptism is a Christ-exalting means of grace that follows the prescription of Christ, pictures the work of Christ, and embraces the promises of Christ.

Like baptism, the Lord instituted Communion as a means of grace to spiritually nourish His people. The Lord's Table is not magical or mystical; it is actually quite practical. When instituting this ordinance Jesus said, "Do this in remembrance of Me" (Luke 22:19). Christ intended for the Lord's Table to instruct us and remind us of the truth of the gospel. It is a visual teaching aid pointing us back to the life-sustaining spiritual truths of the incarnation ("This is my body"), the atonement ("the new covenant in My blood"), and return of Christ ("until the kingdom of God comes") (Luke 22:18–20). In this way, the church is steadied through life's storms with regular reminders and assurance of grace.

All too often people are encouraged not to partake in the Lord's Table if they have sin in their lives. The fact is that if they don't think they have sin in their lives they should be excluded (1 John 1:8-10). Remember, the Lord's Table is proclaiming the Lord's death, not our self-righteousness (1 Cor 11:26). When Scripture says we shouldn't partake in an unworthy manner, it does not mean we should abstain if we're dealing with sin and weakness—no one would ever take Communion if that were the meaning. Instead, these instructions require a person not to take the elements of the Lord's Table if they have not submitted to the Lord. Living in an unworthy manner refers to a heart and conduct that are unwilling to repent and are openly insubordinate to the Lordship of Christ. If you are battling sin and humbly seeking to bring every last lust under the truth, this *is* the fruit of God's work in your life rather than a reason to not partake of the bread and the cup. As you battle to bring your life under the Lordship of Christ, the Lord's Table is a means of grace to help you continue battling. It is designed to remind you that Jesus is sufficient for your salvation, and His work on the cross has done everything necessary for you to be saved (John 19:30). If you are truly believing in Jesus, then the elements of the Lord's Table are a reminder of the assurance of salvation that you have in Him as you battle to obey Him.

The Lord's Table also serves as a gracious reminder that the work and Word of Jesus *is sufficient* for our sanctification: it reminds us that we have all the resources we need to be like Christ because we have Christ! *Communion*, which comes from the Latin translation of the word "sharing" in 1 Corinthians 10:16, reminds believers of our vital and eternal connection to Christ. Through faith we participate in and have communion with Christ, and the Lord's Table is a picture of this inextricable bond we possess with our living Savior.

The Lord's Table also nourishes the body through regular discipline. First Corinthians 5 is very clear that those who continually refuse to be unified under the Lordship of Christ must be disciplined out of the church and excluded from the Lord's Table. They have forfeited their right to assurance, and they have defamed the truths taught through this means of grace. In this way Communion reinforces unity and provides a gracious discipline to protect us from apostasy by compelling us to deal with areas of rebellion on a regular basis. As Christians we should never be content to forsake the Lord's Table. We should crave the nourishment it provides so much that it motivates us to deal with our sin. In this way, along with instructing and assuring us, the Lord's Table is a disciplining means of grace.

In the ordinances of the church we possess vital means of grace for the Christian life. Baptism points to the truth that by faith we have entered into an eternal and unbreakable union with Christ. The Lord's Table points to the truth that by faith we perpetually remain in communion with Christ and benefit from His atoning work. These ordinances have been given as a visible confirmation of God's invisible grace and regular reminders of our membership in the New Covenant. They are Christ-exalting acts of worship that keep our focus and attention on the Person of Christ.

CORPORATE PRAISE

Along with preaching and the ordinances, God uses the corporate praise of the church as an edifying means of grace in the life of the believer. As stated earlier, when we worship as God's people, the Spirit uses that in a unique way to direct our lives. Ephesians 5:18–21 describes the how the Spirit uses the corporate praise of the church to influence the lives of individual believers: "be filled with the Spirit, speaking to one another in psalms and hymns and spiritual songs, singing and making melody with your heart to the Lord; always giving thanks for all things in the name of our Lord Jesus Christ to God, even the Father; and be subject to one another in the fear of Christ." In this passage we learn that the Spirit influences (i.e., fills) your life more fully when you are around other Spirit-filled believers because He ministers to you through their gifts and faithfulness (Eph 4:16; Heb 10:24–25). When we praise the Lord together the Spirit influences us as we speak to one another (Eph 5:19). This certainly applies to the sermon, Bible reading, and prayer, but it also applies as we sing together. When we surround ourselves with believers singing deep truths of the faith, the Spirit encourages and convicts us from within. Hearing fellow believers praise Christ, seeing them offer up the fruit of their lips, and joining together in the bond of redemption and peace strengthens our faith and rejuvenates our spirit and joy in the Lord.

There is a horizontal element to the church's music, not to perform for one another but to edify one another. Make no mistake: there is a vertical element to our corporate singing. Music is first and foremost about the One being sung to. This is why Paul mentions "singing and making melody with your heart to the Lord." He is not speaking about the emotions you feel when you sing, although that may become a rich part of what you experience while praising Him. The heart is who you are at your deepest level. As George Zemek has often referred to it, your heart is your "mission control center." Thus, Paul is saying that Spirit-filled praise must be genuine praise, not measured by the sensations we feel internally, but by spirit and truth (John 4:24). This is the kind of praise that most glorifies God, and it is the kind of praise the Spirit uses as a means of grace to influence you and those around you.

The goal of the church's music is to worship the Lord in spirit and truth, *and* to let the Spirit use us to minister to one another in the process. This has several implications for how we participate in the corporate music of the church. We should focus on aiding the worship of those around us rather than just our own private time with God. We should take joy in the fellowship of singing together as a foretaste of our eternal ministry (Rev 19:1–10). We should be willing to yield our preferences in music for the good of our brothers and sisters in Christ. In all of this, we can trust that the Lord is using our corporate praise as a means of grace in our lives.

THE CHURCH

This brings us to a concluding thought in this chapter about the ordinary means of grace: *they are all found within the context of the local church.* God has promised to use preaching, baptism, the Lord's Table, and corporate praise as means of grace, and He has placed each of these within the confines of the church. As Calvin put it, "In order that the preaching of the gospel might flourish, He deposited this treasure in the church."[6] Grace enables individuals to grow, and the most potent grace for true growth is found in the context of the body of Christ (John 15:5). Christ is the ultimate source of the growth, but He uses the body as a means of grace for that growth. This is the theological truth that undergirds the Bible's instruction for believers not to forsake

[6] John Calvin, *Institutes of the Christian Religion*, trans. Ford Lewis Battles, ed. John T. McNeill, 2 vols. (Louisville: Westminster John Knox Press, 1960), 4.1.1.

"our own assembling together" (Heb 10:25). An emphasis on church attendance is not a legalistic holdover from a supposedly graceless generation; it is the recognition that we need grace, and the church is where God has promised to provide it.

Within the church we actively avail ourselves of the means of grace and simultaneously function as a means of grace in the lives of other believers. God designed you to grow with the body, for the body, and because of the body (Eph 4:15–16). You are designed to grow most effectively as other parts of the body grow with you. Believers "grow by being carefully fitted and held together, rather than growing individually apart from one another."[7] The Lord is not just chipping away at your hardness of heart, He is chipping away at you so that you will be "fitted" together with the other believers around you. In fact, you are not only growing along with the rest of the body, you are also growing *for* the body. God is graciously producing growth in you so that you can be an instrument of growth in the lives of other believers. A measure of grace has been given to each one to be a means of grace to everyone. Every discipleship relationship between believers within the body is a supply line of grace that produces growth when it is working properly. This means you have a responsibility not only to feed on the means of grace within the church, but also to function as a means of grace within the church.

A robust understanding of the God-ordained means of growth plays a vital role in the Christian life, especially in protecting us from the barrenness of legalism and the pitfalls of antinomianism. It guards our hearts from a spirit of legalism by reminding us that we are not earning God's grace by emphasizing spiritual disciplines. Our faith-driven efforts don't remove us from the realm of grace, but plunge us deeper into the storehouses of God's grace. When we pattern our lives according to the commands of Scripture, we are not earning merit; we are simply trusting the Word of the Lord in our lives. A slave who obeys his master has simply done his duty—nothing more (Luke 17:10). The incredible

---

[7] Harold Hoehner, *Ephesians* (Grand Rapids: Baker Academic, 2002), 570.

thing about our Master is that He has graciously designed every one of our duties to be a blessing for us.

At the same time, the disciplines of grace prevent us from the dangers of libertinism by reminding us that God has enlisted us in our own spiritual growth as the opportunity to fulfill what He has equipped us for. He has made us new creatures with a new capacity for spiritual responsibility. He has graciously called and equipped us to obediently follow Him so that His grace will abound in our lives. Practicing sin will not increase grace in our lives (Rom 6:1–2), but practically following Christ will. If we try to shake off the constraints and commands of Scripture, we are fighting against the grace of God and the means He has promised to use for our sanctification. Understanding the means of grace as they are found in the Scripture allows us to root our pursuit of holiness in the free grace of God.

CHAPTER 9

MEANS OF GRACE (PART 2)

GOD will do what He promises in our lives, but we are warned in Scripture to practice what He commands. He is faithful, but we are to be unswerving in our hope-filled efforts to grow (Heb 10:23). While we are "press[ing] on toward the goal for the prize of the upward call of God in Christ" (Phil 3:14), God assures us that He is powerfully working within us to bring our full salvation to its completion (Phil 2:12–13; 3:13–14). There is no contradiction here. God is preserving our faith until we reach glory, but the means by which He does His preserving work is our perseverance in all the commands, urgings, reproofs, and admonishments in His Word. (See chapter 11 for a study of this issue.)

God's grace is a permanent enablement given to His people—always accessible and effective. This is a vital principle for understanding the means of grace. Sometimes believers get confused, thinking that since we are sanctified by grace alone then there can be no place for striving to defeat sin. Human effort, they claim, is the opposite of relying on grace, and therefore is the same as working to merit God's favor—in other words, deadly legalism.

But Scripture frequently bundles God's grace and our effort in the same passage. In Philippians 2:12–13, we "work out [our] salvation with fear and trembling; for it is God who is at work in [us], both to will and to work for His good pleasure." We trust and obey, convinced that through our labor God is doing His will in and through us. When calling us to spiritual battle in Ephesians 6:10, the apostle Paul commands us to "be strong in the Lord and in the strength of His might." The force of Paul's language here is unflinching and commanding—"You be strong"—yet technically the terminology indicates that God is the One who supplies the strength. And there is simply no denying the precise wording of Colossians 1:29, where Paul openly declares, "For this purpose also *I labor, striving according to His power*, which mightily works within me." Admittedly, there is tension in all such paradoxes found in Scripture. So how are we to understand this? John Eadie illuminates our understanding here:

> Though God work and work effectually in us "to will," our will is not passively bent and broken, but it wills as God wills it; and though God work ... effectually in us "to do," our doing is not a course of action to which we are helplessly driven; but we do, because we have resolved so to do .... Lazarus came forth from the tomb by his own act, but his life had been already restored by Him in whom is life. The Hebrews walked every weary foot of the distance between Egypt and Canaan, yet to God is justly ascribed their exodus .... As man's activities are prompted and developed by Him who works in us ... commands are issued, urging him to be laborious and indefatigable; for still he is dealt with as a creature that acts from motive, is deterred by warning, swayed by argument, and bound to obey divine precept. And what an inducement to work out our salvation—God Himself working in us—volition and action prompted and sustained by Him who "knoweth our frame."[1]

All spiritual growth is rooted in the grace and power of Almighty God. But our growth—of any genuine stripe—does not occur without our humble faith in God's Word and yielding our will to it in active submission.

In a supernatural synergy impossible to fully grasp, God is able to work in and through us so that our faith-filled efforts to obey

---

[1] John Eadie, *A Commentary on the Greek Text of the Epistle of Paul to the Philippians* (Eugene, OR: Wipf and Stock, 1998), 134–35.

are wrought by His power alone. One songwriter expressed this truth beautifully in the lyric of a prayer: "Turn my strivings into works of grace."[2] I need not fear that putting forth human effort in sanctification nullifies the work of God to grant me spiritual victories against any temptation, when I walk by faith and strive to humbly obey, saying "not my will but Yours be done," I am assured that God's power is strengthening me past the test into victory. Where I fail, unbelief is always the culprit at one level or another. Where I have defeated sin, faith was genuine and empowered by God. Wonderfully, God has revealed the means He uses to accomplish this work. As we saw in the last chapter, these ordinary means of grace include participation in the public ministry of the local church. Preaching, the ordinances, and corporate praise are part of the weekly rhythm of the Christian life that God uses to shape our soul. In addition to these, God has prescribed several more means of grace that should characterize every believer.

PERSONAL BIBLE STUDY

God designed the Christian life to thrive on a steady diet of truth, which means that personal Bible study is an important discipline of grace. The testimony of the Bible resoundingly confirms its own efficacy in the work of sanctification. God uses the truth to produce courage (Josh 1:7), purity (Ps 119:9), joy (Jer 15:16), discernment (Phil 1:8–11), fruit (Col 1:9–10), maturity (Col 1:28), good works (2 Tim 3:15–17), and Christlikeness (Col 3:10).

The Bible undeniably claims to possess sanctifying power, but how does this power work? How do we explain the case of individuals who know a lot of biblical truth but never experience true change? Doesn't this undermine the assertion that God's Word has the power to sanctify? The answer is no. It is impossible to be sanctified without understanding biblical truth, but it is possible to understand biblical truth without being sanctified

[2] Keith and Kristin Getty, "Holy Spirit," Spotify App (UK & Europe: EMICMG Publishing, 2006), https://www.tym@kingsway.co.uk (accessed July 2016).

by it. In order for your own personal Bible study to have a sancti-fying effect in your life, several key ingredients need to be in place.

For truth to be sanctifying, the Holy Spirit must be at work illuminating and applying it. Bible study is not a way for us to circumvent our dependence upon God for spiritual growth. The fact is, the necessity of truth in the process of sanctification is the necessity of the Holy Spirit. His ministry empowers and enlivens the Scriptures in our hearts. Not only is the Bible the Spirit's book, it is also His chosen instrument for regeneration (1 Pet 1:23) and sanctification (2 Thess 2:13). The Spirit of God uses the Word of God to sanctify the people of God. The Word of God is so connected to the ministry of the Spirit that obedience to Scripture *is* submission to the Spirit. But we must believe what we learn in Scripture for it to have its way in our hearts. Studying the Word while never entrusting yourself to its truth and power feeds pride and leads to spiritual blindness (1 Cor 8:1). As we learn the truth we must respond to the Holy Spirit's illumination and conviction with humble faith and submission. Truth is sanctifying only when you submit to it. If you are not reading the Scriptures with an ear toward submission, you are approaching the Bible with a hermeneutic of arrogance. A mindset like this not only impedes sanctification, it propels us in the opposite direction since the truth either softens or hardens the heart depending on how it is received. If you submissively yield to the truth, it makes your heart pliable to sanctifying change.

Submission to the Spirit by way of submission to Scripture is indispensable in sanctification. However, a person cannot submit to that which he does not understand. This is why the truth must be systematically understood in order to be sanctifying. If you want to grow in your faith, you must understand the substance of your faith because "not knowing what you believe is by definition a kind of unbelief."[3] The bottom line is that sanctifying transform-ation requires an understanding of the truth of the Bible (Rom

[3] John MacArthur, Jr., *The Truth War: Fighting for Certainty in an Age of Deception* (Nashville: Thomas Nelson, 2007), xiii.

12:2). In this way, the Bible is an indispensable means of grace in the daily rhythm of the Christian life.

PRAYER

In conjunction with the Bible, the Lord has provided the practice of prayer as a means of grace for the believer. Prayer is a vital component of the Christian life that allows us to respond to God's Word with words of our own. As Thomas Watson described it, "Prayer is a glorious ordinance, it is the soul's trading with heaven. God comes down to us by his Spirit, and we go up to him by prayer."[4] Through prayer, the believer has been summoned into the fellowship of the King to entreat favor, confess rebellion, and offer thanksgiving. This invitation has not been extended because God needs input on His kingdom matters or because we deserve the undivided attention of the King. By grace, we have been invited into the presence of God because we have been incorporated into the Person of Christ, who stands in heaven as our resurrected High Priest applying the benefits of His completed work for our continued sin. Because we are in union with Him we too have a place before the throne (Heb 4:16).

Some, when they need help and mercy, avoid God in shame rather than run to God for grace. If that is your temptation, remind yourself that you don't need perfection to pray because you have a Priest who, "having been made perfect, He became to all those who obey Him the source of eternal salvation" (Heb 5:9). Others avoid prayer out of love for sin and an unwillingness to forsake it. They don't pray because they know the Spirit will use prayer to convict them of sin and inflict deeper wounds on their conscience. Despite what they might say, they are not avoiding prayer because of a legalistic misunderstanding; they are avoiding prayer to avoid repentance. In either scenario the grace of God beckons us to the throne to receive the mercy and help that we so desperately need.

---

[4] Thomas Watson, *The Ten Commandments* (London: Banner of Truth Trust, 1965), 239.

The only requirement for prayer is faith, which is the God-ordained means by which we receive grace (Matt 21:20-22; Heb 4:16; Jas 1:6; 5:14–18). J. C. Ryle piercingly described the connection between faith and prayer: "The first act of faith will be to speak to God. Faith is to the soul what life is to the body. Prayer is to faith what breath is to life. How a man can live and not breathe is past my comprehensions, and how a man can believe and not pray is past my comprehension too."[5] If you want to refine and mature your prayer life, you must increase your faith. The stronger your faith the more consistent your prayer life will be. This does not mean that your faith must be perfect—there are many occasions when you will need to cry out to God, "Help my unbelief" (Mark 9:24). But even praying for help with unbelief will require some faith. Otherwise, to whom are you praying? Prayer is either an expression of Spirit-empowered faith or a hypocritical act of human effort. Either you pray believing in the presence of our heavenly Father, trusting in the work of Christ the Son and depending on the power of the Holy Spirit, or you pray to be seen by others—a form of self-exaltation (Luke 18:9–14). No matter how weak your faith might be, true prayer is always an expression of faith, communicating to the God you cannot see with conviction in the promises you have only heard.

In addition to being the *basis* for prayer, grace is also the primary *benefit* of prayer. We are privileged to participate in prayer because of God's kindness toward us, and when we pray we experience the benefits of God's kindness more richly. This is why Hebrews 4:16 refers to prayer as approaching "the throne of grace" so we can "find grace." It is a gift of grace that we are permitted to pray, and through prayer we are provided with more grace. Specifically, prayer is a means of grace designed to deepen our communion with God and further our dependence on God.

Our communion with God is deepened through prayer as our faith is strengthened by prayer. As believers, God's presence with us never fluctuates, but our faith in His presence does! This is

---

[5] J. C. Ryle, *Practical Religion* (Edinburgh: Banner of Truth Trust, 2013), 63.

why there are seasons of prayer when God does not "feel" as close. Don't worry, nothing has altered your union with Christ. Your faith was just weak. Weak faith manifesting itself in sinful living will often hinder the effectiveness of your prayers in this way (1 Pet 3:7). Conversely, strong faith manifesting itself through holy living will energize your prayers (Jas 5:16).

Prayer not only deepens our communion with God, it forces us to depend upon Him. He commanded us to pray as a daily reminder that we need Him for everything. By God's design, the discipline of prayer makes a routine out of recounting all the things in life that we cannot accomplish. Thus, when you practice daily prayer you are setting aside time each day to declare your dependence upon God. This is a uniquely humbling grace in our lives, and it is something that God rewards. In fact, sometimes God sovereignly waits to act until we pray so that we will not forget our daily need for his help, providing us with the opportunity to participate in the providential workings of God. In all of these ways, prayer is a vital means of grace in the life of a believer.

TRIALS

In conjunction with the Bible and prayer, God has promised to use trials as a means of grace. This is an exceptional comfort considering every Christian is guaranteed to face various trials throughout their lives. The encouragement believers possess in the midst of this struggle is the fact that God's grace provides the spiritual strength needed to endure these trials (2 Tim 2:1; Jas 1:2–4). Not only does God provide strength *for* our trials, He provides strength *through* our trials. Our heavenly Father promises to use every battle we endure as a means of grace in our lives. The child of God can face every tribulation with the joyful confidence that God has designed our circumstances for the good purpose of conforming us into the image of Christ (Rom 8:28–29; Jas 1:2–4). Through the fiery trials of life's crucible, God reveals our faults and faithlessness and offers His grace as the healing ointment for the wounds graciously inflicted. This refining process is as broad in scope as our sin is, but it works specifically to purify us in several important aspects of the Christian life.

God uses trials to identify the idols in our lives, which threaten the health of our souls by luring us away from grace and enticing us to devote ourselves to something other than God. Thankfully, God is an idol-crushing God who will use any means to crush anything that would hinder us from heartfelt devotion and practical holiness. He would much rather you endure the pain of losing your idol than the injuries caused by idolatry. As the author of Hebrews reminds us, "He disciplines us for our good, so that we may share His holiness" (Heb 12:10). Consider Job. He was a righteous man who had grown in grace beyond any of his contemporaries (Job 1:8), and there were no overt sins dominating his life. However, like all of us, there were idolatrous tendencies hiding in his heart. These seeds of unbelief were secluded in the midst of an otherwise pure heart, but they were present—and dangerous. In Job's case, these idols would have remained hidden from his view if God had not intervened. God squeezed these idols out into the open through the intense pressure of prolonged trial. Only after they were in the open was Job able to humble himself before the Lord and deal with them. Thus, the Lord used affliction to remove the hidden barriers to Job's worship and trust in his God. This is what God does. He uses trials as a means of grace to remove the idols in our lives.

God does not use trials merely to identify our idols; He also works through trials to increase our faith. As we have argued elsewhere in this book, faith is the foundational responsibility in the Christian life. The Lord helps us to fulfill this responsibility and reap the fruits of faith by ordaining trials for us to endure (Jas 1:2–4). Sometimes God allows trials in our lives to give us no other option but to trust Him. He removes the possibility of finding hope in our circumstances so that we are forced to rely on the hope that comes only by faith in the Word. As He did with Abraham, God brings us to "hope against hope" moments (Rom 4:18) so that we have no other option but to rely upon Him. God knows us through and through. He knows what we need and when we need it. There are many occasions when the only way we will walk by faith is when God takes away everything we are trusting in and leaves us with nothing but His promises. He fortifies our faith by leaving us only Himself as our anchor with nothing else to steady us in the storm. We can confidently look at every trial as a gracious opportunity to trust God, strengthen our faith, and deepen our Christian character (Rom 5:3–5).

The manifold purpose for trials does not end with identifying idols and increasing faith; *God also uses trials to improve our ability to minister to our fellow believers.* Scripture provides us with a glimpse of this refining purpose of trials in 2 Corinthians 1:6–7: "But if we are afflicted, it is for your comfort and salvation; or if we are comforted, it is for your comfort, which is effective in the patient enduring of the same sufferings which we also suffer; and our hope for you is firmly grounded, knowing that as you are sharers of our sufferings, so also you are sharers of our comfort." Paul's point is pretty simple: when God safely brings you through suffering, you are equipped to encourage others to trust the Lord in the midst of their suffering. At the same time, He also promises to use your submitted suffering as a means to spread His gospel message to the world (Luke 21:12–13).

For a Christian, bad things in life can be difficult, but they are bearable because we know God is using them as a means of grace to deepen our faith and prepare us for His glory (2 Cor 4:16–18). As Peter teaches us, we share in the sufferings of Christ so that we can share in His glory: "Beloved, do not be surprised at the fiery ordeal among you, which comes upon you for your testing, as though some strange thing were happening to you; but to the degree that you share the sufferings of Christ, keep on rejoicing, so that also at the revelation of His glory you may rejoice with exultation" (1 Pet 4:12–13).

In all of this, the truth that undergirds our expectation of grace in the midst of trials is the doctrine of God's providence. God can faithfully promise to use our trials a means of grace because He fully controls every detail of our lives (Eph 1:11b). Really, apart from God's providence, none of the means of grace would be possible. His preservation and governance of all things ensure the effectiveness of the instruments He has chosen to use and guaranteed to the internal effects He promised to produce within us. Thus, we may not always understand our circumstances, but we do know that God graciously uses every detail of our lives for His glory and our good. To the unbelieving heart such reminders of God's sovereignty might be resisted, but to the regenerate heart—that knows how good, holy, loving, and trustworthy God is—this truth is the source of immense comfort. God's providence guarantees that our lives, no matter what is happening to us in the moment, are in the gracious hands of the sovereign God (1 Pet 4:19). When we are caught in the storms of life, we must anchor our souls to the truth of God's providential care, and diligently hold on to the means of grace He providentially gives us.

CONFESSION AND REPENTANCE

Confession and repentance are necessary for conversion, and they continue to play a vital role as a means of grace in the life of a believer. God intends to make us holy, which includes purging us of all remaining sin. By acknowledging our sin and turning from it, we are submitting to the sanctifying work of God in our lives. In fact, 1 John 1:9 specifically identifies confession as a sanctifying instrument when it promises, "If we confess our sins, He is faithful and righteous to forgive us our sins and to cleanse us from all unrighteousness." This is obviously a necessary element of our conversion, but the context of this passage indicates that this is a promise aimed specifically at believers. In fact, in the previous verse John states that "if we say that we have no sin, we are deceiving ourselves and the truth is not in us" (v. 8). John's point is that true believers do not deny the presence of sin in their lives; they humbly confess it and seek forgiveness for it. This is not the forgiveness that removes the eternal wrath of God—the believer already has that. This is the forgiveness that removes hindrances to communion with God, begins the process of dealing with the consequences of sin, and fulfills a vital role in the removal of that sinful practice. This forgiveness is initiated through confession.

Confession of sin is not an easy spiritual discipline to practice. The very thought of it grates against the pride stored away in the hardened pockets of our hearts. However, the only way to deal with the hubris that hides sin is to humbly get it out in the open through confession. We must be willing to submit to God's assessment of our sins and entrust ourselves to His mercy because "he who conceals his transgressions will not prosper, but he who confesses and forsakes them will find compassion" (Prov 28:13). The wonderful assurance every believer possesses is that God will grant this forgiveness and use our confession as a means of grace to cleanse us (John 13:5–11). God is an amazingly gracious Lord who has chosen to use the mere confession of sin as a means of grace.

It is important to confess our sin, but it would be insufficient to acknowledge sin without also abandoning it. Repentance begins with a changing of the mind that occurs through the influence of inspired truth. There is a change of perspective that recognizes and acknowledges sin as involving personal guilt, defilement, and helplessness. True repentance sorrowfully recognizes sin and submissively obeys truth. There is a convictional element of repentance by which the beliefs and the will of an individual change course from sin to righteousness. Repentance requires a change in disposition informed by the truth of God's Word. This is the most important aspect of repentance, which is indicated in Scripture by the Greek word *metánoia*—which literally means a changing of the mind (Acts 2:38; Rom 2:4). Thus, repentance (like faith) understands the truth about a sin, accepts that truth, and yields to its implications. Repentance is a thorough change to your life stemming from a thorough change in your mind.

Having a truly godly repentance is usually where individuals stumble. Upon seeing sin in their life, they are willing to show remorse for sinning against God, confess it to God, and seek forgiveness from God. However, few are willing to go as far as rooting through the recesses of their hearts to determine the underlying unbelief and lustful allegiances that caused the sin. As a result of superficial repentance, their fruit is often superficial as well. What does thorough repentance look like? Thorough repentance can be summarized with three words: meditation, mortification, and vivification. These words might seem antiquated, but they have a rich biblical heritage worth preserving, and together they encapsulate our responsibility in repentance:

- Meditation: utilizing your new capacity to fill your mind with truth (Col 1:9)

- Mortification: utilizing your new capacity to kill sin (Col 3:5; Rom 8:13; 13:14)

- Vivification: utilizing your new capacity to pursue right-eousness (1 Tim 6:11)

The sweetest fruits of the Christian life are cultivated through godly and thorough repentance, not because fruit is generated through these simple acts of faith, but because God has promised to use them as a means of grace in our life. Through these spiritual disciplines we humbly rely upon God's abundant grace to remove the barriers in our hearts that hinder the Spirit from producing fruit in our lives.

DISCIPLESHIP

The means of grace discussed in this chapter should not be practiced in isolation. They are most effective when they are employed in the context of discipleship, which enhances the impact of all the other means of grace. What is discipleship? Discipleship is helping a person conform their convictions and life patterns to the commands of Christ. We share spiritual life with one another and speak biblical truth in love. Put more simply, discipleship is spiritual influence through relationships; it is the impartation of truth in the context of daily interaction. Jesus made this the duty of every believer when He gave us the Great Commission (Matt 28:18–20). You cannot claim the promise of Christ's presence "even to the end of the age" without accepting the responsibility of discipleship. The work of discipleship requires sharing our lives with others so that we can share the truth of Christ with them. Thankfully, we serve a good and generous Lord, who has designed this duty to benefit us as much as it benefits those whom we are discipling.

When you give your life to the work of discipleship, it forces you to plunge yourself into the depths of God's truth. When you know that the unbeliever you are witnessing to is going to keep asking hard questions, it motivates you find answers from the Bible. When the new believer you meet with on a regular basis is looking to you for wisdom on how to battle specific sins, it drives you back to the Word of God for strategies. When your closest friends are growing in the truth, it challenges and encourages you to pursue the same kind of growth. In all these ways, and more, God uses our obedience in the work of discipleship for the benefit of our own souls.

By ordaining your sanctification to take place in the context of discipleship, God made sure that you will never have to "go it alone" from a human perspective. You might reject God's design and refuse to share your life with other believers around you, but that does not mean God has left you to yourself. God has placed every Christian within the body of Christ so that they can benefit from the spiritual influence and gifted ministry of other Christians.

Discipleship is an organic overflow of the body life of the church, and, as such, will take place in all kinds of varied circumstances. But, as unique as the circumstances might be, the gracious effects of discipleship are consistent. Discipleship graciously influences you to be more like Christ by providing you with practical instruction in the truth, an example of how to live according to truth, accountability to keep you submitted to truth, and encouragement to continue in truth. This, of course, requires that you pursue spiritual relationships that are oriented around the truth of God's Word and focused on becoming more like Christ.

SERVICE

Serving others is one of the simplest but most commonly neglected means of grace in the church. By God's design, there is a sanctifying effect attached to serving. Our measly efforts cannot earn us anything from God since He does not need to be served by us (Acts 17:25). However, in His graciousness, God has promised to use and bless our faithfulness for His purposes and our sanctification. It is easy to lose sight of this reality in the pursuit of personal growth and become inwardly focused in our use of the means of grace. We have been given grace so that we can be a means of grace in the lives of those around us (Eph 4:7, 12–16).

If serving the church is not the practice of your life, it is highly unlikely that spiritual growth is the pattern of your life. In fact, there are specific spiritual dangers associated with a lack of service. The most pressing danger is that if you are not serving the church, you are not serving Christ. As believers, "you were called to freedom, brethren; only do not turn your freedom into an opportunity for the flesh, but through love serve one another" (Gal 5:13). This is the pattern Christ established in His earthly ministry, and it is what He expects from His followers: "Whoever wishes to become great among you shall be your servant; and whoever wishes to be first among you shall be slave of all. For even the Son of Man did not come to be served, but to serve, and to give His life a ransom for many" (Mark 10:43–45). If you do not live the life of service to which you have been called, you cannot expect to grow in grace.

Another danger associated with a lack of service is the danger of becoming inwardly focused. When the pursuit of spiritual growth is detached from service, it will inevitably lead to selfishness. The natural bent of the human heart is to pursue lustful pleasure at all cost (Eph 4:19). Christ saved you from this enslavement to lust and He intends to protect you from the temptation to revert back to it. His command to serve others is designed to protect you from a life of lustful pleasure seeking (Rom 15:1–2). If you ignore your duty to serve the church, you are opening yourself up to all the dangers that come with self-focus.

So many Christians are content to attend a church without getting their hands dirty in the ministry of that church. This kind of spiritual freeloading is not only detrimental to the church as a whole, it is also damaging to the individual believers not engaged in ministry. In most churches you can look around at all the ministry taking place and you will probably see the most mature believers doing most of the work. You might think that the mature are doing most of the serving because they are the most mature—and there is some truth to that. But, more significantly, those who are serving are mature because service is a means of grace God uses in their life. If you are not serving in the church, you are not only cutting the church off from your spiritual gift, you are also cutting yourself off from a vital instrument God uses to mature His children. God has designed us to grow as we give away our lives to the people around us.

There is a common thread running through all the means of grace in the process of sanctification: they drive our hearts toward worship. This is the ultimate goal of sanctification and the end to which the means of grace are working. Man was created for God's glory and the new man is being sanctified into the image of Christ for the same purpose. As Calvin said, "The glory of God is the highest end, to which our sanctification is subordinate."[6]

The right use of the means of grace yields all glory in sanctification to God and equips us to glorify God more effectively. In this sense, you might say that worship is the regulative principle of sanctification. If we think about sanctification and the means of grace in a manner that does not give God glory, we are thinking wrongly. At the same time, if the manner in which we live out our

---

[6] John Calvin, *Commentaries on the Epistle of Paul to the Ephesians*, trans. William Pringle, vol. 21 in *Calvin's Commentaries* (reprint, Grand Rapids: Baker Books, 2005), 198.

sanctification and participate in the means of grace does not result in the glory of God, we are living wrongly. Worship is not only the goal of the Christian life, it is the desired result of the means of grace.

Worship is an important piece in the puzzle of sanctification, especially if we want to understand the relationship between positional and progressive sanctification. God sanctifies us positionally so that we can worship Him. Just as the vessels in the Old Testament temple were sanctified in the sense that they were set apart for worship, we are set apart for the holy service of God. Christians are definitively reconstituted in Christ for God's glory. Progressively, God uses the means of grace to sanctify us and conform us to the image of Christ so that we can more effectively offer Him holy and acceptable worship. Thus, worship is the purpose of both progressive and positional sanctification and the means of grace are instruments God uses to accomplish this purpose (Rom 12:1–2).

In addition to being the fruit of sanctification, worship also plays a key role in the right use of the means of grace. Worship is the ultimate motivation for our effort in sanctification. This is true from a divine perspective since God is ultimately motivated in all things by His own glory. If this is the divine motivation for sanctification, it should be our motivation as well. We should be driven to glorify our God through our actions and attitudes. Our job and our joy should be to make the name of our God great by employing the gracious means He has provided for us.

There are other legitimate motivations from the Scriptures; however, unless all these motivators flow through the filter of worship and devotion to Christ, we run the risk of turning our sanctification into a man-centered endeavor. If I put forth effort in sanctification *only* to be more mature, satisfied, joyful, or to fulfill my obligation, then my motives contradict God's motives. This is not to say that I won't benefit in these ways as I participate in the means of grace, or that these motives are sinful. However, the ultimate goal of my maturity, sanctification, obligatory good works, and joy is God's glory. As Jerry Bridges puts it, "Devotion to God is the mainspring of Christian character and the only foundation upon which it can be successfully built."[7] Too many Christians have languished in a stagnant spiritual life because they have neglected the means of grace or pursued them for selfish purposes. The means of grace have been given to us to make us holy worshipers because God is most glorified in us when we are most sanctified by Him.

---

[7] Jerry Bridges, *The Pursuit of Godliness* (Colorado Springs: NavPress, 1996), 16.

PART 3: DISCERNMENT FOR HOLINESS

CHAPTER 10

DISCERNING PROGRESS

I T was December 2005 when my (Jerry's) daughter finally convinced her fiancé (now husband) to see a doctor about a cough he couldn't seem to suppress over the previous four months. Standard flu symptoms had always made their rounds in our family, so early on nothing seemed beyond the help of some over-the-counter medicine and a good night's rest. Besides, just months earlier the two of them had returned from an exhausting relief trip, helping to clear mold from victims' homes devastated by Hurricane Katrina. Perhaps this was the body's temporary reaction to something in the air or simply a stubborn version of the common cold. Everyone believed this would probably clear up on its own. Most of the time such amateur triage is fairly accurate. But even a slight misdiagnosis in our son-in-law's case would have been disastrous. Along with persistent chest congestion, he began to develop regular fevers and increasing fatigue. These symptoms were similar to severe bronchitis or walking pneumonia, conditions for which an antibiotic protocol might be successfully prescribed.

But at my daughter's strong urging, a chest x-ray was conducted. The attending physician became immediately alarmed and sent our son-in-law to the emergency room. His blood work revealed a dangerously high white blood cell count, and his physical symptoms were becoming noticeably critical by the minute. He was rushed to Miami's Jackson Memorial where a bone marrow biopsy brought instant clarity to all our diagnostic guessing. My son-in-law had acute lymphoblastic leukemia (ALL). Medical personnel rushed to action as doctors determined a treatment protocol and care workers administered the hopeful cure. At that stage of the unfolding drama, nothing was more crucial than a correct diagnosis and corresponding solution. The treatment worked and he's been several years in remission. In the Lord's kind providence, a right diagnosis saved his life.

HEALTHY SPIRITUAL DIAGNOSTICS

In the spiritual realm the stakes are not temporal but eternal. Misdiagnosing the cause of spiritual problems will eventually lead to a weakened spiritual immune system. Persistent confusion about weaknesses will result in the eventual loss of biblical discernment and strong moral convictions. The severity of sin's offense against God diminishes in our minds when we remain ignorant of Scripture's precise definitions of sin. The "counsel of the wicked" (Ps 1:1) becomes more appealing than delighting in "the law of the LORD" (Ps 1:2). It's not long before our conscience is desensitized, leaving us vulnerable to self-deception about our true spiritual condition. In fact, the apostle Paul warns that drifting from "a good conscience and a sincere faith" leaves us without clarity, ever-speculating about truth even though we may feel confident about where we stand (1 Tim 1:5–6). Some Christians become convinced that they have found the remedy to particular sin problems, yet later are devastated when the "cure" gives them no real power over their weakness.

Knowing how to evaluate and accurately diagnose our failures requires brutally honest self-examination *in light of Scripture*—a biblical MRI, if you will. Without the two-edged precision of God's Word (Heb 4:12) helping us see how and why our thoughts and intentions have strayed, we are left guessing in the dark. It is "because of practice" that we have our "senses trained to discern good and evil" (Heb 5:14). Letting the Scriptures define sin, sanctification, and our spiritual responsibilities is how we best troubleshoot our weaknesses. Wishing for an easier path to dealing with sin appeals to our flesh and will only leave us open to remedies outside of God's Word. We must ask well-targeted diagnostic questions. At its root, all sin is unbelief. And all spiritual weakness can be traced to believing lies instead of the truth.

Spiritual Triage

When sin persists in our lives, we must ask ourselves questions that penetrate to the heart level:

- Are all my thoughts and reasonings conformed to the truth (Rom 12:1–2)?

- Have I been a good "Berean" and examined in light of Scripture all the counsel being offered for my spiritual growth (Acts 17:11)?

- Have I understood all that God says about my sin (Rom 7:7, 13)?

- Am I willing to self-indict according to God's view of my guilt (Ps 51:4)?

- Have I confessed all attempts to save face and cover my weakness (Prov 28:13)?

- Do I hand-pick counselors who will not ask the hard questions (John 5:44)?

- Do I gravitate toward remedies that put my sin in a more positive light and require no true brokenness (Matt 5:3)?

- Do I tend to want a relieved conscience rather than a cleansed one through repentance and forsaking sin (Prov 28:13)?

- Has this sin become a pattern of weakness, indicating that I've been "a hearer of the word rather than a doer" (Jas 1:23–25)?

- Am I trying to shift blame for my sin, putting the primary culpability on someone or something else (Gen 3:12)?

Questions like these leave us with no excuses. They hem us in and demand that we measure our spiritual condition by Scripture rather than our subjective assumptions. More importantly, they keep us from the appeal of quick fixes that excuse or flatter our flesh, promising sanctification without strain and struggle. Like our first parents in the garden of Eden, we are prone by our fallen nature not only to blameshift but also to avoid taking personal responsibility for sinful choices. If we can find a "cause" for sin that somehow allows us to admit the weakness in general without pinpointing sinful motives within us, our hearts will go that direction every time.

Haven't you ever wondered why people will often readily acknowledge a wrong but immediately qualify the matter with, "But that was never my intention"? It is because tying our sin to "reasonable causes" is far less incriminating to admit than confessing it was willful. Eventually we may admit we are weak given the "circumstances we've had to undergo," but all of us will stubbornly maintain our innocence at the level of our motives. But we can hardly be objective when our own heart is under the spotlight. The Scriptures are "able to judge the thoughts and intentions of the heart" (Heb 4:12). Spiritual growth is a serious, day-to-day struggle. Asking yourself the toughest questions (as in the list above) and "examining the Scriptures daily" (Acts 17:11) is the best safeguard against spiritual misdiagnosis.

Failure Factors

Suppose someone has become deeply discouraged over frequent failures. According to current evangelical trends about how believers grow, the person should stop "trying to do better" and realize that Christ has already done everything for us. With great relief, this defeated Christian assumes that his problem all along has been the pressure he feels from others who call him to obedience. Despite the counsel of some—that he should turn from besetting sins and be more faithful to God's Word—he continues to blame his failure and discouragement on unrealistic expectations[1] placed upon him by rules and standards instead of relieving his burden with more grace-talk.

Almost immediately, they experience a new "sense" of being liberated from guilt, which they equate with throwing off legalism. They're convinced almost overnight that all exhausted and depressed believers are suffering from the pressure to "perform" for God.[2] This assumption becomes the new grid through which all gospel ministry is evaluated. They begin scrutinizing their local church's sermons, listening for generous helpings of what Jesus already achieved on the cross. Meditating on the grace that justifies, they say, liberates us from the stifling need to "do

---

[1] This is precisely the view presented by David Peterson, *Possessed by God: A New Testament Theology of Sanctification and Holiness* (Downers Grove, IL: IVP Academic, 1995). Peterson confesses to being "troubled" by views of sanctification which speak of spiritual "progress that can lead to ever-increasing measures of holiness" (70). He takes issue with the teaching of nineteenth-century pastor, J. C. Ryle, who taught that assurance of salvation strengthens or weakens depending on the believer's level of diligence in the pursuit of holiness. He raises the concern that Ryle's "approach creates unrealistic expectations and is capable of producing guilt and despair in those who do not perceive the evidence of such progress in their lives" (ibid.). In Peterson's view, it is the "'sense' of God's grace and calling which the Spirit enables through belief in the gospel" that motivates and directs the Christian's "holiness of life" (ibid.). This author's conviction is that Peterson is comparing apples to oranges in his critique of Ryle. Peterson is arguing for a "sense" of assurance deriving from faith in our union with Christ. Ryle, on the other hand, is arguing in the opposite direction: that we gain a "sense" of assurance from our growth in real faith and obedience. Peterson wants to see obedience motivated exclusively by knowing we're united to Christ. Ryle taught that assurance is palpably known through a Spirit-empowered obedience rooted in a faith that strives. For Ryle, the will is rightly activated by true faith in the Spirit's promises—promises not only of union with Christ but also of strength to willingly obey. Both men stand on truth, but only Ryle makes sense of the meaning of true obedience. Peterson's "passive" model renders the will coerced, the conscience an unnecessary burden, and Scripture's imperatives mere hyperbole.

[2] Tullian Tchividjian, *One Way Love: Inexhaustible Grace for an Exhausted World* (Colorado Springs: David C. Cook, 2013), Kindle Electronic Edition: Location 54–78. "Performancism" is a term coined by Tchividjian, describing an alleged overemphasis on conforming to rules and a fear of losing God's love because of failure.

better." Is this the proper diagnosis? Are unfair expectations for obedience the root cause of our lack of victory over sin, frequent doubts, or spiritual lethargy? A right diagnosis of the problem is the only thing that will lead to the right cure. How do we take our spiritual temperature in this case?

One Size Doesn't Fit All

There are many other possible causes behind spiritual lethargy and patterns of weakness. Clichés such as "The Bible is not a book of dos and don'ts" are diagnostic shortcuts that conveniently ignore the whole counsel of God. From beginning to end the Scriptures command us to "do" good deeds and "not do" evil ones. The blame for our failure cannot be laid at the feet of biblical imperatives, as if our inability to obey stems from a false sense of obligation. We are called in Scripture to strive hard after holiness of life—to, in effect, "do better." None of us escapes the Bible's overwhelming emphasis on trusting God and obeying His Word. Indeed, the incarnate Son of God set the bar when He told the tempter that man is to live "on every word that proceeds out of the mouth of God" (Matt 4:4). Live by every word! Straightforward statements like this are commonplace in Scripture, rooted ultimately in God's character.

God's people are to become like Him (Heb 12:14). It was He who said plainly, "Be holy, for I am holy" (Lev 11:44–45; cf. 1 Pet 1:16). Anything less is a perilous shortcut and doomed to failure. We're called as Jesus' disciples to "observe all that [He's] commanded" (Matt 28:20) not in order to merit God's love but as an act of humble worship from a heart of faith (2 Pet 1:5–10). Becoming "holy as He is holy" vindicates the power of His grace and holy character (2 Cor 7:1). Trying to liberate everyone from the shackles of self-merit assumes there are no other reasons for the burden of guilt and failure.

Unnecessary Fears

In some cases, we may fear God's judgment because we've not been clearly taught the freedom of being justified in Christ. Perhaps the church we attend does not have a strong pulpit ministry. Without clear preaching on the essential doctrines of Scripture, we will be vulnerable to confusion and become imbalanced in our application of truth. It is common for new believers to struggle with past fears about not being forgiven by God. This can be true of those who have come from religious backgrounds where the required rituals were more intense and rigorous. The fear is rooted in the struggle to believe that sinners are redeemed by faith alone. Many Christians have spent so many years going through a series of rituals that it is difficult for their life habits to catch up with their newfound faith in Christ. The perfect, forgiving love of our Savior will eventually cast out all the old fears of judgment (1 John 4:18), but healthy doses of Scripture on redemption as well as exercising humble faith is a sure remedy.

Fear of judgment can overtake those from darker pagan pasts, who fear that God could never forgive someone as sinful as they have been. It's not about "forgiving ourselves," as pop psychology has claimed over the years. Clearing our own name accomplishes nothing because, as the apostle Paul admitted, "I am conscious of nothing against myself, yet I am not by this acquitted; but the one who examines me is the Lord" (1 Cor 4:4). And we should never imagine that self-pardon is any kind of real divine pardon. God forgives us solely on the basis of the finished work of Christ on the cross. Self-forgiveness would require that we personally become the basis of our pardon. But Scripture is clear: "God is the one who justifies" (Rom 8:33) and only He can forgive sins (Luke 5:21). A sinner cannot pardon a sinner. When we fear that our sinful past is too heinous for God to forgive, we must remember that the only unpardonable sin is the rejection of Christ. Do you want Christ? Do you want forgiveness on the basis of His sacrifice alone? It is freely offered to all who repent and put their trust in Him. Christ's perfect love continues to drive all old fears away.

FREE TO BE HOLY

Malnourished Faith

Others fear God's judgment because, although they know the doctrine of justification by faith, they struggle to believe it moment by moment. What these dear saints need is to walk by faith and not by sight. They need less leaning on their own understanding and more acknowledging God's truth in spite of their own sense of things. They must exercise their faith muscle by entrusting themselves to the clarity and authority of God's Word rather than craving an earthly, tangible guarantee. There are other believers who, though they don't doubt their justification, are easily overcome by the trials of life. When they don't respond in a godly way to these tests, they compound the problem with a guilty conscience. The objective assurance that comes from trusting God and overcoming temptation eludes them, and they tend to become fearful.

These weary saints need to plead with God for a repentant heart. They must entrust themselves to the Lord's care (1 Pet 5:7) in the various tests ordained by God for the strengthening of our faith (Jas 1:2–4). And they must consider the chastening of conscience and consequences of sin a gift from the Lord to grow their faith and keep them from further disobedience. In the grace of true repentance there is new power to forsake the old sin habits. As they see new patterns of obedience emerging, their assurance will strengthen, their calling and election will grow more certain, and a more settled heart will be "abundantly supplied" to them (2 Pet 1:5–11).

A misdiagnosis of what's behind certain fears will leave people without a clear path to victory. It is spiritual malpractice to tell fearful and fainthearted believers that their conscience is simply overactive, and that they're haunted by years of preaching focused on Law instead of gospel grace. This might be the case for some, but for many who struggle with unnecessary fears, merely contemplating the doctrine of *sola gratia* (grace alone) and waiting for emotional waves of gratitude to compel obedience will offer no long-term help. And what about those who ignore pangs of guilt, speak often of being "free in Christ," and yet use their liberty as a covering for sin? These should be duly warned of the seeds of apostasy, called to genuine repentance, and exhorted to obey the Word of God. Pouring more "grace" on someone's stubborn abuse of it is serious neglect of their true need.

Squandered Grace

There is no question: trusting in Christ's finished work is amazingly freeing! I remember the first moment I understood and believed that God's saving grace in Christ was utterly sufficient to cover all my sin. The resulting euphoria and freedom of conscience were overwhelming. That truth has anchored my soul to Christ again and again through the years, and especially during earlier seasons of failure and doubt. When believers are plagued with guilt over frequent failure, causing doubt about being separated from the love of God, part of the cure is a rich study and deeper understanding of the doctrines of justification and eternal security (e.g., John 10:27–29; Rom 8:29–39; 1 Pet 1:3–9).

It is dangerous, however, to diagnose all struggling believers as self-atoners trying to earn what only grace can give. When we have a guilty conscience we're strongly tempted to seek temporary relief far more than being cleansed through repentance and renewal. It is not surprising that a self-pitying believer loves to hear of *being declared righteous* in Christ (justification) rather than being challenged to actually *walk in righteousness* (sanctification). If they're experiencing real guilt for unforsaken sin, we will be offering them convenient excuses. Quoting Romans 6:14, "you are not under law" will tempt them to ignore Romans 6:2: "How shall we who died to sin still live in it?" But exercising the justification muscle while neglecting an emaciated sanctification will eventually guarantee the atrophy of both. Not all downcast Christians are suffering from the tyranny of pressure to perform in order to gain God's favor. If that were true, God would not have reproved Cain during the lowest point of his life!

In the midst of his depression, Cain's problem was pinpointed:

guilt from a disobedient heart. God asked him, "Why are you angry? And why has your countenance fallen? If you do well, will not your countenance be lifted up?" (Gen 4:6–7). Why would God say such a potentially discouraging thing to someone downcast over his sin? Wouldn't it have been much more liberating for Cain to hear that he was free from having to strive to "do well"? Not at all; God knew Cain's heart. God was setting forth the unbending command ("do well") and pointing to the joy of a clean conscience. Cain was experiencing spiritual "exhaustion," but the root cause was neither oppressive standards for holiness nor any unfair expectation from others. He refused to repent of the murderous jealousy raging within him. A spiritual misdiagnosis when the issue is unrepentance leaves a person without hope for change. We must learn to think biblically about sin and its varying causes.

If our problem is guilt, merely musing on justification could tempt us to ignore the warnings of our consciences. In fact, downplaying biblical commands implies that the conscience has no ongoing function in the life of a Christian. It is as though once justified and free from eternal condemnation (Rom 8:1) we're supposed to stand and shout "Objection!" at our conscience's every charge. But while Scripture reverberates with the reality of our no-condemnation status, it also loudly echoes the truth that failure to obey God's Word brings heaviness upon the conscience (Ps 32:4; 38:1–10, 18; Rom 2:15; 1 Cor 8:12; Heb 12:11–14). When the Spirit's conviction is ignored, guilt compounds, and the conscience becomes dulled and speculative, and leads ultimately to pride (1 Tim 1:5–7). In the absence of true repentance, the result will be spiritual lethargy (exhaustion). What some diagnose as weariness from trying to earn God's love is very often pride and self-pity trying to excuse guilt. The danger here is obvious. If we always comfort someone's weary heart with justifying grace, they will fail to see the squandered sanctifying grace that frequently lies behind their spiritual fatigue.

Even an exhausted believer who has been trying to perform for God shouldn't merely gloss his sorrows with a fresh coat of justification. That will only hide the dry-rot of unbelief that weakens faith at the precise point of temptation. The solution to self-atoning tendencies is not to stop vigorously pursuing righteousness, *but to stop trusting in it.* And in the same way, the solution to patterns of failure is not to stop denying self, but to stop blaming unbelief on commands we find hard to obey. The power of the Spirit against the flesh is not accessed by merely recalling that we're saved by grace. It is ignited by entrusting ourselves to God at the very moment our flesh is crying out for satisfaction. And since obeying the will of Christ is the only sure proof of genuine faith, then we must always fight discouragement, not with less striving, but with greater faith-filled effort.

Doubt Versus Self-Pity

When we hide sin and ignore pangs of guilt, we become distant from the truth, despondent, angry, and quarrelsome (Prov 18:1). We will even attempt to suppress our heavy heart by busying ourselves in ministry, work, educational pursuits, or emotional affirmation. On the outside, a guilt-ridden person's behavior can often mirror that of a doubter under the nagging fear of losing Christ. Both are a flurry of spiritual activity and anxiety, but the underlying cause behind each is very different. In the case of a classic doubter, they struggle to believe in the *permanence* of God's love, thinking that eternal security is based on faithfulness. This is the group most benefitted from today's emphasis on grace. Their spiritual exhaustion is *rooted in sinful fear*—not trusting in God's promise of divine preservation (Rom 8:26–39; Phil 1:6; Jude 24). It's still unbelief at its core, but it is fed by theological ignorance and withered faith rather than a pattern of moral neglect. Classic self-pitiers, on the other hand, have a different kind of unbelief problem. Theirs is a habit of excusing sin and neglecting the disciplines which fortify against temptation. It is a case of spiritual exhaustion from being weighed down with the fruit of disobedience. The burden they carry is rooted, not ultimately in thoughts of earning or losing God's love, but in the repeated *unwillingness* to prefer Christ above the vanities that captivate their flesh.

The solution God set before Cain was repentance from the unbelief that plunged him into failure. The bottom-line diagnosis: Cain had nurtured his self-will into full-blown stubborn rebellion. Sin's mastery was breathing down his neck, but instead of trusting the promises of God he chaffed at not being free to sin without consequence. The result was spiritual depression (Gen 4:7). To emphasize justifying grace when a person is under the burden of unconfessed guilt is to tell only half of God's redemptive story. A physician who has removed a cancerous tumor wouldn't treat other lesions merely by reminding the patient of previous tumors removed. Without the cure for *today's* illness it does him no good. Being justified by grace—freeing as it is from sin's power—doesn't eradicate sin's presence or persistence. Paul never said "therefore there is now no battle for faith and obedience"—only that there is "no condemnation" (Rom 8:1).

Taking Our Spiritual Temperature

As we've explained previously in chapter 2, it is precarious to evaluate our spiritual progress by turning inward for some emotional sense of things. Whenever we have questions and doubts about the genuineness of our motives for obeying the Lord, we must always turn to His Word alone for clarity (Heb 4:12). Our thoughts and intentions are discernible when we measure our words, attitudes, and conduct by the standard of Scripture—the expressed character of Christ. The fogs of doubt dissipate in the steady climate of truth. We must answer all suspicions of the heart with Scripture, for "God is greater than our heart, and knows all things" (1 John 3:20).

Why Don't I Feel Like Obeying?

A common struggle in our daily walk with Christ is those times when we simply are not passionate about obeying. Friends ask us why we seem disinterested in spiritual things, and they want to pull us out of our lethargy. So often during these times we struggle for any real explanation. We know what the Scriptures say, and our theology is tightly wound and unflinching. But when faced with believing truth over lies and walking in obedience, we have no drive, no passion to submit. The popular notion that heightened emotions are the octane of obedience has left Christians with no way to test their motives except by their feelings. A sense of emotional passion has become the only litmus test of a pure motive. Anything less than tangibly felt affection for Christ is not true obedience in the minds of many. But the legitimacy of obedience is never to be measured by the presence or absence of emotion. It is marked by humble faith in Christ and a yielded will. And the opposite is true. When we have merely been conforming in some outward way to biblical commands, with no genuine heart of faith and humility, it will inevitably be followed by an increasing attitude of self-righteousness.

It is crucial to understand that obeying the Lord means submitting to His will. There's no precondition for yielding to Scripture. Obedience does not become genuine when we "feel affectionate toward God." It *is* genuine when we obey "from the heart" (Rom 6:17). What does it mean to obey from the heart? It cannot mean that we must first be carried along by lofty emotions. We may indeed obey at times when our passions are supercharged, but emotions are not a trustworthy gauge of motives or spiritual maturity. Charles Spurgeon once said, "To feel God's love is very precious, but to believe it when you do not feel it, is the noblest. He may be but a little Christian who *knows* God's love, but he is a great Christian who *believes* it when the visible contradicts it and the invisible withholds its witness."[3] Obeying "from the heart" *does* mean that by faith we present the members of our bodies as slaves of righteousness (Rom 6:16–18). We yield to the truth, placing ourselves completely at the disposal

---

[3] Charles Spurgeon, "A Psalm of Remembrance," *New Park Street Pulpit*, Vol 5, https://www.spurgeon.org/resource-library/sermons/a-psalm-of-remembrance #flipbook/ (accessed January 2019).

of the Holy Spirit (Gal 5:16). Yielding in faith is the key to a full-hearted obedience.

You might be saying, *But if I just submit my will when everything in me seems disinterested or resistant, my motives won't be pure and I'll be conforming in hypocrisy.* I understand the challenge of assessing motives for obedience. Let's admit that until we are with Jesus in glory, our motives at any given moment will always be a mixture of selfish man-centered cravings and humble, Godward faith and love. How rich we are to know (1) that our "transgressions are covered" (Ps 32:1), and (2) that the Lord accepts our obedience in Christ despite our mixed motives. Even on our very best day when our obedience seems for the most part genuine, we "are not by this acquitted" (1 Cor 4:4). But God knows our frame, and He turns our meager service and mixed motives into ever-increasing grace trophies for His glory. Whatever meager offering we bring in our striving, He accepts it as loving obedience from one of His beloved children. When you don't feel like obeying, confess to the Lord your feeble and faithless heart, repent and humbly believe that He is worthy, then go forward in faith and submissiveness to His Word.

CHAPTER 11

DISCERNING ASSURANCE

D
EEP, abiding, and full assurance is a sweet grace in the lives of God's children. Knowing you have been saved by grace through faith is a source of inexpressible joy that produces a peace, surpassing bare human understanding. Puritan Thomas Brooks described it as "heaven on earth,"[1] and the familiar lyrics of the hymn "Blessed Assurance" call it a "foretaste of glory divine." The greatest blessing a sinner can ever receive is salvation, and with it, a growing assurance that we are in Christ, which is a treasure to be pursued and enjoyed by God's people. As vital as it is for the Christian life, assurance is not always experienced by every believer. To state it simply, not every true believer possesses the comforts of certainty. Moreover, some who possess the comforts of certainty are not true believers. And since this is such a vital area of our walk with Christ, we need to know how to deal biblically with various types of doubt that come to every believer at one time or another.

WHEN ASSURANCE IS ELUSIVE

Essentially, there are three kinds of assurance we can experience.[2] First, we can have *doubting assurance*, which vacillates on the reality of conversion. If full assurance is "heaven on earth,"

[1] Thomas Brooks, *Heaven on Earth* (London: Banner of Truth Trust, 1961).
[2] See Joel R. Beeke, *Knowing and Growing in Assurance of Faith* (Fearn, Rossshire: Christian Focus, 2017), 55–74.

then constant doubt is the closest a true believer will ever come to the flames of hell. When you question the truth of the gospel or struggle to discern the state of your own heart, the weight of doubt can be soul-crushing. In some of these cases, the fruits of uncertainty are cultivated in hearts that have not fully submitted to the truth. They question the power of the gospel because they have rejected some other doctrine of Scripture they deem "unbelievable." For others, unbelief calcifies in the midst of trials and disappointments so that they question the goodness of God in their circumstances, which opens the door to doubting God's goodness in salvation. There are others, however, who have no doubts about the veracity of the gospel, but they do have a multitude of questions about the genuineness of their faith. They know the Bible is true and God is good, but they cannot discern in their own hearts whether they've actually repented and believed in this true and good God. Usually caused by some distorted doctrine or by a heavily burdened conscience, this kind of doubt cannot find comfort in the promises of the gospel because the person cannot confirm saving faith in their own heart. Disarmed of right thinking and a clear conscience, the soul in doubt has no confidence or clarity when it comes to salvation.

As troubling as doubting assurance can be, *deceived assurance*, which simply assumes assurance without any questions at all, is deadly. This is the person who outwardly claims to be a Christian, yet inwardly remains dead in trespasses and sins. They were told to pray a prayer, or maybe taught about justification by faith, but the dangers of false conversion and apostasy have never crossed their minds. When deceived in this manner, there is a refusal to examine themselves, no matter how much sin might characterize their life. The warnings of Scripture and the call to self-examination fall on deaf ears for the person with deceived assurance; they are blind to their blindness. Make no mistake about it, deceived assurance is not only a possibility to be aware of, it may very well be the most common description of those who consider themselves safe from the wrath to come.

Consider, for example, the teaching of Christ in the parable of the soils (Mark 4:1–8). Four hearts were confronted with the seed of the gospel, but only one bore the enduring fruit of genuine salvation. In other words, in Jesus' parable, two out of three people who actually welcomed the message and professed Christ eventually walked away from Him. This does not mean that exactly two-thirds of the people in the world who profess Christ are not truly saved, but it does indicate that the twin deceptions of false conversion and deceived assurance are not only possible— they are prevalent.

Despite the sobering realities of "assurance" riddled with doubt and deception, true believers can have a very real, *definite assurance*. We can know the immoveable conviction of the truthfulness of the gospel and a personal confidence in its power for daily life. When your soul possesses true biblical assurance, you have confidence in the gospel and clarity about your own faith. God's Word thoroughly demonstrates you can have complete and biblically substantiated confidence that you are in a right relationship with God. Remember, Paul was able to affirm that for the believer "there is now no condemnation for those who are in Christ Jesus" (Rom 8:1). So too, the apostle John wrote his gospel to show you how to be saved (John 20:31), and then he wrote his first epistle to give us assurance of our salvation (1 John 5:13). In fact, certainty of salvation is not only possible, it is commendable (1 Tim 3:13). It is not a sign of maturity to needlessly languish in the uncertainty of lacking assurance. This level of spiritual confidence is both a gracious gift from the Lord, and a personal responsibility for every believer to pursue.

By divine design, firm and full assurance is possible through the objective truth of God's promises and the evident fruit of God's grace in your life. As John MacArthur explains, "The objective ground is *the finished work of Christ on our behalf*, including the promises of Scripture … . The subjective ground is *the ongoing work of the Holy Spirit in our lives*, including His convicting and sanctifying ministries."[3] To frame it another way, the faithfulness of God in Christ is the objective grounds of assurance, while the abiding, fruitful, and humble faith of the believer is the subjective grounds of assurance. Thus, you can know the gospel is true based on the testimony of Scripture, and you can know you have been saved by the true gospel based on the evidence of grace in your life. By looking to the promises of God in humble and obedient faith, doubts can be eclipsed with hope and any tendencies toward presumption can be avoided.

It is possible for us to genuinely know we have been chosen by God, but that knowledge does not come passively. This is where the doctrine of sanctification becomes so crucial in the pursuit of assurance. A biblical paradigm for sanctification gives us clarity on the state of our own souls as we grow in personal holiness. However, a flawed view on sanctification will always produce faulty answers on assurance. In fact, deficient views of the Christian life can often be identified by the deficient answers they provide to doubting individuals. For instance, an antinomian view of the Christian life indiscriminately assures every doubting soul merely on the basis of Christ's finished work without providing any direction or warning for those who might have false faith. Doubters are counseled to simply look at the cross for assurance that salvation has been accomplished, while being encouraged to avoid any serious examination of their lives to see if they *truly believe* in the completed work of Christ. They are taught to regard pangs of conscience as illegitimate moralism, to enjoy their freedom from the endless pursuit of holiness, and to stop worrying about their salvation since "it is finished." At the other end of the spectrum, a legalistic, man-centered view of sanctification invariably questions the assurance of genuine believers, and provides little comfort to those in doubt by pointing to human effort as the sole grounds of personal assurance. Legalism prevents doubting saints from attaining full assurance by cutting

---

[3] John MacArthur, Jr., *The Gospel According to the Apostles* (Dallas: Word, 1993), 164; emphases original.

them off from the grace that leads to certainty. Thus, if antinomianism leads to "easy-believism," then legalism produces "a kind of
'hard believism', looking for evidences that they have no right to
expect. ... They look more at themselves and their works than at
Christ and the promises of God."[4]

Only a view of sanctification that is rooted in the eternal
grace of Christ and regulated by the need for personal holiness
is adequate for navigating the delicate balance between the
objective foundation of assurance and the subjective fruits of
assurance. In fact, the apostle Peter employs this very paradigm
for the Christian life in 2 Peter 1:1–11 to shepherd his readers
toward definite assurance. Peter begins by affirming his own
confidence in the faith of his readers, "who have received a faith
of the same kind as ours, by the righteousness of our God and
Savior, Jesus Christ" (v. 1). For Peter, this confidence begins with
the full assurance of God's sovereign grace, which

> has granted to us everything pertaining to life and godliness,
> through the true knowledge of Him who called us by His own
> glory and excellence. For by these He has granted to us His
> precious and magnificent promises, so that by them you may
> become partakers of the divine nature, having escaped the
> corruption that is in the world by lust (vv. 3–4).

But Peter doesn't leave it at that. Rather, on the basis of God's
gracious provision, he calls on his readers to *diligently pursue the
fruits of faith* in their life as the means of growing in grace and
assurance:

> Now for this very reason also, applying all diligence, in your faith
> supply moral excellence, and in your moral excellence, knowledge,
> and in your knowledge, self-control, and in your self-control,
> perseverance, and in your perseverance, godliness, and in your
> godliness, brotherly kindness, and in your brotherly kindness,
> love. For if these qualities are yours and are increasing, they
> render you neither useless nor unfruitful in the true knowledge
> of our Lord Jesus Christ. For he who lacks these qualities is

---

[4] Beeke, *Knowing and Growing in Assurance of Faith*, 17.

> blind or short-sighted, having forgotten his purification from his former sins. Therefore, brethren, be all the more diligent to make certain about His calling and choosing you; for as long as you practice these things, you will never stumble; for in this way the entrance into the eternal kingdom of our Lord and Savior Jesus Christ will be abundantly supplied to you (vv. 5–11).

These instructions from the pen of Peter reveal that certainty of salvation is attainable, but it is not automatic. God's sovereign grace requires nothing from you, but personal assurance will require grace-empowered diligence ("be ... diligent"), endurance ("as long as you practice"), and faithfulness ("you will never stumble"). From this it is evident that divine "calling and choosing" are objective facts, but being certain of His calling of you is a subjective reality that must be diligently pursued.

Personal assurance is not as simple as "once saved always saved," although that is certainly true. An individual truly converted by the redeeming grace of God can never be lost to the clutches of sin and death. However, the security of salvation does not automatically grant assurance that we are saved—it only guarantees that those who believe in Christ will be fully and finally saved. There is a difference between the doctrine of eternal security and the reality of assurance in the life of a believer. Eternal security teaches that salvation is eternally secure for the one who believes in Christ. This security rests on the promise of God's faithfulness, the securing power of God's grace, and the sovereign glory of God in salvation. Assurance, on the other hand, is the firm conviction that God's grace has saved you, which grows with Christian faithfulness, manifests itself by increasing holiness, can be shaken by a violated conscience, and will wane with patterns of neglect and rebellion.

From a theological perspective, the security of the believer and personal assurance are best understood as the difference between the *preservation* of God and the *perseverance* of the saints. The Scriptures repeatedly and clearly call the believer to a faithful obedience and an enduring devotion to Christ. Behind such a call, however, is the related but distinct promise of God's preservation of the saints. On the one hand, believers are commanded to strive in obedience if they want to enjoy the comforts of full assurance, yet security is never ultimately grounded in personal effort, but rather in God's gracious work. God is the One who secures salvation, and, by His grace, saints are empowered to persevere in salvation. Thus, the grounds of personal assurance rest on both divine preservation (objective) and diligent perseverance (subjective).

DIVINE PRESERVATION

Security in salvation is the result of divine preservation, which is the ceaseless grace of God that keeps His children eternally safe, protecting their souls and preserving their faith. In other words, the same grace that regenerates dead sinners and redeems guilty rebels continues to work in the life of a believer to ensure they will receive all the benefits of salvation. The same grace that initially justified you guarantees that you will ultimately escape eternal wrath and permanently enjoy a reconciled relationship with God (Rom 5:9–11). Believers predestined by God, purchased by Christ, and sealed by the Holy Spirit will not fall away, but will be kept in an eternal state of grace (Eph 3:1–14). He will not choose you to lose you! In moments of weak faith, or as a result of poor teaching, you might be tempted to doubt this reality and question whether eternal life is really eternal. However, the Bible provides convincing and objective reasons never to doubt the certainty of divine preservation.

The Character of God

To begin with, you can be confident in the certainty of divine preservation because of the character of God, whose nature and perfections assure us of the certainty of salvation. You can be certain that His infinite goodness will not run dry before He has fulfilled every saving promise He has ever made (Exod 34:6–7a). As the gospel demonstrates, man's sinfulness cannot outpace

God's goodness. Additionally, God's immutable faithfulness guarantees He will never change His mind about salvation (Mal 3:6). Not only is He infinitely good to grant you salvation, He is irreversibly decided about this grace. God is not capricious, fickle, and impossible to please. When He promises to pour out His goodness in a person's life, He will not change His mind. Thankfully, the unchangingly good God is also an omnipotent God able to keep every one of His unassailable promises. As Jude asserted, He is "able to keep you from stumbling, and to make you stand in the presence of His glory blameless with great joy" (Jude 24). There is no created power capable of thwarting the electing love of the Creator; nor is there any temporal circumstance able to frustrate the eternal plan of the Almighty (Rom 8:31–39). When God promises grace to a sinner, He will not change His mind and there is nothing outside of Him that can keep Him from fulfilling His Word.

The Work of Christ

In addition to being established by the character of God, divine preservation is secured by the completed work of Christ. Through His priestly work of incarnation and intercession, Christ has accomplished everything necessary for salvation. He provides the righteousness sinners need to stand before a righteous God, and through His death on the cross He served as the ultimate and atoning sacrifice for sin. Christ's priestly work on behalf of believers continues to this day in heaven through His ministry of intercession. He is at the throne of grace interceding for His people and affirming the application of His blood to every sin they commit. He prays for His followers to be protected, and whatever Jesus requests of the Father He will receive (John 11:22, 41–42). Consequently, all those the Father has given to Christ out of the world will be kept in Him and sanctified unto eternal glory (John 17:6, 9, 11, 17, 19–26). Christ has done everything that is necessary to secure salvation and secure His sheep in that salvation. He is the Great Shepherd who gives eternal life to His sheep, and nothing is able to remove them from His protective care. Apart from Christ's work, assurance would be impossible because salvation would be impossible.

The Ministry of the Spirit

Along with the character of God and the work of Christ, divine preservation is sealed by the ministry of the Holy Spirit. At conversion, the believer is "baptized into Christ" by the Spirit (Rom 6:3; 1 Cor 12:13), and "sealed in Him with the Holy Spirit of promise" (Eph 1:13). The Spirit serves as God's signet ring, securing a soul in union with Christ—He is the down payment of eschatological blessing that guarantees final payment. His work of regeneration and His indwelling presence within us guarantees that God will dwell with us eternally (Rev 22:4), because the same Spirit who carries us into Christ assures that we will be kept in Christ. There is no doubt: the Father will jealously guard His Spirit-sealed possessions (Jas 4:5), and will not let them fall into the hands of someone else.

The Nature of Salvation

In addition to the perfections of the Triune God, divine preservation is established by the very nature of salvation. Redemption takes its shape from the imprint of God's nature, who designed salvation to be secure. Robert Culver rightly concludes, "There is hardly an aspect of soteriology from election to glorification that is not employed in some passage of the New Testament to give believers assurance and thereby support for the doctrine of perseverance."[5]

Take, for instance, *election*, which guarantees every other aspect of salvation, including preservation. There is an unbreakable chain of salvific effects, which have their ultimate cause in the electing love of God (Rom 8:29–30). The believer has been set apart for all time (Heb 10:16–18) and chosen for the purpose of perfected

[5] Robert Duncan Culver, *Systematic Theology* (Fearn, Ross-shire: Mentor, 2005), 769.

holiness (Eph 1:4). God will not miss the mark on the aim of election—not one who has been chosen will be rejected.

Furthermore, those whom God has justified cannot become unjustified. The divine act of *justification*, whereby God declares the sinner righteous and acceptable before Him on the basis of Christ's holy self-offering and propitiatory death, is a comprehensive declaration and cannot be reversed (2 Cor 5:21). Once the sinner is covered, through repentance and faith, by the imputed righteousness of Christ, the condemnation of the Law is removed by the finished work of the cross (Col 2:13–14).

Along with election and justification, the believer's *adoption* into God's covenant blessing requires the doctrine of preservation. The believer has been declared a child of God, an heir according to the promise, and a permanent part of God's family (John 1:12–13). Being members of God's household (Eph 2:19), believers are preserved and sustained by God, made part of the body of Christ (Rom 8:29), and destined for the glorious inheritance reserved in heaven (1 Pet 4). Adoption into the family of God cannot be revoked and will not be rescinded.

Ultimately, every aspect of salvation is tied to the believer's vital *union with Christ*, which also undergirds the doctrine of preservation. At conversion, the believer has been "crucified with Christ" (Gal 2:20), becoming "united with Him in the likeness of His death" (Rom 6:5). Since, therefore, "Christ was raised from the dead through the glory of the Father" (Rom 6:4), the resurrection of all true believers is secure (Rom 6:5b, 8). Union with Christ removes the condemnation of the Law (Rom 8:1), freeing the believer from slavery to sin's relentless power (Rom 6:6–11). Paul outlines "every spiritual blessing in the heavenly places" as grace-gifts of God found only "in Christ" (Eph 1:3). To be chosen and blessed "in Christ" is to have guaranteed preservation. Our life is "hidden with Christ in God," and so we must be revealed with Him at His coming (Col 3:3–4). In fact, union with Christ makes the Father's love for us just as certain as the Father's love for His Son:

> For I am convinced that neither death, nor life, nor angels, nor principalities, nor things present, nor things to come, nor powers, nor height, nor depth, nor any other created thing, will be able to separate us from the love of God, which is in Christ Jesus our Lord (Rom 8:38–39).

By the design and work of the Triune God, preservation is required by the very nature of salvation.

The Promises of Scripture

In addition to the character of God and the work of salvation, divine preservation is confirmed by the promises of Scripture, which leaves no doubt about the efficacy or certainty of salvation. Psalm 37:24 asserts of the believer that "when he falls, he will not be hurled headlong, because the LORD is the One who holds his hand." The prophet Jeremiah established the sole reason why true believers never fall away, namely that God has put the fear of Himself "in their hearts so that they will not depart from [Him]" (Jer 32:40). Jesus also affirmed the permanent sufficiency of His saving work, proclaiming that "he who believes in Me will never thirst" (John 6:35b), that everyone given to Him by the Father "will certainly not [be] cast out" (John 6:37), and that every true believer will be raised up "on the last day" (John 6:39–40).

Simply put, the Bible promises that if you repent and believe in Christ, you will be saved. It is a great comfort to the believer that salvation can neither be lost nor preserved by human effort. We know that our own failings, our sinful habits, and our anemic pursuit of righteousness cannot thwart the saving purposes of God. Redemption is grounded in the saving character and holy design of Almighty God. Beloved, in Christ we are objectively secure!

DILIGENT PERSEVERANCE

When the Bible assures that all who call on the name of the Lord will be saved, you can be absolutely certain of the eternal reality of this promise. Divine preservation, however, does not

automatically lead to personal assurance. The majority of rebel-
lious men will reject the gospel outright, and many will perish in
hell even though they thought they were saved. This is why you
must "test yourselves to see if you are in the faith" (2 Cor 13:5). If
you want to experience the comforting rest of personal assurance,
you must completely expose your life to the truth of Scripture
in the pursuit of clarity about your own soul (Heb 4:11–13). This
means you must look closely at your life to see if it matches the
description of a saved person found in the Bible. In other words,
you must examine your heart to see if you possess genuine, saving
faith. Faith alone is required for justification, which is why you
must see the evidences of faith in your life to have any assurance
that you are justified.

Through Examination

As you search your inner man for the assurance of faith, keep in
mind that saving faith is a gift from God (Eph 2:8–9). Through
the regenerating work of the Holy Spirit, the child of God is
given a new capacity to trust Christ and follow after Him. This
new capacity for faith is not only the means by which you are
converted, it is also how "the Spirit Himself testifies with our
spirit that we are children of God" (Rom 8:16). If you are convinced of the truth of Christ, it is because of the ministry of the
Holy Spirit in your inner man. This assuring testimony of the
Spirit is not a mystical feeling or a new revelation that comes at
some point after your conversion to confirm your adoption. The
Spirit testifies to our inner man that we are God's children by
convincing us of the truth of Scripture and thereby empowering
us to recognize the Lordship of Christ (1 Cor 12:3), trust in the
graciousness of the Father (Gal 4:6), and turn away from our
previous enslavement to sin (Rom 8:14–15). Thus, when you are
searching your soul for faith, you are looking for *confirming
evidences of the Spirit's saving grace in your life*. The presence of
faith is a necessary ground for personal assurance because it is
what God requires for salvation, and it is what He produces in

a saved life. But this raises another question: *How can you know that your faith is genuine?*

The definitive litmus test of genuine faith is that it perseveres all the way to the end, while imposter faith inevitably falls away. Examining the doctrine of eternal security might tempt you to think that you can be passive about your faith and unconcerned with your endurance. You might even wonder, *If God is preserving me, do I need to diligently persevere?* If you are wondering this, the answer is emphatically *yes*, especially if you want to experience the joy of assurance in your life. The Bible consistently demands that you endure in your faith until the end in order to enter God's eternal kingdom. No less than Jesus Himself declared that "the one who endures to the end, he will be saved" (Matt 24:13). Hebrews 10:36 even indicates that this endurance includes obedience to the will of God: "For you have need of endurance, so that when you have done the will of God, you may receive what was promised." Of course, this also implies that those who do not endure in faith-filled obedience have no assurance that they will be saved. This is precisely what Hebrews 10:26–27 teaches: "For if we go on sinning willfully after receiving the knowledge of the truth, there no longer remains a sacrifice for sins, but a terrifying expectation of judgment and the fury of a fire which will consume the adversaries." Statements such as these are predicated on the reality that a life that rejects the authority of God's truth and defects from faith in Christ is the product of an "evil, unbelieving heart" (Heb 3:12). You simply cannot turn away from devotion to Christ or reject His Lordship over your life and expect to reign with Him in eternity—loyalty to Christ and submission to His will are necessary fruits of saving faith. To shrink back from diligent perseverance calls into question the reality of divine preservation in your life, because one never exists without the other.

Through Enduring Faith

In order to balance these realities in your thinking, you must remember that God's preserving grace is directed at your enduring faith. In other words, diligent perseverance is not an attempt to work for your salvation apart from grace, but is the purpose and product of divine preservation. In the same manner that God gifted you with initial faith, He continues to pour out His preserving grace in your life to empower your persevering faith. This is why, from a human perspective, you must "work out your salvation with fear and trembling" (Phil 2:12), because God "is at work in you, both to will and to work for His good pleasure" (Phil 2:13). In this way, both divine preservation and diligent perseverance make up the "way the entrance into the eternal kingdom of our Lord and Savior Jesus Christ will be abundantly supplied to you" (2 Pet 1:11). You must make every effort knowing that all of your faith-driven effort is the product of God's grace in your life.

The need for perseverance does not imply that you can keep yourself safe by your own power, but it does mean that wherever the grace of divine preservation is present you will see signs of diligent perseverance. Additionally, your persistence in following Christ does not add to or usurp the imputed righteousness of Christ as the basis for your standing with God. Justification is a decisive, transactional reality, but the faith that leads to justification does not become inactive once we're justified. Once you are saved you will always be saved. Persevering faith doesn't earn you entrance into the kingdom any more than initial faith merits justification, but it is just as necessary for final and abundant entrance into the kingdom as that initial faith. We simply cannot enter into the kingdom unless, having believed, we keep believing in Christ. This is in no way inconsistent with the free grace of the gospel. Rather, diligent perseverance is a grace in the life of a true believer that, because of divine preservation, can never be completely absent, making it absolutely essential for assurance.

God does not preserve His people apart from means. Remembering this truth is crucial to grasping how perseverance functions in our lives. Just as God's sovereign grace employed temporal means to convert you to Christ, so He has provided ordinary means of grace to keep you in Christ. Thus, when it comes to preservation, God is keeping you in accordance with His eternal decree and by means of His providential instruments—including your faith-fueled endurance. Notice how 1 Peter 1:3–5 points to your faith as a means employed by God in your preservation:

> Blessed be the God and Father of our Lord Jesus Christ, who according to His great mercy has caused us to be born again to a living hope through the resurrection of Jesus Christ from the dead, to obtain an inheritance which is imperishable and undefiled and will not fade away, reserved in heaven for you, who are protected by the power of God *through faith* for a salvation ready to be revealed in the last time.

The omnipotent power of God employs our faith as a means of safeguarding our salvation to be revealed in the last time. This, of course, is not out of necessity on God's part—He does not need our contribution to accomplish anything. However, Peter could not be more clear: God preserves the saints "through faith." He is keeping you in the faith (Jude 24), in part, by you keeping your faith (Jude 21).

Understanding the fact that God uses our humble faith as a means to preserve us to the end helps us understand the various warnings about apostasy in Scripture (2 Cor 13:5; Col 1:22–23). God will do what He promises in salvation, but we are warned by God to practice what He commands, especially if we want assurance (Heb 10:23). In these passages, God graphically warns professing believers of the ultimate results of unbelief in order to protect their faith. These warning passages alert readers to the possibility of being self-deceived by false assurance, but they are also intended to forge an active and passionate growth in His grace, to test levels of faithfulness, and to cause sober reflection on the genuineness of our faith. These warnings are God's gracious "red lights" that stop us in our tracks and call us to greater diligence and enduring faith. As Calvin explained, "it pleased the Lord by such threats to arouse to repentance those whom he was terrifying, that they might escape the judgment they deserved for their sins."[6] If we blow through these "red lights" in the pursuit of gratification, we can be certain that our assurance will waiver. To neglect clear biblical warnings leaves us vulnerable to deception and false assurance because God uses our perseverance as a means to preserve us, and if we are not persevering we cannot enjoy biblically-grounded assurance. The securing grace of God ensures and employs the diligent perseverance of every believer, which is why enduring faith always leads to growing assurance. The faith God provides for conversion and requires for salvation always endures to the end—that's how you know it is genuine. Really, the question you must ask when seeking assurance is, *Since only genuine faith will persevere to the end, how can I know if my faith will persevere to the end?* Or, to borrow the language of the Puritans, *How can I know I will die well?* The faith that you die with is the faith you will stand before God with, because that is the faith you had all along.

Through Fruitfulness

If the only way to know that your faith would endure was to wait until you approach death, then assurance in this life would be impossible. Thankfully, though, God has designed enduring faith to manifest itself in several other demonstrable ways so that it can be tested and proven genuine now. Specifically, you can discern the provenness of your faith by its accuracy and its fruitfulness. Proven faith must be accurate because the gospel is the only saving message, and it must be fruitful because God's grace is always effective. Genuine, God-given, saving faith not only perseveres until the end, it also produces fruit in accordance with the truth. God designed it this way so that He would be glorified by our faith-filled works, and so we can have assurance as we see the fruits of proven faith in our lives. This means that if you want to prove the genuine and enduring character of your faith, confirm your election, and have genuine assurance, you must

[6] John Calvin, *Institutes of the Christian Religion*, trans. Ford Lewis Battles, ed. John T. McNeill, 2 vols. (Louisville: Westminster John Knox Press, 1960), 1.17.14.

pursue faith-filled obedience to God's inspired Word. Or, to put it another way, you can prove the genuineness of your faith now through diligent perseverance in the truth, especially in the midst of trials and temptations (1 Pet 1:6–8).

The radical change in belief required by conversion will not leave your life unchanged: spiritual fruit will always accompany a change in your spiritual condition. This, of course, is why Jesus said you can identify false teachers by their fruit (Matt 7:20). No one is a more adept hypocrite than a false teacher, and yet even the most polished fraud will eventually be identified by the fruit of his life. In the same way, the fruit of your life always indicates the genuineness and enduring character of your faith. A spiritually idle and fruitless life will never lead to the clarity and confidence that is necessary for assurance because there is no proof that person knows Christ (2 Pet 1:8). In contrast, however, a life characterized by fruits that can be produced only by the Holy Spirit demonstrates the reality of redemption in a person's life. Many individuals needlessly fret about whether or not they are among the elect. While you cannot know the secret will of God, you *can* see the evidences of His redemptive will in your life. God elects His people unto holiness, gives them grace for holiness, and they gain assurance through practical holiness. If you are growing in holiness it is because the Father chose you and the Spirit effectually called you, and if you are not growing in holiness, you will have no assurance that you will see God (Heb 12:14). Fruit is necessary for assurance, which is why James says "I will show you my faith by my works" (Jas 2:18).

When the Bible commands you to examine yourself to see whether you are in the faith, this is the kind of faith that you should be looking for in order to enjoy personal assurance. This does not mean you need to reach some perfected level of holiness in your life before you can credibly claim to be a Christian. The mere presence and increasing growth of fruit demonstrates the nature of the tree, no matter what kind of yield it produces. How many oranges are required on a tree in order to prove that it is orange tree? If you see even an orange blossom on a tree, it is an orange tree.

Self-examination that is not rooted in biblical truth will inevitably devolve into proud introspection. However, when you examine yourself under the light of Scripture to look for the fruits of faith in your life, you will gain clarity on the condition of your soul. Saving faith is a gracious gift from God that is always accurate, productive, and enduring. Faith that ultimately believes something other than divine truth, or fails to produce any spiritual fruit, or falls away into rejection of Christ, was never genuine faith in the first place. The subjective grounds of assurance rests on tested faith that has been proven to be consistent with the gospel, productive in the church, and unwavering toward Christ. God has ordained our obedience as a reliable source of assurance—"If you continue in My word, then you are truly disciples of Mine" (John 8:31)—which is what makes discerning assurance possible.

CHAPTER 12

DISCERNING A WAY FORWARD

BESIDES the good news of the gospel, the very best news
a child of God could ever hear is that our freedom from
sin's bondage also gives us the power to be conformed to
the image of our Savior. In a word, the best news is that in Christ
we are free to be holy. This is not only the ultimate end of God's
work in and through us—to "share His holiness" (Heb 12:10)—
but it should be the highest passion and pursuit of our lives (Eph
1:4; 1 Pet 1:15–16). There are some today who teach that communion with God is somehow a higher goal than striving to be holy
like our Lord. But this confuses the issue. Make no mistake, to
be holy *is* to commune with God in the fullness of His joy (John
15:10–11; 17:13, 17). Our ultimate communion with God will occur
when, perfected in holiness, we will behold the Lord Jesus Christ
in all the fullness of His glory (John 17:24). How is it that we can
stare with unveiled face into the blazing majesty of the Lord of
lords and not be consumed? Because we will be sinless, having
finally experienced the complete eradication of our unredeemed
humanity and free to be in the presence of our holy God without
fear of judgment. To be holy as He is holy is to enjoy perfect communion with Him, and eternal communion with Him demands
that we be made completely holy (Heb 12:14).

I don't believe it is biblical, let alone helpful, to distinguish
between the fullness of communion with God and becoming holy
and blameless before Him. In Scripture, the two are essentially

the same spiritual reality. We may speak of communion with
God from a relationally-oriented vantage point, which is true and
correct. But we also find in Scripture the ground and purpose of
our redemption, which is God in Christ, by His Spirit, quickening
our dead hearts so that we may be presented by Him "holy and
blameless and beyond reproach" (Col 1:22). Relationally speaking,
to be with God in a state of holiness is to have entered into the
most intimate communion possible.

Our lives, therefore, should be focused primarily on "the
surpassing value of knowing Christ Jesus" (Phil 3:8) by entrusting
ourselves to Him in humble faith so that His Holy Spirit may
transform us into His image (Eph 1:4; 1 Pet 1:14–15). We should
strive to be holy, which is the same as saying we should strive to
enter into the most intimate communion with Him. To have an
ongoing growth in grace and the knowledge of Christ we must
be more than just gospel-centered. We must pursue more than
merely a higher contemplation of grace. Living in light of the
gospel is essential, and understanding the grace of our justification is the drivetrain of a sanctified life. But these alone are not
the end of our redemptive power and progress. We must also put
sanctifying truth at the center of our life. And we must live each
moment by faith, humbly pursuing Christlikeness in the power
of the Spirit. Nothing short of all these essentials could really
be called gospel-centeredness. This is the way forward in today's
debate over sanctification. Finding the balance between God's
work of grace and our holy diligence is achieved only by knowing
the truth and aligning our hearts with it.

A WORD-CENTERED LIFE

A gospel-centered life is a Word-centered life. It means living
by every word that proceeds from the mouth of God (Matt 4:4)
and longing for God's revelation as a babe hungers intensely for
his daily milk (1 Pet 2:1–2). A truly gospel-centered approach to
Scripture will always include several indispensable and overlap-
ping disciplines.

Listen to the Word

Word-centered lovers of the gospel have spiritual ears to hear the Word. They study the Bible with a mind and heart open to the Spirit's every confrontation, challenge, encouragement, admonition, and warning. "Listening" to the truth is not about mystically waiting to "hear" some audible voice or strong inner impression. It's simply acknowledging our need for the mind of Christ on every issue, praying fervently that the Lord would have His way, and desiring every new understanding the Spirit brings to our minds and hearts.

Embrace the Word

To be Word-centered is to gladly and gratefully embrace the sanctifying implications of biblical truth. Many profess to be gospel-centered but refuse to accept what Scripture is revealing about their flaws. They are like hearers of the Word only, who ignore the definitive truths of the Bible in favor of gospel generalities (Jas 1:22–25). Trafficking in the murky waters of subjectivity is far less convicting than thinking deeply on the specific pathology of our weaknesses. Hungry Christians learn to love the precision and inflexibility of Scripture.

Confess the Word

A Word-centered life is a confessional life. There's no way to truly embrace the heart-penetrating implications of the truth without also fully confessing personal culpability. King David's renowned confession—sung for generations in Israel's corporate worship (how would you like your guilt put to music for the church?)—set the example for genuine, unvarnished confession: "Against You, You only, I have sinned and done what is evil in Your sight, so that You are justified when You speak and blameless when You judge" (Ps 51:4). Gospel-centered, Word-centered living always exonerates the righteous character of God and His just dealings with men. Someone claiming to adore the gospel while habitually minimizing God's holiness and sin's offense is either deceiving or being deceived.

Obey the Word

Word-centered believers obey the Word. Many professing believers faithfully attend "gospel-centered" churches, read many blogs in a single day, duke it out on numerous online theological forums, and quote their favorite teacher's pithiest zingers, but their private lives are often a chronicle of dominating weaknesses for which they have become adept excuse-makers. Tired and irritated, their lives seem to reflect one edgy, non-conformist lifestyle choice after another. It's as if their response to frequent failure has become resignation—a settled giving up on God's promises and the Spirit's sufficient power. Yet a truly Word-focused life is one of both confessed weakness and increasing spiritual strength. What's the evidence of a genuinely gospel-centered life? It's the fruit of the Spirit in obedience to God's Word (Gal 5:16).

A claim to gospel-centeredness is an empty boast if it isn't marked by an increasing devotion to the Word of God. To be gospel-centered is to be "biblocentric." If you even mildly scoff at Scripture's precision and authority, you can't talk of loving the gospel. If you would rather live in gospel generalities than explore "all the treasures of wisdom and knowledge" (Col 2:3) revealed in Christ, you have totally missed the bullseye. You may be truly saved by grace, but God will not rest until He's taught you to love His *instruments and crucibles* of grace. Many newly-Reformed brothers and sisters will quote books and theologies because the "gospel-centered" verbiage captures their thrilling discovery of grace. What's sad is how many are swinging hard away from pursuing the fruit which saving grace promises.

Conferences on gospel grace and passion for Christ are standing room only. But conferences on separation from the world (2 Cor 6:14–7:1) and obedience to the commands of Christ (Matt 28:20; John 14:15, 23–24; 15:10; Rom 2:7)—not so much. How can that be the case? If gospel-centeredness is our banner, then shouldn't Christ's *every word* be our most precious treasure? We can't be selective, seeing only the emphasis we want to see (or feel is right) in Scripture. And the current trend of defanging the force of Greek imperatives is not healthy. People are trying to redefine biblical commands as "delightful invitations" or "gentle urgings," and this just won't do. After all, what are commands but expressions of the will of Christ? Undoubtedly, Jesus is in perfect harmony with His divine will. He can do no less than love what He wills. Therefore, the question is, do you love the will of Christ? Is He worthy of your ardent submission to it? No one is truly gospel-centered when he is indifferent toward Jesus' teaching to "observe all that ... [He] commanded" (Matt 28:20).

A FAITH-CENTERED LIFE

In addition to being Word-centered, a gospel-centered life is a faith-centered life. We have discussed the role of faith in the Christian life in this study at length. However, it remains surprising that when talking about spiritual growth so many in the current gospel-centered movement don't use the term *faith*. Or if they do, it is an afterthought to emotional, visceral, and subjective descriptions of the Christian life.

Dire Need for Faith

When speaking of sanctification, we should not be leaving out the Bible's more common terminology of walking by faith (2 Cor 5:7), being controlled by the Spirit (Eph 5:18), and hoping in God (1 Pet 1:21). Is it possible that the pendulum has swung beyond Scripture's balance on how we live the Christian life? In their desire for a vibrant walk with Christ, many evangelicals are missing what the Scripture teaches about growing in Christlikeness. A truly sanctified life is a *faith-centered* life. Putting anything else *before* faith, especially emotions, eliminates the need for truth or faith. I could experience emotional passion before believing truth, and human emotions could just as well be rooted in unbelief as in belief. Expecting some experience to *cause* me to believe and obey is like wanting to taste and enjoy fruit before peeling it and taking a bite.

Waiting for emotional joy to inspire obedience inevitably leads to discouragement, particularly when life's frequent trials leave us in an emotionally low state. Christians do not live at either end of the emotional scale. We do not trust in excited emotions, nor do we assume that downcast feelings signal disobedience or faithlessness. Iain Murray writes of a time Charles Spurgeon told a dying congregant that his diseased body and low spirit did not mean he had weak faith: "'Do not be cast down by your feelings,' [Spurgeon] told him. To which the man at once replied, 'No, sir, I am in no danger of that, for when I have had the most joyful feelings, I have never rested in them. You have taught me that a soul can only lean on eternal verities, and these I know come from the mouth of God, and never from the changing feelings of the flesh.'"[1] Spurgeon would later remark: "Do not rise upon feelings, and you will not sink under them. Keep to believing: rest all your weight upon the promises of God, and when heart and flesh fail, God will be the strength of your heart and your portion for ever."[2]

We don't deny that emotions can become more sanctified and more intensely "felt," but the Scriptures teach that obedient faith begins and ends with knowledge of, and humble submission to, the truth. The Bible's path to spiritual growth is not uncharted: "We walk by faith" (2 Cor 5:7). Understanding that will keep us from depending on the uncertainties of emotion and experience.

A HOLINESS-CENTERED LIFE

In addition to being Word-centered and faith-centered, a gospel-centered life will always be a holiness-centered life. God poured out His sovereign grace into our lives so that we would be holy—and we honor the purpose of the gospel by pursuing holiness. This is the very thing that God's grace has transformed us to do. Even on our best day as an unbeliever, morally speaking, we produce only more sin, more guilt, and greater condemnation. But now, in Christ, we have a miraculous new inclination that leads toward holy desires and godly fruit (Rom 7:6). Christians are identified as

[1] Iain H. Murray, *The Forgotten Spurgeon* (London: Banner of Truth Trust, 1972), 33–34.
[2] Ibid., 34.

those who walk "according to the Spirit" (Rom 8:4), meaning His grace and power are coursing through our spiritual veins. Simply stated, no one can claim to be gospel-centered who is not also appropriating the power of the gospel in holy striving.

A HUMILITY-CENTERED LIFE

In addition to being Word-centered, faith-centered, and holiness-centered, a gospel-centered life will always be a humility-centered life. A life driven by the *solas* of the gospel is a completely self-depreciating life. This is the gospel-centered reality that seems to be lost in the current resurgence of Reformed theology. One thing that's particularly alarming about the current Reformed movement is the haughty attitude with which many often champion their "gospel-centeredness." Defeating our pride is a lifelong battle, especially early on in our Christian life when the Spirit has had little time to crush it. And unless a newborn Calvinist spends those early years aggressively putting self-importance to death, he will merely transfer worldly boasts to theological ones. The Bible repeatedly warns against using theological knowledge and giftedness to make ourselves prominent (1 Cor 3:3–4; 4:6, 19; 8:1–3; 1 Tim 3:6; 6:4). True gospel-centeredness, by definition, always seeks to magnify the name of Christ—not multiply personal followers.

The first fruit of saving faith is genuine brokenness over sin. In fact, the moment we first believed in Christ alone for salvation was a grace-enabled moment of true humility. Pride was supernaturally shattered the very second we rightly saw our desperate need for a Savior. God granted us repentance and faith, and in that moment we were *truly gospel-centered*. At its core, being "Reformed" is not merely aligning with historic confessions or theological camps. Nor is it simply shedding old Arminian notions and learning to articulate the doctrines of grace. These may be important steps toward an orthodox understanding, but without the death of self they just end up as notches on the belt of personal significance. Why do many young Christians today—humbled by the grace of the cross—seem unaware of their utter lack of either grace or humility?

Dangers of Preeminence

In a day when godly character is urgently needed in the pulpit and the pew, so many are preoccupied with self-branding, and flouting the slightest caution about their lifestyle. Even men—some fresh out of seminary—fearlessly ascend the sacred desk with neither careful study of texts nor transformation of their own heart. Preaching has become much more about theological musing, turning phrases, and comedic timing. There seems to be a new level of hubris in the air within evangelicalism. Biblical counsel from experienced and wiser Christians is readily dismissed by those who need it most. We are a fast growing subculture of the quick-to-speak and slow-to-hear. Humilty, in the classic biblical sense of it, has given way to narcissism and a love of preeminence. The reasons for this dramatic shift are many, but two in particular should be noted.

Rhetoric Without Renewal

Pragmatic-driven preaching has conditioned people to assume that communicating truth is exclusively about style and technique. Lip-service is given to content, but a speaker's captivating manner is becoming king. Rather than stick to the particulars and principles *clearly* rising from a passage of Scripture, preachers today will extemporaneously muse on a theological theme, almost appearing to make it up as they go. The authority is tied to the talent and wit of the preacher rather than the rightly-divided meaning of the inspired text. Tragically, audiences today are learning to focus on the speaker's style and quotables.

Even in conservative churches, some pastors seem free to teach contradictory and often outlandish things with no biblical pushback. Apparently, if it sounds biblically-based no one is allowed to pour water on that flame by asking hard questions about interpretation. We've lost both our discernment and our nerve! Too many have become teachers, and too few are willing to keep them in line for fear of being reproached. This trend has served only to embolden the most frequent offenders. They scoff at theological critiques and anyone who won't get in line. This is *not* shepherding "the church of God which He purchased with His own blood" (Acts 20:28). We can't be gospel-centered when the Chief Shepherd's heart is eclipsed in His church by those who love to have preeminence (3 John 9).

Every word of God *exclusively* "performs its work in you who believe" (1 Thess 2:13). No one is saved or sanctified apart from Scripture (John 15:5; 17:17). And we should not conclude that affirming doctrinal statements, reciting confessions, joining coalitions, or ardently defending pet theological truths equates to spiritual growth. Such privileges amount to nothing without knowing what Scripture actually says, grasping what it truly means, and humbly submitting to it in genuine faith. In the minds of many today, the Bible is a book of theological topics to be articulated, pondered, and confessed, but not a set of implications and demands to take to heart. Context and details of Bible verses are considered minutiae, only lightly mentioned on the way to the preacher's inspiring words.

Evangelicalism has raised a generation that follows what's popular and culturally acceptable. Some even speak boldly of the authority of Scripture for ministry, but their lifestyle and choices are patterned after the latest fads. Tragically, this is the very opposite of gospel-centeredness. This is nothing but unvarnished love of preeminence and fear of man. When fear of man displaces fear of God in pulpits, ministries will be infused with self-assured theological rhetoric and very little Word-centered clarity or true renewing power.

Notoriety Without Responsibility

Technology is the younger generation's tool. They developed it. They have the cutting-edge talent to use it in a way to promote themselves. So why not develop a personal brand, gradually cultivate a social media audience, and publish their theological insights to the masses? It's fast and easy, and it requires no proven character, no theological testing and affirmation, and no public repentance for harmful errors perpetrated against the church. Worse, there's no remedial training or character change required before going public. But here's the reality: if this generation of evangelicals were being used to do great things for Christ, we would see them vigorously fleeing the slightest whiff of self-glory. There would be fear, trembling, and a holy hesitation about shepherding God's sheep. We'd observe a reluctance to offer spiritual counsel in areas of stubborn weakness not yet successfully challenged. Instead, many are rushing to "weigh in" on any topic currently trending, afraid that someone else's perspective will be heard first and steal the recognition. These things ought not be this way! Truly gospel-centered people hate "even the garment polluted" by pride (Jude 23).

The apostle Paul taught us how to be useful, even when we might not have a lot of life experience. Instead of clamoring for preeminence or demanding to be heard over others, we are to live in such a way that our lack of experience is made up for in proven character. First Timothy 4:12 says: "Let no one look down on your youthfulness, but rather in speech, conduct, love, faith and purity, show yourself an example of those who believe." Some today want to have influence in the lives of others, but they've chosen to demand it rather than earn it. Paul tells his young apprentice, Timothy, that speaking beyond your years isn't something you stipulate. It comes gradually as others observe your conduct. When the church hears edifying speech from young believers, when they see patterns of exemplary conduct, humble love, robust faith, and moral purity, the church becomes less reluctant to pass the baton to them. God makes a person increasingly "useful to the Master" as they "abstain from wickedness" (2 Tim 2:19, 21). Take personal inventory of your life. Have you influenced others toward holiness? Is your counsel wise and not mere opinion? Is there an immoveable integrity in your dealings with others? And have you strengthened the faith of others? I am afraid that for all the passion and theological sparring that goes on, the church may be at an all-time low on Paul's list of exemplary character qualities. Where are the young, *reverent*, and Reformed of today?

Development of Humility

The church needs servants committed to being just that—servants. God gives grace to the humble, not those who proudly seek after their own interests. If you're going to be greatly used of God, you must cultivate humility. Toward that end, here are several contemporary resolutions aimed at going from restless and proud to reverent and meek:

1. Memorize the second half of 1 Timothy 4:12, and nurture each quality in your heart and conduct *before* you demand that older believers respect what you have to say or write.

2. If you have a voice of influence in the lives of others, ask yourself how many of the principles you have taught others have you deeply studied and nurtured into maturity.

3. If you know (and most do but rarely admit it) that you secretly love the sense of personal significance you get from having influence over others (particularly through social media), then wean yourself from the pride of it all. Stop promoting yourself, whether online, in ministry, or in any forum. "Decrease" for the "increase" of Christ until the idolatry of significance is killed and the preeminence of Christ floods more than your speech and emotions. Let it flood your heart first (Ezra 7:10; John 3:30).

4. Never establish and flaunt lifestyle choices of a controversial nature, in the name of the gospel, before nurturing a blameless conscience and the sacrificial love enough to control those choices. Many young believers are simply unaware that their attitude is in direct defiance of Romans 14:13–23 and Galatians 5:13. This is merely pride and bondage cloaked as gospel freedom.

5. If your talent is in demand, remember that with privilege comes massive culpability (1 Cor 4:2; Jas 3:1). When others thank you for your spiritual knowledge, it doesn't mean you've mastered what you can articulate. Praise from others tests a man (Prov 27:21). For most of our Christian lives we'll be explaining truths we have trouble consistently living. That reality alone is an astounding grace! Technology affords greater opportunity for wider influence, but it has no power to make us godly.

6. Serve your local assembly without seeking recognition, and humbly submit to your leaders in the ministry (Heb 13:17). Don't spend time with only your peers, but find ways to sacrificially minister to needs across the generational spectrum. Make this a much higher priority than influence in all other arenas.

Above all, remember that being gospel-centered means being humility-centered. One cannot exist without the other.

* * *

If today's grace-wielding enthusiasts were *wholly centered* on the redemptive work of Christ, there'd be a swing away from worldliness *so drastic as to prompt the astonishment of all.* In other words, wherever God's people get lost in the wonder of Christ's grace, their lives become centered on Christ's holiness. Honoring the righteousness and purity of the Master becomes our highest love and daily ambition (2 Cor 5:9), and the sinful world around us is caused to both wonder and fear (Acts 5:11, 13). Saving grace never leaves us comfortable in old grave clothes. It schools us in holiness, teaching us how to "deny ungodliness and worldly desires and to live sensibly, righteously and godly in the present age" (Titus 2:12). Gospel-centered people set their minds on "the things above, where Christ is" (Col 3:1). We begin to manifest the Savior's heart and character. We love not only Jesus, but we also love holiness and hate sin. Gospel grace never produces contempt for Scripture's commands and indifference toward worldliness. We are "predestined to become conformed to the image of [Christ]" (Rom 8:29). When we cut through the modern nomenclature and allow the Bible to shape our thinking, a gospel-centered life is a Word-centered, faith-centered, holiness-centered, and humility-centered life.

APPENDICES

APPENDIX I

HOW DOES GOD FEEL?

A T its core, spiritual growth begins with offering our entire life to God as a sacrifice of praise. According to Romans 12:1, it is the only reasonable and rational response to the "mercies of God" given in Christ. There is simply no more worthy way to live. If someone claims to have experienced salvation in Jesus, yet sneers at God's commands, Paul says that such hypocrisy is irrational. It is unworthy of the calling with which we've been called, and the most incongruous response imaginable. How could anyone who claims to worship Christ live each day for the honor of something other than His will? We are called to offer our entire lives—our mind, will, emotions, affections, motives, imaginings—to God as a living, adoring sacrifice. Nothing is held back. To worship God is to become a living sacrifice by dying to self in everything. There's no other way to soften what is commanded in this passage.

Paul is concerned primarily with the nerve center of our entire Christian experience. Romans 12:1 is the call to lay our entire lives on the line for Christ. Verse 2 is the way it is accomplished. This is not a call to feel something. It's not a call to turn inward and evaluate levels of emotional delight and love for God. Feelings of joy over the truth are a wonderful part of the image of God in man. But true faith, not emotional stirrings, is the instrument through which the Spirit transforms us. Paul's urgent call here is—dare I say it—a command. It's not an option or even merely an invitation in order to avoid a sense of obligation.[1] Paul writes that *we must not* be "conformed to this world, but be transformed by the renewing of [our] mind[s]." The Christian life involves transformation from one thing into something else. There can be no spiritual growth without real, substantive, spiritual change. Some claim that we should be passionate about Jesus and not concern ourselves with His commands. But a passion for Christ is a passion for His will (John 14:15). The two are inseparable. And Paul is crystal clear as to the means of grace involved in this transformed life of worship. This may shake up the contemporary paradigm for how we change and grow, but Paul isn't focused on only one dimension of our inner man, such as how we feel about being close with God. He's not interested in what our emotions are or are not experiencing. There is only one entry point, one channel for igniting this transformation: the *renewal of our minds*. Since whole-life worship is Paul's concern, he gathered all of our inner life dynamics into one expression for spiritual change: mind renewal. This is the one habit of life, the nerve center from which everything flows. It is our *reasonings and convictions* that Paul is urging us to offer as worship.

The command to be transformed is the opposite of remaining conformed to this world. Our pre-Christian heart was steeped in the morality and self-exaltation of a godless existence. Our thought life was consumed only with hedonistic cravings and the pride of life. A justified life is a worship-centered life, and to be worship-centered is to be transformed from earthly to heavenly convictions and conduct. We are no longer to think and

[1] While Scripture is clear that God's commands are not burdensome (1 John 5:3), I cannot agree with today's overemphasis on grace which softens biblical imperatives. The will of God is freighted with His ultimate authority. We love God and long to please Him, to be sure, but we're also unworthy slaves "bought with a price" and "not [our] own" (Luke 17:10; 1 Cor 6:19–20). We serve God from both a heart of genuine love *and* reverence for His Lordship. He's not only the supreme object of our affections, He is also the sovereign Lord of our mind and will. If Christians were merely invited to joyfully align with God, then Scripture's imperatives would not include the warnings which so often follow.

reason according to our old self-exalting ideologies. And mark it down: no amount of emotional stirring will change worldly thinking into Christlike convictions. Faith in the truth and denial of fleshly desires manifest the Spirit's powerful work in us. How we feel at any given moment in our worship of God is not a reliable measure of spiritual growth. The great news is that Christ is always working in us, through His grace, to renovate our inner life. Through the Spirit, we've been given "the mind of Christ" (1 Cor 2:16). When we entrust ourselves to the truth (i.e., exercise faith)—"taking every thought captive to the obedience of Christ" (2 Cor 10:5)—sinful perspectives give way to righteous ones. The result is the spiritual renewal of our affections, motives, emotions, and will. We discern truth from lies (Heb 4:12; 5:14), we experience power over the flesh (Rom 8:4–13; Gal 5:16), we grow strong in faith (Rom 4:18–21; 2 Pet 3:18), we know a deeper love and intimacy with the Lord (Eph 3:16–19), our pride is subdued (1 Pet 5:6–10), and we are drawn upward in richer worship (Rom 12:1–2).

Jonathan Edwards—dubbed by some as the father of "Christian Hedonism"—was very alert to the danger of nurturing a faithless dependence upon feelings and aesthetics:

> A natural principle of self-love may be the foundation of great affections towards God and Christ, without seeing any thing of the beauty and glory of the divine nature. There is a certain gratitude that is a mere natural thing. Gratitude is one of the natural affections ... and there is a gratitude that arises from self-love, very much in the same manner that anger does. Anger in men is an affection excited *against*, or in opposition to, another, for something in him that crosses self-love: gratitude is an affection one has *towards* another, for loving or gratifying him, or for something in him that suits self-love. And there may be a kind of gratitude without any true or proper love .... Of this gratitude Christ declares, (Luke vi.) *Sinners love those that love them*; even the publicans, who were some of the most carnal and profligate sort of men, (Matt. v. 46.).[2]

[2] Jonathan Edwards, *A Treatise Concerning Religious Affections, In Three Parts*, in

Earlier in this same work Edwards expressed that

> There are two sorts of hypocrites: one such as are deceived with their outward morality and external religion ... and the other, such as are deceived with false discoveries and elevations. These last often cry down works, and men's own righteousness, and talk much of free grace; but at the same time make a righteousness of their discoveries ... and exalt themselves to heaven with them.[3]

The Scriptures teach that faith is the divinely-ordained instrument through which we are commanded to know God and experience life in Him (Heb 11:6). God's grace is granted by His power alone, and with it comes the illumining power to go from a dead mind and heart to knowing and clearly perceiving the truth (1 Cor 2:12–16). He grants the power to fully receive it to yield in obedience (John 17:8; 1 Thess 2:13). Faith is the instrument that actively dispenses to us what His grace grants. But the sanctification talk today doesn't mention faith very often. Bible passages are cited where God commands us to delight in Him, love Him, and to rejoice. In response to these texts, I heartily say amen! But obedience to a command—even to rejoice and delight in the Lord—begins with believing God's Word and yielding my will to Him (John 15:10; Heb 11:6). Defining or evaluating our spiritual condition by internal sensations brings no further clarity, as Iain Murray rightly observed: "To live by faith in Christ is not the same as to live by feelings."[4] I'm concerned that the church is nurturing a generation of Christians whose framework for knowing, communing with, and obeying God revolves around an emotional sense of their spirituality. We do experience emotions, but do we understand them rightly, and have we put them in their proper biblical place?

The Works of Jonathan Edwards, 2 vols. (Peabody, MA: Hendrickson, 1998), 1:275; emphases original.

[3] Ibid., 258.

[4] Iain H. Murray, *Evangelical Holiness and Other Addresses* (Edinburgh: Banner of Truth Trust, 2013), 33.

HOW DOES GOD FEEL?

The Bible doesn't define emotions like a dictionary would, but it describes them being expressed both by God and human beings. When trying to understand the "emotions of God," or the relationship between divine affections and human ones, we should tread very carefully. The Scriptures speak of God expressing divine affections (e.g., delight, love, anger), but our understanding of how His "emotions" function in light other attributes, such as His immutability,[5] is severely limited. The Bible declares that God's affections "are ultimately inscrutable"[6] (Rom 11:33; Eph 3:19). God's nature includes emotional realities, in so far as He describes them as such. But unlike us, He is without flaw in the expression of them. We are given to mood swings, "involuntary passions,"[7] and irrational, often out-of-control affections.[8] God is not subject to any such things. The divine affections "are never passive and involuntary, but rather always active and deliberate."[9] And Scripture indicates the varying ways God's "feelings" can be observed and, at times, actually change.

> Behold My Servant, whom I uphold, My chosen one, in whom My soul delights (Isa 42:1).

> The LORD your God is in your midst, a victorious warrior. He will exult over you with joy, He will be quiet in His love, He will rejoice over you with shouts of joy (Zeph 3:17).

[5] God reveals Himself to be immutable (eternally unchanging), yet He expresses divine emotions. Theologians through the years have immediately recognized the dilemma: since God cannot change (Mal 3:6), how are we to understand texts such as Genesis 6:5–6, where God is said to be grieved in response to seeing the great wickedness of man? The debate is beyond the scope of this book, but it bears noting that though God's passions and ours may be described similarly in Scripture, they are far from exact parallels.

[6] Phillip R. Johnson, "A God Without Mood Swings," in *Bound Only Once: The Failure of Open Theism*, ed. Douglas Wilson (Moscow, ID: Canon Press, 2001), 114.

[7] Ibid., 117.

[8] Ibid.

[9] Ibid.

> My purpose will be established, and I will accomplish all My good pleasure (Isa 46:10).
>
> Then LORD saw that the wickedness of man was great on the earth … and He was grieved in His heart (Gen 6:5–6).
>
> Do not grieve the Holy Spirit of God, by whom you were sealed for the day of redemption (Eph 4:30).
>
> God is a righteous judge, and a God who has indignation every day (Ps 7:11).
>
> There are six things which the LORD hates, yes, seven which are an abomination to Him (Prov 6:16).
>
> Just as a father has compassion on his children, so the LORD has compassion on those who fear Him (Ps 103:13).

These texts declare God's emotional response toward various people and circumstances. It is important to affirm that His emotions are always in accord with His perfect will rather than coerced reactions to an outside influence. In other words, He genuinely responds emotionally in some sense, but always according to His own sovereign will and glory rather than being compelled or obligated by anything He's created. God's emotions are not from shifting convictions nor any kind of overpowering passion exercised upon His will. They are driven by His thoughts and perfect purpose for each given situation.

PUT FEELINGS IN THEIR PLACE

Because God made us in His image, we reflect these same capacities of sense and experience. In a word: we are emotional beings. What a thrilling gift to humanity. I've always thought how tragically different life would be without the profound ability to feel life's most moving experiences. Having said that, and though we bear the marks of God's "emotional" capacities, our expression of them is far different from His. Ours fluctuate dramatically. We experience emotions rooted in shifting convictions and inclinations. We also experience passions that seem to rush upon us so suddenly and without warning that we allow them to sway our thoughts and choices. It can seem as though our feelings have simply taken over, but behind all human emotions is a complexity of reasonings and motives. Our emotions need sanctifying much like our thoughts and choices need sanctifying. Understanding the two following truths will help us put our emotions in their proper place.

First, human emotions are limited by God's design. Our emotions are designed to respond to thoughts and convictions, so that we're not ruled by them. Emotions are responses to what we know and believe. God created us to know the truth, believe it, and live by those convictions. Everything about us begins with our minds, our ability to reason (Rom 1:20–21). As convictions become settled in us, we have the capacity to respond with deep emotion. God never intended for us to bypass our minds as though emotional experiences should be the basis of what we know. In fact, since nothing we think or believe originates in our emotional senses, we shouldn't allow biblical thoughts and convictions to be overrun by a flash flood of unsanctified passions we've not yet learned to restrain.

Revelation, by definition, assumes our capacity to understand, to reason, and to believe. Some Christians become dangerously dependent on emotions from moment to moment. Through years of spiritual neglect, they allow their choices to be controlled by powerful physiological sensations rooted in unrestrained thoughts and cravings. Rather than subduing their passions with robust faith and biblical convictions, they are allowing the velocity of uncrucified lusts and swirling emotions to drive their choices and worldview. Seventeenth-century pastor Thomas Brooks warned of the spiritual black hole resulting from living by the senses: "We walk by faith and not by sight .... And, verily, he who makes sense and carnal reason a judge of his condition, will be happy and miserable, blessed and cursed, saved and lost, many times in a day, yea, in an hour."[10]

---

[10] Thomas Brooks, quoted in C. H. Spurgeon, *Smooth Stones Taken from Ancient Brooks* (New York: Sheldon and Company, 1860), 41–42.

Truth is apprehended with the mind, which, when believed, gives us the clearest view of ourselves (Heb 4:12), as well as the purest alignment of our emotions to God's will. Many who refer to having joy in the Christian life speak of it as though it were a bare emotional sensation rather than a conviction forged by faith. I agree that the terms used in the Old Testament refer to the full range of inner life experience (joy, grief, dread, hope, etc.), but many people confuse the issue by equating these things *merely* with emotions. Scripture doesn't give such a narrow picture of the inner life of man. It encompasses far more than what we're sensing and feeling.

Our inner life is a complex control center made up of thoughts, emotions, motives, reasonings, beliefs, and the will (Gen 6:5; Josh 24:15; Ps 37:4; 139:23; Prov 4:23; Matt 23:37; Gal 5:16–26; 1 Tim 1:5; Heb 4:12). The biblical terminology describing our inner man is rich and varied. The "heart" of man is the seat of his rational, volitional, and emotional activity. Applied to worship, for example, our entire inner life is to be engaged if it is to be genuine. Emotions should not be made the sole, or even primary, gauge of genuine obedience and love for Christ. There are many complex causes behind hypocritical worship. For instance, when we give mere lip service to God without humble faith, it is false worship regardless of the presence or absence of emotions (Isa 29:13; Matt 15:8). To express passion without knowing the truth is vain worship (John 4:22). When we claim to have faith in the truth but rationalize disobedience, our worship is feigned. If we sing praises to God while exalting self, it is false worship. The presence or absence of recognizable emotions is only one small part of the equation. Drawing spiritual conclusions based on feelings proves nothing.

Second, human emotions are limited by depravity. Our emotions are fallen. The effects of the Fall on the mind have darkened every way we reflect the image of God. Therefore, we can't be trusted. Our entire inner man is wholly infected with self-worship (Rom 1:18–23). Appraisal of our spiritual condition should always come from what Scripture alone declares. I'm burdened that many believers today doubt the authenticity of their obedience to Christ merely because they're not feeling the emotional sensations they've been told they should always be experiencing. Even after gaining victory over sin by faith, some question their progress because they "didn't feel like obeying." God's Word warns of the danger of drawing our own conclusions about our spiritual condition (1 Cor 4:3–5). Left to ourselves, we cannot rightly evaluate our walk with God. Apart from the truth of Scripture, it is foolish to take our own spiritual pulse and make a final diagnosis based on inner sensations. Only God's Word brings the clarity we need (John 17:17; Heb 4:12). God alone is "the Heart-Knower" and "Heart-Transplanter."[11] First John 3:18–20 teaches that our hearts become more assured of our belonging to God when, in His power, we love others "in deed and truth," despite how our own hearts raise doubts and condemn us. God's Word and work in our daily lives are the only sure way to a strengthened faith and joyful rest in His faithfulness.

[11] George Zemek, "Theology III" (unpublished course notes, The Expositors Seminary, n.d.), 131.

A PURITAN VIEW OF
FAITH, FEELINGS, AND AFFECTIONS

TODAY'S emphasis on subjective emotions has risen to such prominence that it has overshadowed the biblical place of faith in the process of sanctification. Believers are encouraged to look to their "sense of things," their "satisfaction," their "delighting," and their being "affected," rather than the straightforward biblical language of faith. As we have argued in this volume, obedience does not depend on any state of the emotions. And wherever there is affection or emotion, they will be sanctified only as a result of faith and a yielded will. This is not a new perspective, as an examination of Puritan writings will demonstrate.

Some have appealed to the Puritans in order to support an affections-driven approach to sanctification. This is unfortunate because the sense of the language of the Puritans simply does not support such a view. Indeed, the Puritans often used language we might view as visceral, like *affections*. But when they use that terminology, it is intended in one of two senses: 1) that which is detached from faith and is thus merely visceral; and 2) more commonly, that which is understood as an inclination of the will or a synonym for faith.

Thomas Brooks (d. 1680) speaks poignantly on the necessity of not just feeling convicted, but continually *believing*, as the key to Christian endurance:

Ah! sinner, remember this, there is no way on earth effectually to be rid of the guilt, filth, and power of sin, but by believing in a Savior. It is not resolving, it is not complaining, it is not mourning, but believing, that will make thee divinely victorious over that body of sin that to this day is too strong for thee, and that will certainly be thy ruin, if it be not ruined by a hand of faith.[1]

Thomas Watson (d. 1686) shows that *duty*—the language of believing and yielding to Scripture—comes before the believer experiences sanctified feelings:

When Christians abate their fervency in private devotions, God abates their peace. If you slacken the strings of the violin, the music is spoiled; so, if a Christian is slack in duty, they spoil the sweet music of peace in their souls. As the fire decays, the cold increases; so, as fervency in duty abates, our peace cools.[2]

Thomas White (d. 1672), a formidable Presbyterian non-conformist, taught that *meditation*—the act of looking at truth, thinking on its implications, and yielding your will to obey it in faith—must come before sanctified affections: "By it [i.e., meditation], the Christian improves his knowledge, quickens his affections, and excites practice."[3]

Thomas Manton (d. 1677) uses the language of *faith* and *trust* as prerequisites to happiness and a settled contentment in the Christian life:

If a man would lead a happy life, let him but seek a sure object for his trust, and he shall be safe: "He shall not be afraid of evil tidings: his heart is fixed, trusting in the Lord." He hath laid up his confidence in God, therefore his heart is kept in an equal poise.[4]

---

[1] Thomas Brooks, *Precious Remedies Against Satan's Devices* (London: Banner of Truth Trust, 1968), 220.

[2] Thomas Watson, *A Body of Divinity* (London: Banner of Truth Trust, 1958), 264.

[3] Thomas White, *Instructions for the Art of Divine Meditation* (Coconut Creek, FL: Puritan Publications, 2013), 11.

[4] Thomas Manton, *The Complete Works of Thomas Manton* (London: James Nisbet, 1874), 42.

Manton is keen again on faith being that which drives spiritual disciplines: "Faith is the fountain of prayer, and prayer should be nothing else but faith exercised."[5]

John Owen (d. 1683) refers to affections as a synonym for the faith that comes before our desires turning toward spiritual things:

> If our principal treasure be, as we profess, in things spiritual and heavenly, (and woe unto us if it be not so!) on them will our affections, and consequently our desires and thoughts, be principally fixed.[6]

Owen emphasizes faith in Christ according to the Scripture as the key to individual revival:

> A steady view of the glory of Christ, in his person, grace, and office, through faith, or a constant, lively exercise of faith on him, according as he is revealed to us in the Scripture, is the only effectual way to obtain a revival from under our spiritual decays, and such supplies of grace as shall make us flourishing and fruitful even in old age.[7]

Here again, Owen demonstrates that true sanctification will occur only when we do what we feel like least—working to mortify our lusts:

> The choicest believers, who are assuredly freed from the condemning power of sin, ought yet to make it their business all their days to mortify the indwelling power of sin.
>
> So the apostle, Col. iii.5, "Mortify therefore your members which are upon the earth." Whom speaks he to? Such as were "risen with Christ," verse 1; such as were "dead" with him, verse 3; such as whose life Christ was, and who should "appear with him in glory," verse 4. Do you mortify; do you make it your daily work; be always at it whilst you live; cease not a day from this

[5] Thomas Manton, *A Practical Commentary, Or an Exposition with Notes on the Epistle of James* (London: R. Gladding, 1840), 420.

[6] John Owen, *The Grace and Duty of Being Spiritually Minded* in *The Works of John Owen*, Vol. 7, ed. William H. Goold (n.p., Johnstone & Hunter, 1850–53; reprint, London: Banner of Truth Trust, 1967), 302.

[7] John Owen, *Meditations and Discourses on the Glory of Christ* (Fearn, Ross-shire: Christian Focus, 2004), 286.

work; be killing sin or it will be killing you. Your being dead with Christ virtually, your being quickened with him, will not excuse you from this work.[8]

Owen went on:

Let not that man think he makes any progress in holiness who walks not over the bellies of his lusts. He who doth not kill sin in his way takes no steps towards his journey's end. He who finds not opposition from it, and who sets not himself in every particular to its mortification, is at peace with it, not dying to it.[9]

Stephen Charnock (d. 1680) refers to resolutions—which is the language of a believing will—as that which empowers holy living:

Frequently renew settled and holy resolutions. A soldier unresolved to fight may be easily defeated. ... The weakness of our graces, the strength of our temptations, and the diligence of our spiritual enemies, require strong resolutions.[10]

Henry Scougal (d. 1678) brings severe warnings against putting emotions or visceral affections before faith. He wrote on what he terms "affectional emotionalism" and how it ruins true faith:

Others again put all religion in the affections, in rapturous hearts and ecstatic devotion; and all they aim at is, to pray with passion, and think of heaven with pleasure, and to be affected with those kind and melting expressions wherewith they court their Saviour, till they persuade themselves they are mightily in love with him, and from thence assume a great confidence of their salvation, which they esteem the chief of Christian graces.[11]

---

[8] John Owen, *Of the Mortification of Sin in Believers*, in *The Works of John Owen*, Vol. 6, ed. William H. Goold (n.p., Johnstone & Hunter, 1850–53; reprint, London: Banner of Truth Trust, 1967), 9.

[9] Ibid., 14.

[10] Stephen Charnock, *The Complete Works of Stephen Charnock* (London: J. Nichol, 1866), 286.

[11] Henry Scougal, *The Life of God in the Soul of Man*, in *The Works of Henry Scougal* (Glasgow: William Collins 1830), 38–39.

Scougal goes on to contrast the previous statement with this:

> The root of the divine life is faith …. Faith has the same place in the divine life, which sense hath in the natural, being indeed nothing else but a kind of sense, or feeling persuasion of spiritual things; it extends itself unto all divine truths; but in our lapsed estate, it hath a peculiar relation to the declaration of God's mercy and reconcilableness to sinners through a Mediator; and therefore, receiving its denomination from that principal object, is ordinarily termed faith in Jesus Christ.[12]

Obadiah Sedgwick (d. 1658) states a similar idea in a volume on assurance:

> The value of that piety still advances according to the quantity of true faith, as the ring is more considerable with the diamond. I cannot conceive of a more compendious way for any Christian's full and constant revenues than this: to get faith, and still to use it; the sum or product of which would be this: grace and glory, heaven and earth are ours.
>
> Satan well knows what a serviceable channel faith is for all our traffic, whether for our ship to launch out into duties or for God's ship to come laden in to us with mercies; and, therefore, there is no grace which he batters and conflicts so with as with faith. If we weaken or shake foundations, this has a spreading influence into the whole building. A Christian's faith cannot be wronged, but presently all the spiritual frame becomes sensible of wrong and loss.[13]

Jeremiah Burroughs (d. 1646) uses language of trembling at the Word, irrespective of one's circumstantial disposition:

> A gracious trembling is a habitual trembling, a trembling of heart that is habitual in the heart, not all of a sudden only. … But the trembling at God's Word that the Lord so highly esteems is a constant, habitual disposition of soul. … Many men will tremble at God's Word in time of their sickness and affliction,

---

[12] Ibid., 48.

[13] Obadiah Sedgwick, Dedication in *The Doubting Believer* (Morgan, PA: Soli Deo Gloria, 1993), vii.

but let them have quiet and outward peace and ease and their trembling is gone. But a gracious heart trembles at the Word of God even when it has a most quiet conscience.[14]

J. C. Ryle (d. 1900), often mistaken for a Puritan, should be heard as well. Faith is the good fight:

> There is another warfare of far greater importance than any war that was ever waged by man. It is a warfare which concerns not two or three nations only, but every Christian man and woman born into the world. The warfare I speak of is the *spiritual* warfare. It is the fight which everyone who would be saved must fight about his soul.
>
> This warfare, I am aware, is a thing of which many know nothing. Talk to them about it, and they are ready to set you down as a madman, an enthusiast, or a fool. And yet it is as real and true as any war the world has ever seen. It has its hand-to-hand conflicts and its wounds. It has its watchings and fatigues. It has its sieges and assaults. It has its victories and its defeats. Above all, it has consequences which are awful, tremendous, and most peculiar. In earthly warfare the consequences to nations are often temporary and remediable. In the spiritual warfare it is very different. Of that warfare, the *consequences*, when the fight is over, are unchangeable and eternal.
>
> It is of this warfare that St. Paul spoke to Timothy, when he wrote those burning words: "Fight the good fight of faith; lay hold on eternal life."[15]

Ryle finishes this thought with the emphasis on faith:

> In this respect the Christian warfare is utterly unlike the conflicts of this world. It does not depend on the strong arm, the quick eye, or the swift foot. It is not waged with carnal weapons, but with spiritual. Faith is the hinge on which victory turns. Success depends entirely on believing.
>
> A general faith in the truth of God's written Word is the primary foundation of the Christian soldier's character. He is

[14] Jeremiah Burroughs, *Gospel Fear* (Orlando, FL: Soli Deo Gloria, 1991), 38.
[15] J. C. Ryle, *Holiness* (Moscow, ID: Charles Nolan, 2001), 62; emphases original.

what he is, does what he does, thinks as he thinks, acts as he acts, hopes as he hopes, behaves as he behaves, for one simple reason—he believes certain propositions revealed and laid down in Holy Scripture. "He that cometh to God must believe that He is, and that He is a rewarder of them that diligently seek Him" (Heb. 11:6).[16]

Last, let us observe Jonathan Edwards (d. 1758), who is often cited as the primary illustration of a believer needing to experience visceral affections for their progress in holiness to be genuine. Unfortunately, appealing to Edwards for support of this position misunderstands his teaching on progressive sanctification. Edwards distinguishes between the disciplined habit of "holy affection" (involving our faith and will) and circumstantial, temporal emotions:

> Upon the whole, I think it clearly and abundantly evident, that true religion *lies very much in the affections*. Not that I think these arguments prove, that religion in the hearts of the truly godly, is ever in exact proportion to the degree of affection and present emotion of the mind: for, undoubtedly, there is much affection in the true saints which is not spiritual; their religious affections are often mixed; all is not from grace, but much from nature. And though the affections have not their seat in the body, yet the constitution of the body may very much contribute to the present emotion of the mind. The degree of religion is to be estimated by the fixedness and strength of habit exercised in affection, whereby holy affection is habitual, rather than by the degree of the present exercise: and the strength of that habit is not always in proportion to outward effects and manifestations, or indeed inward ones, in the hurry, vehemence, and sudden changes of the course of the thoughts. But yet it is evident, that religion consists so much in the affections, as that without holy affection there is no true religion.[17]

---

[16] Ibid., 69.

[17] Jonathan Edwards, *A Treatise Concerning Religious Affections, In Three Parts*, in *The Works of Jonathan Edwards*, 2 vols. (Peabody, MA: Hendrickson, 1998), 1:243; emphasis original.

One pastor says, on this quote, and after reviewing multiple volumes in a quest to understand how Edwards thought about emotions and affections,

> Interpreters are divided about whether he [Edwards] used the term "affections" to refer to and include the emotions, or whether he saw this as a function of the inclination, or will. … By examining … [Edwards] in his own words, we will find that he does not regard the affections as emotions, but rather a function of the will. In order to stir the affections, … [he] preached for faith, by seeking to make truth clear to the mind.[18]

Edwards demonstrates again that white-hot feelings of happiness are not a prerequisite for true obedience: "I made a solemn dedication of myself to God, and wrote it down; giving up myself, and all that I had to God; to be for the future, in no respect, my own; to act as one that had no right to be himself, in any respect. And solemnly vowed to take God for my whole portion and felicity; looking on nothing else, as any part of my happiness, nor acting as if it were; and his law for the constant rule of my obedience; engaging to fight with all my might, against the world, the flesh and the devil, to the end of my life."[19]

A sampling of Edwards' resolutions, written at age nineteen, reflects his thoughts on true "religious affections." These resolutions prove he saw duty, the will, and faith—not a visceral experience—as the key to progress in holiness:

> 7. Resolved, Never to do any thing, which I should be afraid to do, if it were the last hour of my life.

> 10. Resolved, When I feel pain, to think of the pains of martyrdom, and of hell.

> 12. Resolved, If I take delight in it as a gratification of pride, or vanity, or on any such account, immediately to throw it by.

---

[18] Jonathan Anderson, "A Passionate Pulpit: Jonathan Edwards' View of Emotions and Its Implications for the Pulpit" (unpublished PhD paper, The Southern Baptist Theological Seminary, 2016), 1.

[19] John E. Smith, Harry S. Stout, and Kenneth P. Minkema, eds., *A Jonathan Edwards Reader* (New Haven, CT: Yale University Press, 1995), 38–39.

37. Resolved, To inquire every night, as I am going to bed, wherein I have been negligent,—what sin I have committed,—and wherein I have denied myself;—also, at the end of every week, month, and year.

47. Resolved, To endeavour, to my utmost, to deny whatever is not most agreeable to a good and universally sweet and benevolent, quiet, peaceable, contented and easy, compassionate and generous, humble and meek, submissive and obliging, diligent and industrious, charitable and even, patient, moderate, forgiving, and sincere, temper; and to do, at all times, what such a temper would lead me to; and to examine strictly, at the end of every week, whether I have so done.

55. Resolved, To endeavour, to my utmost, so to act, as I can think I should do, if I had already seen the happiness of heaven and hell torments.

57. Resolved, When I fear misfortunes and adversity, to examine whether I have done my duty, and resolve to do it, and let the event be just as Providence orders it. I will, as far as I can, be concerned about nothing but my duty and my sin.

62. Resolved, Never to do any thing but my duty, and then, according to Eph. vi. 6–8. to do it willingly and cheerfully as unto the Lord, and not to man: "knowing that whatever good thing any man doth, the same shall he receive of the Lord."[20]

In summary, all of the above quotes point to the language we see in Scripture: for sanctification to be real, a person does not need an emotional stimulus in order to obey genuinely. It must begin with faith, for "without faith it is impossible to please Him" (Heb 11:6). Our emotions and experiences cannot be trusted. Some moments of faith may be joined with sensations of happiness, but if they do not, it is no measure of genuineness. When we simply walk in humble faith despite our emotions, we find our purest moments of Christlike faith (Heb 12:1–5).

---

[20] Jonathan Edwards, *Resolutions*, in *The Works of Jonathan Edwards*, 2 vols. (Peabody, MA: Hendrickson, 1998), 1:lxii–lxiv.

SELECTED BIBLIOGRAPHY

Bavinck, Herman. *Saved by Grace*. Grand Rapids: Reformation Heritage Books, 2008.

Beeke, Joel R. *Knowing and Growing in Assurance of Faith*. Roshshire: Christian Focus, 2017.

Berkouwer, G. C. *Faith and Sanctification*. Grand Rapids: Eerdmans, 1952.

Brooks, Thomas. *Precious Remedies Against Satan's Devices*. London: Banner of Truth Trust, 1968.

Eskridge, Larry. *God's Forever Family*. New York: Oxford University Press, 2013.

Ferguson, Sinclair B. *The Christian Life: A Doctrinal Introduction*. Edinburgh: Banner of Truth Trust, 2001.

———. *The Holy Spirit*. Downers Grove, IL: InterVarsity, 1997.

Kevan, Ernest F. *The Grace of Law*. Ligonier, PA: Soli Deo Gloria, 1993.

Lloyd-Jones, D. Martyn. *Spiritual Depression: Its Causes and Cure*. Grand Rapids: Eerdmans, 1965.

MacArthur, John, Jr. *Faith Works: The Gospel According to the Apostles*. Dallas: Word, 1993.

———. *Slave*. Nashville: Thomas Nelson, 2010.

————. *Strange Fire*. Nashville: Nelson Books, 2013.

————. *The Truth War: Fighting for Certainty in an Age of Deception*. Nashville: Thomas Nelson, 2007.

Marshall, Walter. *The Gospel Mystery of Sanctification*. Grand Rapids: Reformation Heritage Books, 2013.

Murray, Iain H. *Evangelical Holiness and Other Addresses*. Edinburgh: Banner of Truth Trust, 2013.

Owen, John. *The Grace and Duty of Being Spiritually Minded*, in vol. 7 of *The Works of John Owen*. Edited by William H. Goold. N.p., Johnstone & Hunter, 1850–53. Reprint, London: Banner of Truth Trust, 1967.

————. *Of the Mortification of Sin in Believers*, in vol. 6 of *The Works of John Owen*. Edited by William H. Goold. N.p., Johnstone & Hunter, 1850–53; reprint, London: Banner of Truth Trust, 1967.

Ryle, J. C. *Holiness*. Moscow, ID: Charles Nolan, 2001.

————. *Practical Religion*. Edinburgh: Banner of Truth Trust, 2013.

Sproul, R. C. *The Holiness of God*, rev. and exp. ed. Wheaton, IL: Tyndale, 1998.

Watson, Thomas. *The Ten Commandments*. London: Banner of Truth Trust, 1965.

Wells, David F. *God in the Whirlwind*. Wheaton, IL: Crossway, 2013.

INDEX OF SCRIPTURE REFERENCES

Genesis

1:26	20
2:3	18
3:12	165
4:6–7	172
4:7	174
6:5	218
6:5–6	215n., 216
15:6	58

Exodus

3:14	19
28:2	20
36:6–7a	183
40:13	20

Leviticus

11:44–45	24, 168
19:2	18
20:7–8	20
26	93

Deuteronomy

28	93

Joshua

1:7	145
24:15	218

Ezra

7:10	205

Job

1:8	150

Psalms

1:1	164
1:2	88, 164
7:11	216
32:1	176
32:1–2	74
32:4	172
34:11–14	115
37:4	122, 218
37:24	187
38:1–10, 18	172
45:7	16
51:4	165, 197
51:7–10	16
103:13	216
119:9	145

Psalms (cont'd)

119:18	90
119:29	90
119:72	90
119:77, 92	88
119:97	85, 87
119:97, 113, 163, 165	90
119:142	90
139:23	218

Proverbs

3:5	58
4:23	218
6:16	216
18:1	173
27:21	206
28:13	153, 165

Isaiah

6:3	18
29:13	218
40:29	125
42:1	215
45:22	102
46:10	216
53:4-10	95
64:6	74

Jeremiah

3:15	132
13:23	109
15:26	145
31:33	21, 98
32:40	187

Zephaniah

3:17	215

Malachi

3:6	184, 215n.

Matthew

3:15	22, 88
4:4	168, 196
5:3	165
5:16	17, 105
5:17	95
5:46	213
5:48	24
6:5, 16	6
6:9-13	xvii
6:24	135
7:18	109
7:20	193
13:3-8, 18-23	124
14:26-31	39n.
15:8	218
16:23	107
16:24	67
21:20-22	148
22:37-40	63
23:25	39
23:37	218
24:13	189
28:19	135
28:19-20	xix, 8, 155
28:20	168, 198, 199

Mark

1:15, 35-39	131
1:24	22
4:1-8	179
9:24	62, 148
10:43-45	156
12:30-31	98

Luke

4:18	23
4:34	22
5:21	169
6	213
16:31	49
17:10	xix, 140, 212
18:9–14	148
21:12–13	151
22:18–20	136
22:19	136
22:42	71

John

1:12–13	186
1:14, 17	61
3:16	92
3:20	93
3:30	205
4:19–24	21
4:20	50
4:22	50, 218
4:24	44, 50, 64, 139
5:44	165
6:35b	187
6:37	187
6:39–40	187
6:69	22
8:12	106
8:31	194
8:58	22
10:27–29	171
10:36	23
11:22, 41–42	184
13:5-11	153
14:6	61
14:15	212
14:15, 23–24	198

John (cont'd)

14:20–21	75
14:23	110
15:5	139, 203
15:10	214
15:10–11	195
16:8	91
16:22	15
17:6, 9, 11, 17, 19–26	184, 214
17:8	195
17:13, 17	130, 131, 203, 219
17:17	130, 131, 203, 219
17:19	23
17:22–23	105
17:24	195
19:30	137
20:29	44, 67
20:31	179

Acts

2:37–38	135
2:38	153
5:11, 13	206
6:4	131
10:15	99
10:47–48	135
17:11	165, 166
17:25	156
20:28	203
26:18	55

Romans

1:4	53
1:5	218
1:17	53
1:18–23	218

Romans (cont'd)

1:18–32	105
1:20–21	217
2:4	153
2:5	74
2:7	198
2:12	104
2:15	172
2:29	99
3:19	89
3:19–20	93
3:26	58
3:31	95
4:2–5	74
4:3	75
4:4–5	75
4:18	150
4:18–20	50
4:18–21	48, 54, 213
4:20	38, 39n.
5:3–5	151
5:9–11	183
5:12–20	77
5:13–14	93
5:20	78
6:1	77, 79
6:1–2	141
6:2	79, 171
6:3	185
6:3–4a	135
6:4	79, 125, 135, 186
6:4–7	75
6:4–11	70
6:5	75, 186
6:5b, 8	186
6:6	83
6:6–11	xviii, 77, 186
6:8–9	76

Romans (cont'd)

6:9	76
6:10	76
6:11	76, 120
6:11–20	28
6:12	75, 82
6:12–13	80
6:13	83, 84
6:14	82, 90, 94, 97, 171
6:16	123
6:16–18	175
6:16–19	75
6:17	94, 175
6:18	123
6:19	123
6:21, 23	107
6:22	29
6:22–23	124
7–9	105
7:5	106, 107
7:6	94, 200
7:7–11	91
7:7, 13	165
7:7–13	121
7:8–13	93
7:12	90
7:13	93
7:21, 23	103
7:25	103
8:1	103, 172, 174, 179, 186
8:2	6, 103
8:2–14	67
8:3	104
8:3–4	95
8:4	21, 89, 105, 201
8:4–13	54, 213
8:5	107
8:6	21, 107

Romans (cont'd)

8:7	109, 111
8:8	111
8:9	110, 111
8:10	112
8:10–11	112
8:11	21
8:12	70, 113
8:13	xviii, 16, 21, 29, 69, 80, 81, 114, 115, 154
8:14–15	188
8:16	112, 188
8:23	112
8:24–25	67
8:26–39	173
8:28–29	147
8:28–30	70
8:29	xix, 9, 15, 21, 186, 207
8:29–30	185
8:29–39	171
8:31–39	184
8:33	169
8:38–39	58, 187
9:31–32	94
10:3	94
10:4	87, 88, 95
10:9–10	135
10:17	61, 132
11:33	215
11:36	89
12:1	21, 211
12:1–2	130, 158, 165, 213
12:1–3	54
12:2	28, 83, 146–7
13:8	97
13:8–10	95
13:9	96
13:9–10	97

Romans (cont'd)

13:10	97
13:14	154
14:13–23	205
14:17	16
14:23	57
15:1–2	157
15:13	63
16:25–27	134
16:26	10

1 Corinthians

1:2	24, 105
1:30	24
2:12–16	214
2:14	109
2:16	16, 54, 213
3:3–4	201
3:17	99
3:19	xxv
4:2	206
4:3–5	219
4:4	71, 169, 176
4:6, 19	201
6:9–11	25
6:17	75
6:19–20	122, 212n.
8:1	146
8:1–3	201
8:12	172
9:24	29
9:26–27	79
10:13	125
10:16	137
10:31	15, 84
11:26	136
12:3	188
12:13	185

1 Corinthians (cont'd)

13:2	65
14:1	27
15:12–26	83
15:50–54	30
15:58	30

2 Corinthians

1:6–7	151
1:20	95
3:18	39n., 64
4:6	28
4:16	112
4:16–18	151
5:7	55, 67, 72, 199, 200
5:9	206
5:17	79
5:21	74, 75, 186
6:14–7:1	79, 198
7:1	23, 27, 29, 168
10:5	54, 213
13:5	188, 191

Galatians

1:23	58
2:20	67, 186
2:20–21	55
3:11	74
3:24	91, 93, 94
3:25–27	136
4:4	104
4:6	188
4:10	21
4:19	7
5:4, 5, 6	64
5:13	79, 156, 205
5:14	96
5:16	7, 51, 54, 71, 176, 198, 213

Galatians (cont'd)

5:16–24	16
5:16–25	28
5:16–26	218
5:18	97
5:19	7
5:22	28, 97, 111
6:2	95

Ephesians

1:3	186
1:3, 11, 14	105
1:4	17, 18, 31, 63, 105, 186, 195, 196
1:11b	152
1:12	125
1:13	185
2:3	74
2:4–5	109
2:5, 9	2
2:8	55
2:8–9	70, 188
2:10	15, 54, 80, 81, 128
2:19	186
3:1–14	183
3:16–19	54, 213
3:19	215
4:7, 11	133
4:7, 12–16	156
4:11–12	132
4:12–24	28
4:13–16	133
4:14	133
4:15–16	140
4:16	138
4:19	156
4:23	83
4:24	15, 79

Ephesians (cont'd)

4:30	216
5:8, 10	87
5:18	71, 199
5:18–21	138
5:19	133, 138
5:25–27	25, 31
5:26–27	18, 105
6:6–8	229
6:10	xviii, 144
6:10ff	xviii
6:13	xviii
6:13–17	129
6:16	6, 57

Philippians

1:6	54, 71, 125, 173
1:8–11	145
2:7	104
2:12	3, 4, 80, 190
2:12–13	3, 4, 80, 190
2:13	54, 71, 81, 190
3:8	196
3:9	74
3:12	73
3:13–14	29, 143
3:14	143
3:19	16, 107
3:21	29
4:8	83

Colossians

1:9	154
1:9–10	145
1:10	29
1:13	102, 135
1:15	22
1:21	16

Colossians (cont'd)

1:22	196
1:22–23	191
1:28	145
1:29	9, 144
2:3	198
2:10–17	21
2:12	135
2:13–14	74, 104, 186
3:1	206
3:1–12	9
3:3–4	186
3:5	115, 154, 223
3:10	16, 145
3:16	133
3:17	84

1 Thessalonians

1:10	83
2:13	203, 214
4:7–8	16
5:15	27
5:21–24	125

2 Thessalonians

2:13	146

1 Timothy

1:5	218
1:5–6	164
1:5–7	172
3:6	201
3:13	179
4:6	131
4:12	205
6:4	201
6:11	27, 154
6:12	xviii

2 Timothy

1:12	130
2:1	114, 130, 149
2:19, 21	204
3:15–17	145
4:2	131

Titus

2:7, 14	29
2:11–12	29
2:12	6, 23, 206
2:13	83
3:5	110

Hebrews

1:3	22, 76
2:9–11	105
2:14	76
3:12	189
4:2	120
4:11	99
4:11–13	188
4:12	54, 164, 166, 174, 213, 218, 219
4:16	147, 148
5:9	147
5:14	54, 164, 213
7:26	22
7:27	99
8:10	21
10:1–10	21
10:1–18	59
10:11–14	22
10:12	76
10:16	98
10:16–18	185
10:19–39	59
10:23	143, 191

Hebrews (cont'd)

10:24	29
10:24–25	138
10:25	140
10:26–27	189
10:35–36	56
10:36	189
10:39	59
11:1	35, 48, 58, 59, 66, 130
11:1ff	48
11:1–3	23
11:1–40	10
11:3–40	67
11:6	5, 55, 56, 57, 109, 214, 227, 229
11:24–26	67
11:24–28	62
11:27	68
12:1	2
12:1–5	229
12:2	70, 125
12:4	29
12:10	31, 150, 195
12:11	15
12:11–14	172
12:12–17	79
12:14	24, 27, 168, 193, 195
12:14–17	28
13:8	22
13:17	206

James

1:2–4	149, 150, 170
1:6	148
1:22–25	197
1:23–25	165
1:25	95
2:8	21, 95

James (cont'd)

2:17	62, 69
2:18	193
2:19	56
3:1	206
4:5	185
4:12	135
5:14–18	148
5:16	149

1 Peter

1:1–2, 14–16	105
1:3–5	125, 191
1:3–9	171
1:6–8	193
1:8–9	64
1:14–15	196
1:14–16	16
1:15	20
1:15–16	22, 24, 195
1:16	90, 168
1:17b–19	125
1:21	199
1:23	146
2:1–2	196
2:9	23
2:11	45
2:11–12	17
2:16	79
2:21–23	66
2:22	23
3:7	149
3:15	22
4	186
4:11	125
4:12–13	151
4:19	152
5:6–10	54, 213

1 Peter (cont'd)

5:7	170

2 Peter

1:1–11	181
1:3	xviii, 51
1:5	5, 29, 130
1:5–10	168
1:5–11	170
1:8	193
1:9–11	124
1:11	190
3:17–18	29
3:18	xviii, 27, 54, 79, 130, 213

1 John

1:6–7	106
1:8–10	136
1:9	152
1:10	29
2:6	106
2:17	83
3:2	83, 105
3:3	29, 105
3:20	124, 174
4:18	71, 169
5:13	179, 212n.

2 John

1:6	106

3 John

9	203

Jude

21	191
23	204
24	73, 173, 184, 191

Revelation

3:7   22
4:8   19

Revelation (cont'd)

19:1–10   139
22:4   185